The Soviet Union as an Asian Pacific Power

The Soviet Union as an Asian Pacific Power

Implications of Gorbachev's 1986 Vladivostok Initiative

edited by
Ramesh Thakur
and Carlyle A. Thayer

Routledge
Taylor & Francis Group
LONDON AND NEW YORK

First published 1987 by Westview Press, Inc.

Published 2019 by Routledge
52 Vanderbilt Avenue, New York, NY 10017
2 Park Square, Milton Park, Abingdon, Oxon OX14 4RN

Routledge is an imprint of the Taylor & Francis Group, an informa business

Library of Congress Cataloging-in-Publication Data
The Soviet Union as an Asian Pacific power.
(Westview special studies in international security)
Bibliography: p.
1. Asia—Foreign relations—Soviet Union.
2. Soviet Union—Foreign relations—Asia. 3. Soviet Union—Foreign relations—1975- . 4. Soviet Union—Politics and government—1953- . 5. Gorbachev, Mikhail Sergeevich, 1931- . I. Thakur, Ramesh Chandra, 1948- . II. Thayer, Carlyle A.
III. Series.
DS33.4.S65S69 1987 327.4705 87-21686

National Library of Australia Cataloguing-in-Publication Data
The Soviet Union as an Asian Pacific Power
Includes index.
ISBN 0 333 43078 6.
1. Soviet Union—Foreign relations—Asia. 2. Soviet Union—Foreign relations—Pacific Asia. 3. Asia—Foreign relations—Soviet Union. 4. Pacific Area—Foreign relations—Soviet Union. I. Thakur, Ramesh Chandra, 1948- . Thayer, Carlyle A.
327.4705

ISBN 13: 978-0-367-29615-5 (hbk)

ISBN 13: 978-0-367-31161-2 (pbk)

Contents

1

Introduction

Ramesh Thakur and Carlyle A. Thayer

According to one scholar of the USSR, "[t]he coming to power of any new top leader in the Soviet Union changes, to a greater or lesser extent, the correlation of forces among the various institutional interests, opinion groupings and issue networks which exist within both the domestic and foreign policy making realms."[1] The case of Mikhail Gorbachev has proved no exception to this rule. The turnover of General Secretaries has been unexpectedly frequent in the Soviet Union in recent years. However, Yuri Andropov and Konstantin Chernenko lacked both health and time to leave a mark upon Soviet history.

Mikhail Gorbachev by contrast has seized the opportunity, if not with relish, then at least with evident vigour to try and reshape Soviet society both domestically and in its international relations. In so doing, Gorbachev has defied early predictions of maintaining the tradition of "[c]ontinuity, caution and consensus" characteristic of "a system revolutionary in doctrine but deeply conservative in practice." Consequently, continued the *New York Times* editorial, "whatever his ambitions, Mr. Gorbachev is unlikely soon to make waves."[2]

If "we base our conclusions on the course of events since 1949," Geoffrey Barraclough has noted, then "it would be ... easy and ... plausible to argue that the world was moving not into an Atlantic but into a Pacific age."[3] Europe has been a settled if divided continent since the Second World War. In the Pacific theatre, the war began earlier and ended later. It was the Pacific war which ushered in the nuclear age; it is the Pacific which remains the scene of competing claims, great power rivalry, and residual regional tensions, some of which predate both world wars.

In 1986, Mikhail Gorbachev, General Secretary of the Communist Party of the Soviet Union (CPSU), journeyed to the Soviet Far East Maritime Kray to present the Order of Lenin to the city of Vladivostok.

While in this seaside city, he delivered a major policy speech which touched on both domestic and foreign policy issues. The General Secretary's remarks were broadcast live on 28 July 1986 by Soviet television and by Radio Moscow's home service.

Russian encounters in the Far East were not the happiest at the turn of the century, nor immediately after the establishment of the Soviet state. For all that, in July 1986 Gorbachev served notice that the USSR would engage in international relations as an Asian-Pacific power as much as a European power. In the eastward-looking approach adopted by Gorbachev at Vladivostok, the General Secretary may be said to have launched his own, or at least the Soviet, version of *ostpolitik*. Jerry Hough has noted that the "vast majority of men of the Brezhnev-Gromyko generation were born between 1900 and 1910 and were almost all thrust into high positions in the wake of the purges of 1937-1938. Men of this generation remember World War I; their fathers may have fought in the Russo-Japanese War and reminisced about it; they, themselves, were high officials in World War II."[4] In his Vladivostok Initiative, as indeed in other remarkable aspects of his foreign policy, Gorbachev perhaps reflected the fact that he was the first Soviet leader "too young to have been an active participant in the Second World War, which had such a profound effect on the thinking of his predecessors ...."[5]

At the same time as the Pacific is the scene of much contemporary tension, it also contains some of the most dynamic economies of the post-war period. Even the US trade with Asia-Pacific surpassed that with Europe in the 1980s. It was appropriate therefore that Gorbachev's call at Vladivostok for improved international relationships in the Asian-Pacific area were preceded by calls for economic development of the Soviet Far East. That is, the Soviet Union's identity as an Asian-Pacific power is critical to Gorbachev's twin concerns of the security of the USSR and the rejuvenation of its economy.

Ambassador Evgeni Samoteikin's chapter seeks to explain and interpret the meaning of the Vladivostok address, and to respond to critical reactions in the West to aspects of the speech. It is an interesting statement for being simultaneously an affirmation of superpower legitimacy for the Soviet role in the Pacific, and an attempted reassurance against any military or other anti-Western designs in the South Pacific.

An early indication of Gorbachev's firmness of intent and search for new directions was the scale of personnel changes in the highest echelons of party and state organs, a subject which is discussed by Graeme Gill. Dissatisfaction with the intractability and durability of problems had perhaps suggested to the General Secretary that fresh minds ought to be brought to bear on them. More importantly, though, a new General Secretary uses early opportunities to replace the old guard by his own nominees as a tried and tested method of consolidating his position at the apex of the Soviet leadership. Gill suggests how an urgent task for any new General Secretary is to establish his authority, and that personnel changes - what Jerry Hough terms "the politics of building coalitions and neutralizing opposition"[6] - are an important and early item on the agenda of authority building. Personnel changes are more significant in the foreign policy realm than in the domestic because of the relatively fewer people who occupy key positions, and who can therefore be made more readily responsive through a tightened chain of command to the policy preferences of the General Secretary.

Another characterisitc of the Gorbachev approach seems to be to make the political environment more receptive to the possibility of fundamental change by engaging in bracing rhetoric at the declaratory level prior to policy innovations at the operational level. Changes both in the climate of opinion and in personnel can be prerequisites to policy innovations. The Vladivostok address confirmed Gorbachev's reputation as an impressive salesman of ideas who through a masterful campaign of public diplomacy can set the agenda for international affairs and force opponents into a reactive role.

The characteristic Gorbachev style has been much in evidence in the arms control sphere: bold pronouncements, challenging visions and unilateral initiatives which not only made Soviet foreign policy uncomfortably unpredictable, but also created a superpower and international climate of opinion more conducive to concluding a historic nuclear disarmament agreement in September 1987, earlier false starts notwithstanding. On this "question of questions," Gorbachev was not interested in mere cosmetic changes at the margins of the nuclear balance; he wanted fundamental progress. He was not willing to negotiate away strategic parity with the USA; but he was prepared to contemplate strategic parity at a significantly lowered threshold.

In a prescient piece of scholarly journalism, Adam Ulam noted that "a younger man could be expected to be impatient with the immobilism that has characterized the Soviet economy and society in the last decade or so and be inclined to look at the risks and costs of expansionism and the arms build-up."[7] The Vladivostok speech too underlined the impression that Gorbachev believes that mere tinkerings will not suffice to achieve long term fundamental goals in either the economic or the foreign policy realm. The General Secretary attacked what we might term the intellectual inertia which has produced a lag between the security requirements of the 1980s and the state of the world's nuclear arsenals. He called accordingly for a fundamental break with many conventional approaches to foreign policy, a break with the axioms of political thinking on the problem of war and peace, a break with the entrenched assumptions of individual and international security policies. In so doing, he acknowledged the special responsibility of the superpowers in the management of world order, which is the necessary corollary to their privileges flowing from that status.

Furthermore, Gorbachev has been an evident believer in the linkage argument. A deteriorating international environment was less conducive to the pursuit of economic prosperity because it diverted scarce financial and human skilled resources to the less productive sectors of defence. As he said almost a year before the Vladivostok Initiative, "[i]f the main thing for us Soviet people is the development of the economy, social relations and democracy, this also determines our interests in the international arena and our foreign policy issues - above all our interests in peace, in a stable international situation that would make it possible to focus attention and resources on peaceful, creative matters."[8] Not surprisingly, the linkage re-emerged at Vladivostok. There is thus an economic logic to the fervour with which Gorbachev has pursued arms control and disarmament negotiations. Vladivostok was a clear affirmation by Gorbachev that even a superpower cannot live in security by military means alone.

The result of such linkage for analysts is to raise questions about the sincerity of proposals to reduce international tensions in their own right. Richard Armitage, the US Assistant Secretary of Defense for International Security Affairs, remarked that what "we are seeing is the addition of political and economic elements to the growing [Soviet] power projection capability in East Asia and the Pacific, a capability clearly aimed at the US and its regional friends and allies."[9] Paul Keal in his chapter too draws attention to the fact that many of Gorbachev's "initiatives" were in fact self-serving and therefore foredoomed.

The Vladivostok address was important also for confirming that in the Gorbachev strategy, high-level overtures to Europe, Asia and the Pacific were meant to complement relations with the United States. If one was not a substitute for the other, then it could not be hostage to the other: relations with Asian-Pacific countries could be delinked from the state of superpower relations. Nevertheless, the USA too was explicitly acknowledged as a fellow-Pacific power, with legitimate superpower interests in the region.

If the Vladivostok Initiative was a bluff, then can it be shown up as such without being called? If the address contained a genuine offer of accommodation with Asian-Pacific countries, then what responses should be forthcoming from these countries? How, in other words, can the countries that were the objects of Gorbachev's courtship at Vladivostok respond positively while minimising security risks to themselves? Questions such as these are addressed by all the contributors. While there is, not surprisingly, no unanimity, there does seem to be a general feeling that the Soviet overtures deserve cautiously optimistic treatment rather than uncritical embrace or outright rejection.

In the 1970s, the Sino-American *rapprochement* profoundly realigned the world's power relations. A normalisation of relations between China and the Soviet Union would usher in a similarly profound process of readjustment, not just regionally, but globally. A major, if not the major, object of Gorbachev's Vladivostok address was therefore the People's Republic of China. The nature, meaning and significance of his remarks, as also the likely Chinese responses, are analysed by Gary Klintworth. He describes the accelerating pace of inter-governmental contacts between Moscow and Beijing since Gorbachev came to power, and notes some genuine concessions made by Gorbachev at Vladivostok on the obstacles to Sino-Soviet normalisation. Perhaps we will witness the development of a less antagonistic and more pragmatic relationship between China and the USSR during Gorbachev's stewardship of the Soviet state. If so, then that would surely represent a major prize of Soviet diplomacy.

But it would also entail complications in some other relationships. The notion of a general system of Asian-Pacific security was revived by Gorbachev at Vladivostok, with the important difference from the discredited proposal of Leonid Brezhnev that it was not so transparently aimed at China. The centrality of China to the entire Asian-Pacific region is attested to by the fact that it borders upon or is proximate to, and certainly relevant to, all the relationships touched upon by Gorbachev, from Afghanistan in the Southwest to Korea and Japan in the Northeast.

Not surprisingly, therefore, the importance of the Sino-Soviet relationship is discussed in virtually all the chapters. Thus China will be a key actor in determining the shape of the eventual solution of the Afghanistan problem. Amin Saikal discusses the implications of the Vladivostok Initiative for the conflict in Afghanistan, and is generally sceptical of the "initiatives" in terms of their novelty, sincerity, significance, or likely success. In South Asia, China is a looming presence rather than an integral player. The central actor there is India, which is a neighbour to every other country in the region; Pakistan and Afghanistan are the only two other countries to share a border. While Saikal's analysis brings in the Pakistan factor, Ramesh Thakur gives it a more central place in his account of the relationship between the USSR and India. Moscow's link with New Delhi is the only unqualified success story for the USSR of any note in the entire non-communist world; and it is some success. Yet Thakur notes the constraints to the relationship as well as the mutual benefits. Gorbachev could easily have had the Indo-Soviet relationship in mind as a model when he spoke of improved bilateral relations with the countries of Asia-Pacific. But even the Indo-Soviet relationship could be dramatically affected by major changes in the Sino-Soviet relationship.

China is of course much more directly concerned about and involved in the Southeast and Northeast Asian regions. Carlyle Thayer analyses in some detail recent moves concerning the problem of Kampuchea, noting in particular possible shifts in nuances in the Soviet position in and since the Valdivostok Initiative. Topics such as confidence-building measures, nuclear-free zones and Helsinki-type conferences are covered for Southeast Asia and Northeast Asia by Robyn Lim and Paul Keal repectively, both of whom are less than confident about major progress resulting from the Vladivostok Initiative. Lim argues that the non-communist countries of Southeast Asia may be willing to concede legitimacy to the USSR as an Asian-Pacific power, but are unlikely to enter into an arms control regime which disadvantages American strategic interests in the region. But the Americans do have to devise appropriate responses to the freshly fashioned moral-political challenge posed by the Soviet Union.

Given the location of the symposium, it is not surprising that the South Pacific in general, and Australia in particular, receive separate and detailed treatments by Richard Herr, Stuart Harris and David Charles. Herr argues that the era of strategic denial of the South Pacific to the Soviet Union may have passed, and that it may be time to work out a new *modus vivendi* of peaceful coexistence which acknowledges a Soviet fishing, and possibly a Soviet diplomatic, presence in the island countries of the South Pacific. Harris and Charles assess the Gorbachev initiatives from an Australian perspective of cautious optimism: it may be that one can detect a note of greater caution in one than in the other.[10]

Not long after its delivery, it became apparent that Gorbachev's Vladivostok speech carried with it implications extending far beyond his domestic audience. Yet outside analysts differed in their assessments and interpretations of the address. Some argued that the speech was mainly rhetorical and designed for propaganda purposes. Others argued that references to the development of the Far East were merely an example of wishful thinking. Still others noted a mischievous flavour in certain sections, especially those dealing with nuclear-free zones, foreign bases, and the conflict in Afghanistan. Yet, however much Gorbachev's speech was discounted, it became clear that it was a significant policy address which warranted careful attention and close study.

The idea to host a one day symposium on Gorbachev's Vladivostok speech arose from discussions held in October 1986 by members of the Department of Politics at the newly created Australian Defence Force Academy (ADFA). An organising committee, consisting of Anthony Bergin, William Maley and Carlyle Thayer, successfully obtained financial backing and moral support from Professor G. V. H. Wilson, the Rector of University College; Professor Ian McAllister, Head of the Politics Department; and Dr W. H. Smith, Director of the Australian Defence Studies Centre at ADFA. Major General Peter Day, Commandant of the Defence Academy, provided logistical and other support.

It was decided to convene the symposium in March 1987 in order to allow sufficient time for retrospective analysis and judgment. In this, the organisers proved wise. In the weeks preceding and following the symposium, Eduard Shevardnadze made his first visit as Soviet Foreign Minister to Southeast Asia and Australia. On the eve of the symposium, Kim Beazley, the Australian Minister of Defence, released a White Paper, the first in a decade. Accordingly, interest in the topic was high and the symposium attracted a gratifyingly large audience, including many members of the diplomatic corps and the defence establishment based in Canberra.

Although the symposium was weighted in favour of the foreign policy sections of the Vladivostok speech, domestic implications were not ignored. The organisation of the symposium took the following form. Keynote addresses were delivered by Dr Stuart Harris, Secretary of Australia's Department of Foreign Affairs, and His Excellency E. M. Samoteikin, Ambassador of the USSR. Then followed two separate presentations, the first, by Graeme Gill, dealing with the interrelationship between domestic politics and foreign policy, and the second, presented by Gary Klintworth, covering the Sino-Soviet relationship.

The second half of the symposium consisted of three panels. The first considered the implications of Gorbachev's Vladivostok Initiative on a region by region basis: Paul Keal on Northeast Asia, Robyn Lim on Southeast Asia, Ramesh Thakur on South Asia, and Richard Herr on the South Pacific. The second panel examined the prospects for a negotiated settlement of on-going regional conflicts: Amin Saikal on Afghanistan, and Carlyle Thayer on Kampuchea.

The symposium concluded with a panel of specialists who were asked to comment on the day's proceedings and to draw out the implications of Gorbachev's initiative, if any, for the region and Australia. The government and opposition were represented by David Charles and Andrew Peacock respectively. Other panelists included Nancy Viviani, Director of the Centre for the Study of Australian-Asian Relations, Griffith University; Air Marshall David Evans (ret.), former Chief of the Defence Force Staff; and Denis Warner, editor of the *Pacific Defence Reporter*.

After the symposium, the organisers concluded that the written papers were of such high quality that they should be made available as soon as possible to a wider audience in published form. One factor which influenced this judgment was the publicity accorded by the Soviet press, which ran features on page one of *Pravda, Izvestia* and *Krasnaia Zvezda*. The *Washington Times* too reported portions of the address by the Soviet Ambassador. It was agreed to ask contributors to update their papers for publication, and to invite Ramesh Thakur to co-edit this volume because of his previous relationship with Westview Press, his experience in producing camera-ready books for Westview, and his status as the inaugural Visiting Fellow of the Department of Politics at ADFA in 1986.

The text of Mikhail Gorbachev's Vladivostok address is reproduced in the appendix. While it is almost entirely the BBC version that we have published, we have supplied our own section headings for ease of reading convenience. We have also on rare occasions checked words or passages, which seemed to be not entirely clear, against the edition published by Novosti Press,[11] and substituted the latter version if it seemed to clarify the meaning more readily. But for practical purposes it remains the BBC version, and we are grateful to the organisation for permission to reproduce it.

NOTES

1. Archie Brown, "Change in the Soviet Union," *Foreign Affairs* 64(Summer 1986), p. 1060.

2. As reprinted in the *International Herald Tribune*, 13 March 1985.

3. Geoffrey Barraclough, *An Introduction to Contemporary History* (Harmondsworth: Penguin, 1967), p. 22.

4. Jerry F. Hough, "Gorbachev's Strategy," *Foreign Affairs* 64(Fall 1985), p. 45.

5. Roderic Lyne, "Making Waves: Mr Gorbachev's Public Diplomacy, 1985-6," *International Affairs* 63(Spring 1987), p. 206.

6. Hough, "Gorbachev's Strategy," p. 42.

7. Adam B. Ulam, "Gorbachev: A Strange Soviet Sequence May Now Give Slow Change a Chance," *International Herald Tribune*, 13 March 1985.

8. In an interview on 30 September 1985; quoted by Lyne, "Making Waves," p. 208.

9. As reported in the *Australian*, 27 February 1987; cited in Amitav Acharya, "The Asia-Pacific Region: Cockpit for Superpower Rivalry," *World Today* 43(August/September 1987), p. 156.

10. The Harris and Charles addresses to the ADFA symposium were also published in the official *Australian Foreign Affairs Record* 58(March 1987), pp. 111-119 and 122-124 respectively.

11. *Speech by Mikhail GORBACHEV in Vladivostok, July 28, 1986* (Moscow: Novosti Press, 1986).

2

The Goals of Vladivostok

Evgeni Samoteikin

If we put aside all technical and secondary questions, the main point to discuss and argue about is whether the Soviet Union is sincere in its aspirations. What are the reasons for and goals of the Vladivostok Initiative?

To answer this question I have to begin from relevant general aspects of the Soviet policy.

Last year the Party Congress, the highest forum of Soviet society, set forth our vision of the world, our philosophical concept of its present and future. We did not just proclaim a pure theoretical doctrine but formulated a definite political platform for an all-embracing system of international security. This is a system based on the principle that one's own security cannot be ensured at the expense of others; it is a system that organically links all the main areas of security - the military, political, economic and humanitarian.

We consider this system to be an essential international background for the process of restructuring and accelaration which has been launched on such a large scale in our country. The reasons here are quite obvious - we simply won't be able to reach our goals at home in a hostile international environment, spending material and intellectual resources of our society on arms race and confrontation.

Restructuring, which is a dominant factor of our domestic life, cannot but affect the foreign policy of the USSR. The thesis about the need for a new political thinking, a new outlook put forward by the Soviet leadership is not a tribute to a fashion. It is a reflection of our understanding and recognition of the fact that with the stockpiling and sophistication of nuclear armaments the human race is no longer immortal, that international relations and the policies of governments and states must, without delay, be brought into line with the realities of the nuclear age.

Recent political actions of the Soviet government in the international arena are clear evidence that we take this plain truth into full account. It is virtually impossible to name a sphere of international policy where the USSR has not put forward major proposals and initiatives, the main features of which are realism, constructiveness, and boldness. That is what makes them so attractive to the public worldwide.

The Vladivostok Initiative attracted special attention here in Australia, because it is aimed at the solution of problems in Asia and the Pacific - regions of direct national interest to this country.

The title of the symposium contains a question whether this initiative is something new? In a sense it will not be absolutely correct, because many ideas which are an integral part of the proposal have been known for years. What is really new is the comprehensive character of the initiative, its balanced approach to all complex problems of the vast region. The main idea which underlies the whole Vladivostok speech is that all the problems can be solved if there is political will and joint efforts of all the states.

Let me very briefly outline the main points of the Soviet Union's proposal for integrating the Asian-Pacific region into the general process of establishing a comprehensive system of international security.

First of all, the Soviet Union intends to invigorate its bilateral relations with all countries in the region without exception. Certainly, we are prepared to expand ties with Australia and all South Pacific Islands countries, as well as with our neighbours - the People's Republic of China, Japan, the United States and others.

Secondly, we advocate joint efforts for finding settlements to regional issues, such as Afghanistan, Kampuchea, Southeast Asia and Korea. In our view there are good possibilities for not only quickly stopping bloody violence and relieving dangerous tensions in these areas, but also for establishing mutually acceptable relations between the countries concerned.

Thirdly, we suggest concrete measures on scaling down military preparation in the Asian-Pacific region, including, in particular, prevention of a proliferation and build-up of nuclear weapons, establishment of nuclear free zones, bringing down the level of naval activity in the Pacific, resumption of talks on establishing the Indian Ocean as a peace zone, reduction of armed forces and conventional armaments in Asia, and practical discussion on confidence-building measures and the non-use of force in that region. In this respect simpler measures - for instance, measures for the security of sea lanes in the Pacific, and for the prevention of international terrorism - could serve as the beginning.

Clearly, sometimes there can be a considerable time lag between the formulation of ideas and their implementation. But what is important is to identify the objectives and start moving towards their attainment. It is also clear that no one country has or can have instant prescriptions for dealing with all existing problems. This requires the collective wisdom of nations. This is exactly why the Soviet Union proposes - even though not as an immediate objective - that following a series of bilateral and regional negotiations, a Helsinki-type conference be held with the participation of all the countries gravitating to the Pacific Ocean.

It must be noted - and this was specifically emphasised by the General Secretary in his speech in Vladivostok - that the Soviet Union does not seek any special rights or privileges for itself in the Asian-Pacific region. What it desires is to jointly build new and equitable inter-state relations in this part of the world too. And, of course, the Soviet approach is based on the recognition and understanding of the existing realities.

We are prepared to examine most carefully considerations and proposals by other countries of the Asian-Pacific region concerning ways to strengthen security and develop international cooperation in the area. In particular, we approve of the South Pacific Nuclear Free Zone established on the initiative of Australia and some states of Oceania. We are open-minded about the idea of "Pacific Economic Cooperation" and are willing to join in outlining possible foundations of such cooperation, provided, of course, that it is not conceived in terms of a bloc anti-socialist scheme imposed by somebody, but as the result of a free discussion without any discrimination whatsoever.

Sceptics might say that good declarations are fine, but what about concrete deeds to support all these far-reaching statements?

This is exactly what I would like to address now. Any objective observer will agree that the Soviet Union did not lack concrete actions in practical realisation of its concept of normalisation of the situation in the Asian-Pacific region since the Vladivostok Initiative was put forward.

I will not outline the chronology nor go into details. Let me just mention that six Soviet regiments from Afghanistan and more than one division from Mongolia have been or are being returned home. A certain improvement has been reached in Soviet-Chinese relations. The Soviet Union became the first nuclear power to sign protocols to the Treaty of Rarotonga. In November 1986, the USSR for the first time took part as an observer in the fifth meeting of the Pacific Economic Cooperation Conference.

Yet another proof of our firm determination to translate into action the Soviet concept of guaranteeing peace and security in Asia and in the Pacific region was recent official visits by the Soviet Foreign Minister Eduard Shevardnadze to Australia, Indonesia and countries of Indochina.

The talks he held here with Australian partners were of an open, straightforward and, one could say, constructive nature. Both sides gave particular attention to a broad range of questions relating to stronger peace and security in the Asian-Pacific region. We understand that our ideas on normalisation of the situation in the region became clearer to the Australian government.

The visit coincided with another important initiative by the USSR aimed at the elimination of medium range missiles in Europe and their drastic reduction in Asia.

The Soviet government decided to single out the question of medium range missiles, to delink it from the well-known Reykjavik package, and to treat that issue separately. According to our proposal of 28 February 1987, all American and Soviet missiles of this range in Europe should be eliminated. At the same time we are prepared to limit the number of those missiles in the Eastern part of the USSR to just 100 warheads - and that is a fraction of the existing number (33 missiles).

As Eduard Shevardnadze said at his press conference in Canberra, the Soviet Union is in favour of eliminating any nuclear systems in Asia on a mutual basis. We also favour radical reductions of conventional forces and armaments in all regions of Asia, and we propose to move towards this step by step, beginning with partial measures first.

Even brief reference to what has been done since the Vladivostok speech shows that our words are confirmed by deeds. All of them are an integral part of measures of universal character aimed at freeing the world from nuclear and other mass annihilation weapons and the creation of a truly secure peace on our planet.

REGIONAL CONFLICTS

Now let me say a few words about regional conflicts. Their settlement is an important priority for the Soviet Union, and the best way towards this is an active dialogue between states in the region. Any other attempt, any other way can only cause complications and prolong tension and bloodshed. There exists of course the question of confidence, the question of trust. In other regions the countries have already tested certain specific confidence-building measures of a military and political character, and we believe they can be used also in the Asian-Pacific region. That is the reason why we proposed the convening of a regional conference to discuss these matters. And frankly speaking, we are surprised when we hear that the time is not yet ripe for a general Asian dialogue, that there are still obstacles in the way of an overall Asian dialogue. Well, we say that dialogue is needed precisely in order to remove those obstacles. We see no reason why the process of strengthening Asian and Pacific security and cooperation could not get under way, taking as a basis for a point of departure the principles of the Delhi declaration and of the Helsinki final act. Each of those principles could be filled with specific content acceptable not just to any one country but to all countries.

Our views about security in the Asian-Pacific region did not come out of thin air. They take into account the experience of the past and of today. Nor do they ignore the lack of trust towards the Soviet Union on the part of many countries of the region. Of course we can take offence, or start arguing. But instead we are trying to explain our position, and we do not have any forbidden themes.

So let me touch upon some so called contentious aspects of the Soviet policy, which cause so much concern in the western world, and here in Australia as well.

Afghanistan

We used to hear that the Afghan problem is the main obstacle to an Asian dialogue. In his Vladivostok speech, the General Secretary made it absolutely clear that as soon as a political settlement is finally worked out, the recall of all Soviet troops from Afghanistan, which started last year, can be accelerated. Schedules for their stage-by-stage recall have been agreed upon with the Afghan leadership.

The outline of a political settlement in Afghanistan is a policy of national reconciliation which is being pursued so actively by the Afghan government. We have information that after 15 January 1987, after the cease-fire announced by the government more than 25,000 refugees have returned home, more than 10,000 armed men who were engaged in the armed struggle against the authorities have now decided to join the process of reconciliation. And this is only a beginning of the process which, we hope, will bring about genuine national reconciliation and peace in Afghanistan.

Unfortunately, as we see, those who wage an undeclared war against the people of Afghanistan do not as yet seem ready to grasp the olive branch of peace extended to them by the Government of Afghanistan. However, their designs, as has already been the case in the past, will be upset by reality. The Afghan people's yearning for a peaceful, tranquil life is too strong to be thwarted by such obstacles.

As a result of bold, constructive initiatives undertaken by the Afghan government, certain progress has been achieved at the Afghan-Pakistani talks held through the mediation of the representative of the Secretary General of the United Nations.

The Soviet Union supports the policy of the present Afghan leadership aimed at national reconciliation and at widening the social base of the National Democratic Revolution. This includes unilateral cease-fire, talks that are open to all Afghan forces for the creation of a government of national unity, and speedy return of refugees.

The joint efforts of the Afghan and Soviet governments to ensure the earliest political settlement must be answered by the curtailment of outside interference in the affairs of the Democratic Republic of Afghanistan.

Kampuchea

As to the problem of Kampuchea, it too can be resolved quite quickly. Compromise proposals for the resolution of the Kampuchean problem were put forward by the Ministers for Foreign Affairs of the countries of Indochina. They contain the time-frame for the withdrawal of foreign troops from Kampuchea, provided that outside interference in the internal affairs of Kampuchea is terminated. Vietnam and Kampuchea offered to have a direct dialogue with the ASEAN countries.

The Kampucheans invited the opposition forces to participate in a coalition government. And Vietnam proposed to the Chinese that a direct dialogue be entered into on all questions, including Kampuchea. All this surely opens up the prospect of establishing peace in that region. But a quest for forms of diffusing the conflict situation by political means is not a unilateral action. It is a reciprocal process which requires definite movement from the other side as well.

As we discuss today the issues of peace and security in this region, I would like to touch upon one more question which is quite often exploited by certain forces in the west for sowing mistrust towards Soviet policy in the Asian-Pacific area. Recently they found another pretext for their accusations against the USSR which were uncritically picked up by some Australian journalists. They have given broad publicity to so-called authoritative reports and even photoreconnaissance pictures allegedly taken from space, while frank and detailed information on this score made public by Soviet military authorities was almost completely ignored. What I mean is speculation about some Soviet "superpowerful naval base" at the port of Cam Ranh Bay in Vietnam, a base which allegedly poses a threat to sea lanes and straits.

In this regard I must emphasise that the USSR has no naval base at Cam Ranh Bay in the sense in which it is customary to define such bases, namely, ones with complete structure. What exists over there is only a point for the material and technical supply of the Soviet navy. Ships call there to replenish the stocks of water and food or to make minor repairs on their own.

The point at Cam Ranh Bay can in no way be compared with the US naval base at Subic Bay in the Philippines, nor with any of the 350 US military bases scattered around the region.

We do not really understand why those who so vigorously defend the right of US ships to make calls at the ports of the allied countries simultaneously deny the equal right for Soviet ships.

South Pacific

Now briefly about the so-called "Soviet threat" to the South Pacific. What has been said and written about our policy here will be familiar. In my opinion, this is the most vivid example of political hypocrisy that I have ever met during my diplomatic career of more than thirty years.

We make no secret of our intention to develop relations with the island states. Mikhail Gorbachev in his Vladivostok speech said that to envisage the process of establishing international security and peaceful cooperation in the Asian-Pacific region, the Soviet Union will try, first of all, to invigorate its bilateral relations with all countries in the region without exception. I repeat, without exception. All we are doing, or have already done in Oceania, must be viewed through this particular prism. Nothing more and nothing less.

As Ambassador of the USSR, I act on the basis of instructions I receive from Moscow. I must emphasise that there is nothing in those instructions that can be construed as the slightest hint of evil designs or threat towards countries of the region.

It is difficult to predict what will be the nature of our relations with the South Pacific nations in future. It all will depend on what those countries want. If we have expanding trade and economic cooperation with those countries, and a growth in tourism, athletic and cultural exchanges, then that will of course mean increased Soviet presence. But in no case will the result be a Soviet *military* presence.

During consultations with his Australian counterpart, Eduard Shevardnadze emphasised once again that the Soviet Union is entitled to have an interest in tranquility and stability in the region of the Pacific and Indian oceans, not the least because there are sea lanes of communication here that are important for the USSR. But in a more general way we are concerned about the region because it is potentially an area of military threat against us. That military threat results from American military presence in Japan, in South Korea, in the Philippines, in Micronesia, and also results from the policy of Japan itself which has recently stepped over the threshold of responsible moderation in increasing its military forces. Naturally the expansion in the region of the US navy, which has long-range sea-launched cruise missiles there, and the policy of Washington here, all of this must be of concern to us. There is also the problem of the security of our friends in Southeast Asia, to whom we have political and moral obligations. This is also a factor in our policy.

On the whole the Pacific region has not as yet been militarised to the extent that Europe has. But the potentialities of its militarization are truly immense, and the consequences could be extremely dangerous. That is why we urge everybody to reverse the policy of tension, to replace it with the policy of cooperation and dialogue.

We do not pretend to have a monopoly on political wisdom. We are ready to listen to counter arguments, to discuss different options. Our growing political dialogue with Australia is another proof of this.

Australian Foreign Minister Bill Hayden said at the lunch for Eduard Shevardnadze:

> Each of us has our different vision of how the future should be shaped but underlying each of those different visions there are common basic themes and aspirations
>
> - that humanity will go on
> - that the species will survive
> - that the glories of the earth and human civilisation will continue to delight the eye and the mind of man.

Let me assure you that the Soviet Union is ready to use its international prestige and all its power to secure these noble goals. It needs reiterating that there is only one way to achieve these objectives, namely patient dialogue, discussion, and a joint search for untying knots of conflict and international tension. This is what we call the new political thinking.

It is a must if we wish to survive.

3

Power, Authority and Gorbachev's Policy Agenda

Graeme Gill

In the period since Mikhail Gorbachev was elected General Secretary of the Central Committee (CC) on 11 March 1985, events have been moving swiftly in the Soviet Union. One of the principal forces behind such movement has been the attempt on the part of the General Secretary and his allies to consolidate his position by building up both his power and authority. This chapter will outline the broad strategy for strengthening power and authority which Gorbachev has adopted, and it will indicate how his Vladivostok speech of 28 July 1986 fits into this strategy.

THE GORBACHEV QUEST FOR AUTHORITY

Upon his election, a General Secretary is confronted by a situation which belies the popular conception of this post as the most powerful in the world. Initially, the new party leader is constrained by the effects of the Soviet succession process and by the nature of elite politics. The new leader is not in a position whereby he can easily choose a new leadership team, wiping the slate clean and starting afresh. Instead the General Secretary inherits a leadership team from his predecessor. Moreover it is this leadership team which has chosen him and, in the likely event that this choice was not unanimous, it will include not only his supporters but people who may in varying degrees be opposed to him. The level of fluidity that this situation creates in elite relations is reinforced by the absence of firm institutional buffers for the position of General Secretary itself. Although this post possesses various rights and prerogatives, the crucial considerations which would make for its formal institutionalisation, regulations relating to tenure, extent of power and means of choosing and removing the incumbent, are lacking.[1] Precedents and conventions are important for structuring the post in these regards, but the absence of formalised rules nevertheless injects a sense of uncertainty into a situation in which the power politics are already sufficient to create some ambiguity in Soviet elite relations.

The practical effect of the sort of situation which the General Secretary inherits is that, upon election, he must set about consolidating his position. This means that he must build up both his power and his authority. In crude terms, power can be defined as the ability to get one's way, while authority is that quality whereby people obey because they believe that the person giving orders has a right to give those orders and they have a duty to obey. Authority implies legitimacy, but power need not. Nevertheless, the two are closely linked. Power can stem from authority in that an increased sense of authority can translate into increased effective power. Indeed, it is only through the generation of authority that power can be stabilised and the position of a political leader rendered secure in the long term.

Students of Soviet politics have long recognised the importance of power, and in particular the power of the individual leader, for their subject. But brought up under the shadow of Stalin, they have been slower to recognise the role that authority has played throughout the life of the Soviet system. Fortunately that situation is now being remedied.[2] Any attempt to understand the place of the General Secretary that ignored the question of authority would be partial in the understanding it achieved. This is particularly clearly shown by looking at the period of Gorbachev's tenure.

Most students have approached the question of the power of the General Secretary through analysis of personnel disposition. They have sought to ascertain the extent of the power of the General Secretary by his ability to move supporters into positions of influence throughout the political structure, and particularly in the elite political institutions. With some reservations noted below, this methodology is useful; a General Secretary's power can be seen to be reflected in his ability to move supporters into responsible positions. How has Gorbachev fared in this regard?

Significant personnel changes have taken place in the Soviet political structure in the first two years of Gorbachev's tenure as General Secretary. Of the eleven full members of the Politburo in March 1987, five have entered that body since March 1985.[3] Six of the eight candidate members[4] and nine of the twelve CC secretaries[5] took up their positions over the same period. This represents an unprecedented rate of turnover within the first two years of a General Secretary's incumbency; 52 percent of the political executive, consisting of full and candidate members of the Politburo and CC secretaries, were not members of those bodies at the time of Gorbachev's election. Significant changes have also taken place within the CC apparatus.

The extent of personnel change has also been significant at lower levels of the political structure. At the 27th Congress of the CPSU in February-March 1986, 40.7 percent of the full members of the newly elected CC were new, while 59 percent of those who had been elected in 1981 and were still living were re-elected to this body. This is the highest level of renewal of the CC since 1961.[6] Six republican party first secretaries have been replaced,[7] significant numbers of oblast first secretaries in the RSFSR have been removed,[8] while rates of turnover of lower-level party officials has also been high. This has been most marked in Uzbekistan, Kazakhstan and Turkmenistan, where wide-ranging purges have been conducted during this period.

Significant changes have also occurred in the state sector. A new Chairman of the Council of Ministers (prime minister, Nikolai Ryzhkov) and Chairman of the Presidium of the Supreme Soviet (state president, Andrei Gromyko) have been named, while almost 50 percent of the membership of the Presidium of the Council of Ministers was changed in the first year of Gorbachev's tenure. Large numbers of government ministers and chairmen of state committees have been pushed into retirement or resignation,[9] and shake-ups have occurred at the lower levels of the central state administrative apparatus; there has been some organisational restructuring (such as the creation of Gosagroprom, the State Agro-Industrial Committee, and the restructuring of foreign trade) and at least two state ministries, Foreign Affairs and Interior, have been subject to purge. Similar sorts of developments have occurred at the republican level.

The extent of the personnel changes has been remarkable for such a short period of time. The established assumptions of Sovietology would lead us to conclude that such a spate of personnel changes should reflect the strengthening and consolidation of the General Secretary's position. But the extent of the changes may be more a reflection of the circumstances of the Gorbachev succession, following the stasis of the last Brezhnev years and the ageing of the Soviet elite that was such a feature of that period,[10] than of the intrinsic strength of Gorbachev's position.

Both Nikita Khrushchev and Leonid Brezhnev were able to consolidate their respective positions at the top of the party structure by ensuring that those with whom they had career connections were promoted into positions of responsibility throughout the political system. The career link was usually connected to patronage considerations, which in turn were translated into support for the leader. But these two leaders were at a distinct advantage in this regard compared with Gorbachev. Both had been geographically mobile in their careers, thereby multiplying the range of contacts they had and expanding the potential reservoir of supporters they could later promote. In contrast, all of Gorbachev's career until called to Moscow in 1978 (with the exception of his years at Moscow State University) was spent in the Stavropol' area. The range of personal contacts open to him was therefore much more restricted than it had been for his two predecessors. Consequently, in filling the many positions that have become vacant, Gorbachev has been able to utilise established personal contacts and thereby build up a solid patronage basis far less than we might have expected. Of course some of those promoted do have links with Gorbachev: for example, CC Secretary Viktor Nikonov was USSR Deputy Minister of Agriculture while Gorbachev was CC Secretary responsible for agriculture, CC Secretary Georgy Razumovsky served in the neighbouring Krasnodar krai while Gorbachev was in Stavropol' and spent some time in the Council of Minister's Agro-Industrial Complex department while Gorbachev was CC Secretary with responsibility for agriculture, CC Secretary Anatoly Lukyanov was at MGU with Gorbachev, and Gosagroprom head Vsevolod Murakhovsky succeeded Gorbachev as first secretary in Stavropol'. But more important, at least in terms of numbers, than those with career associations with Gorbachev, are recent promotees who come from Leningrad and Siberia. The top echelons of Soviet politics now contain a significant number of people who have spent time in these areas, and although there is no evidence of either group consolidating itself into a coherent political bloc,[11] their career experiences are geographically far removed from that of Gorbachev.

The weakness of Gorbachev's support base, at least as defined in terms of the promotion of those with established career links with the General Secretary, is reflected in the fact that neither of the other two most important men in the administration, Egor Ligachev and Nikolai Ryzhkov, have long-standing career associations with him. Certainly both were promoted by Gorbachev, and this could be a source of some sense of obligation on their part to the General Secretary. But promotion alone is a weak basis upon which to construct a solid patronage connection and the associated sense of obligation and support,[12] as Khrushchev discovered. It is much more likely that while Gorbachev may have clients in the more traditional sense of the word within leadership circles, the more important and powerful members of the elite are probably better seen as allies who retain a degree of autonomy from the General Secretary. If this is so, and

Gorbachev is much less certain of a solid foundation of patronage-based support, then the authority question becomes much more important.

One of the principal planks in Gorbachev's programme[13] for the construction of authority has been to counter-pose the contemporary administration with that of the last years of Leonid Brezhnev. Criticism of the state of affairs which had existed under the former leader has peppered Gorbachev's speeches and been reported widely in the press. It has even been given programmatic status by the inclusion in the new party Programme adopted at the 27th Congress, albeit without mentioning Brezhnev, of criticism of the emergence in "the 1970s and early 1980s [of] certain unfavourable trends and difficulties in the country's development. To a great extent these were due to failure to assess promptly and appropriately changes in the economic situation and the need for profound transformations in all spheres of life, and to lack of persistence in carrying them out."[14] More pointedly, an article commemorating the eightieth anniversary of Brezhnev's birth criticised the "many negative phenomena" and shortcomings and the failure to respond adequately to the problems that arose during Brezhnev's last years.[15] Many of the contemporary problems being faced by the Soviet Union were blamed on the sense of drift and malaise which was attributed to the final stages of the Brezhnev period; the bureaucratic inertia and slackness, covered up by the falsification of results and official corruption, combined to produce a dispirited society and an ailing political and economic mechanism.[16] What Gorbachev and his allies have been doing has been constructing a negative example; if the conservative and indolent Brezhnev administration had got the Soviet Union into its current predicament, what was needed was an innovative and enthusiastic administration with vigorous and appropriate policies to reverse this process. It is this sort of image which Gorbachev has tried to project.

Economic Reform

Central to Gorbachev's programme for reviving the Soviet Union has been the question of economic reform. Although recognition of the need for substantial economic reform has been evident for some time in academic and some other circles in the Soviet Union, it was not until this was taken up by Gorbachev, in the form of calls for "restructuring," that it moved into a central place on the political agenda; indeed, many of his proposals are echoes of previous reform attempts. Gorbachev has spoken of the need for a "radical reform" in the economic sphere,[17] but exactly what he has in mind has not been spelled out in a single, coherent statement. Nevertheless some of the elements of the reform can be pieced together from official statements and measures already introduced.

The essence of the economic reform strategy is to loosen up the constraints that currently hinder economic advance.[18] An important element of this, in Gorbachev's view, is the strengthening of both central planning and enterprise autonomy. This apparent contradiction is to be resolved by a shift in the focus of planning concern away from the close, daily supervision of production towards strategic perspective planning. In the process of strengthening both the apex and the base of the productive structure, it is the middle levels which will be squeezed, and in particular the state ministries.[19] But what is of most interest about this plan is the changes in the conditions in which the productive units, the enterprises, must operate.

An attempt was begun in 1984 to broaden the economic independence of enterprises. This experiment has since been expanded, reflecting dissatisfaction with the limitations of the initial measure. Increasingly the emphasis has fallen upon the need for enterprises to become self-financing[20] rather than relying upon subsidies from the centre to underwrite their continued operation. The main mechanism for achieving this is to be the retention by the enterprise of a guaranteed proportion of the profits that it generates. The incentive would thus be created for enterprises to maximise profits in order to be able to inject more funds into enterprise performance and development and into the pockets of the workers. Furthermore, the criterion of enterprise success is to be the satisfaction of the demands of the customers rather than the meeting of quantitative plan targets; sale rather than simply production. Prices should reflect production costs and demand rather than being artificially set in the plan.[21] The new need to satisfy customers has also meant an emphasis upon the production of higher quality goods. This is reflected in the moves to encourage wholesale trade in producer goods between enterprises (as opposed to allocation by the centre through the plan) and to fine suppliers which are late in their deliveries, both aimed at eliminating some of the causes of the practice of "storming" in the factories, and the introduction of quality control investigators independent of the enterprises.[22] Productivity and performance are also to be improved by granting enterprises greater flexibility in the hiring and firing of labour; labour shedding can be carried out to increase efficiency and productivity, with the money saved from the shed labour being directed into production and shared among the workers who are still employed.[23] In addition, workers' pay levels are to be linked to their performance,[24] and enterprises are to be given the right to sell any unused material and to keep the proceeds.

These measures to increase enterprise autonomy and encourage improved efficiency and productivity have been accompanied by continual demands that managers become more efficient. Along with this, they are also to become more accountable, so that they are no longer able to hide their failings behind falsified production results as in the past. Measures to strengthen the role of labour collectives early in Gorbachev's tenure and provision for the election of enterprise managers are part of this.

These steps toward freeing the production units, the enterprises, from the strait-jacket of centralised plan control have been matched in the agricultural sector. There have been moves to strengthen the private plots and kolkhoz markets.[25] Kolkhozy and sovkhozy have been given the right to do what they like with any goods produced above the plan target, including selling them on the open market.[26] At the same time Gorbachev has supported the introduction of a contract and piece-work system of payment on the farms whereby teams, groups and families would have means of production (including land) assigned to them for a specified contract period, and their income would be determined by the results that they achieved. As in the factories where the pay of the workers is to be dependent upon their performance and the income of the factories would reflect their performance, so on the farms; income, and therefore material well-being, is to be linked to results.

This attempt to stimulate individual enthusiasm and initiative is also reflected in what is perhaps the most controversial of Gorbachev's economic reforms, the law on individual labour adopted in October 1986.[27] This provides for the operation of private enterprise in the service sector (including the provision of consumer goods, services and catering) and is clearly motivated, in part, by a desire to bring under control certain aspects of the unofficial economy. The law provides for family enterprises which do not hire workers outside the family to be established in a range of walks of life. Provision has also been made for the transformation of these into cooperatives of from five to fifty workers if this was appropriate; a tax incentive has been foreshadowed to facilitate such a transformation. While many aspects of this measure remain uncertain (for example, where the family firms/cooperatives are to obtain the materials they need to function, how they are to dispose of their product), the legalisation of private enterprise that this involves, with the as yet unseen social consequences, constitutes a very important change to the Soviet economic system and potentially may have revolutionary implications for the development of Soviet society.

Gorbachev's message on the economy is not restricted to these measures promoting structural change in the economic system. He is also promising improved economic performance in the short-medium term through a process of "acceleration." Investment is to be concentrated in heavy industry and engineering, principally in order to re-equip industry with modern technology. The emphasis is upon re-equipment of existing capacity, bringing it up to date with modern technology, rather than the construction of new capacity.

But there is also an emphasis upon re-invigorating the system, both for short term improvement and long term reform, through the "human factor." One side of this campaign is positive, offering incentives. The proposals for workers' incomes to be determined in accord with the quality of the work they do is one form of incentive, although it clearly has its negative side as well. Another is the proposal to give workers a greater role in the management of the factory. But also important is the promise about improved supplies of consumer goods. A major programme for the supply of consumer goods was adopted in October 1985,[28] and since then there have been constant exhortations about improving the supply and fulminations against producing goods of inferior quality. Although the balance of investment in the Twelfth Five Year Plan in favour of industrial development makes significant improvement in the consumer goods sector unlikely,[29] such promises are nevertheless designed in part to stimulate harder work and consequent economic improvement.

But there has also been another side to the attempts to improve economic performance; this relates principally to the demands for discipline. This whole strand of the Gorbachev programme constitutes an attempt to construct an ethical basis for the changes that the leadership desires.

Social Reform

A continuing theme of the Gorbachev leadership has been the sense of social malaise which has beset Soviet society. This theme is reflected principally in complaints about the weakness of social and work discipline and the presence of corruption, but it also appears in such things as references to the drug problem, alcoholism, crime, prostitution and youth unrest. This social malaise must be combated, and a new sense of civic ethos, personal commitment and moral fibre engendered. As with many observers on the right in Western society, a chief means of doing this is perceived to be discipline.

The Gorbachev leadership has built on the beginning made under Yuri Andropov to tighten up both social discipline generally and labour discipline among Soviet workers.[30] Penalties have been increased for absenteeism and lateness, and demands have been stepped up for the improved quality of on-job performance on the part of individual workers, with the threat of job loss or income reduction if such improvement is not forthcoming. Important too has been the drive against alcoholism and drunkenness,[31] with increased penalties for drunkenness, and limitations upon the production and sale of alcohol and an expanded propaganda campaign. But perhaps the most important aspect of this campaign has been the drive against unearned income.[32] Directed against such things as speculation, black marketeering and moonlighting, this is designed to eliminate what was a real growth area during the last years of the Brezhnev period, the privately-based second economy. Along with the measures to legalise certain types of private enterprise referred to above, this constitutes an attempt to shift certain aspects of economic activity out of the grey shadows of society into the legal sphere where they can be controlled and taxed. It is also an attempt to eliminate some forms of such activity.

Particularly important in this regard has been the drive against corruption. Although the anti-corruption campaign had begun before Brezhnev died, its most spectacular results have been achieved under Gorbachev. People from all walks of life at all levels of society up to and including members of the Politburo and state ministers, have been accused of corrupt practices and dismissed from office. The party machines in Uzbekistan, Kazakhstan and Turkmenistan have been purged on the grounds of corruption, while party committees across the country have had their conduct scrutinised to see how they have measured up in this regard. Furthermore, the drive against corruption and abuse of official position has led to the questioning of the right of party leaders to enjoy the sorts of privileges which are unavailable to ordinary citizens.[33] The main thrust of this campaign is aimed against the possession by some of a privileged position in Soviet society, an aim which accords with the basic principle behind the economic changes Gorbachev has sponsored: success or failure must be a result of one's own efforts.

The push against privileged positions is reflected in the legal sphere also. Much has been made of the need for the party to work within the law and for party members and officials not to consider themselves nor to be considered above the law.[34] The legal system is to be reorganised and legal bodies are to observe the tenets of socialist legality in the way they handle themselves and conduct the law. Furthermore, protection is to be provided for citizens against arbitrary treatment, including the capacity to pursue through the courts any party officials who wronged them.[35] The rejection of a privileged position for some was publicly symbolised by the sacking of a KGB officer in the Ukraine who had abused his power by locking up a journalist involved in a piece of investigative journalism which he considered to be unacceptable.[36]

Gorbachev has also proposed changes in the political realm designed to combat the development of privilege and the abuse of power by those in authority. At the January 1987 CC plenum he called for the democratisation of electoral procedures throughout the country.[37] The changes that he proposed were the introduction of multi-candidate elections (with the party committee retaining the right to nominate candidates) and election by secret ballot. If introduced, these measures would render party leaders, leaders of state organs and even factory managers subject to scrutiny and judgment by below them in a way which they have generally not been before. Such measures were tried out in a number of Komsomol elections before Gorbachev enunciated them at the plenum.[38]

Important also in the struggle against abuse of position has been the policy of *glasnost,* or openness. This has been clearest in the more vigorous and open press in the Soviet Union since Gorbachev came to power. The official media has handled a whole range of issues which were previously closed to it: economic reform, party privileges, corruption, drugs, prostitution, natural disasters and the Afghanistan conflict have all been discussed in the press in ways that were undreamt of under Brezhnev. The sort of investigative journalism that led to the fall of the KGB officer referred to above has also become a feature of the Soviet media. So too has the reproduction of articles by Western politicians and critics of the Soviet Union. Such developments make the media a much more exciting and compelling source for those interested in Soviet affairs, both inside the country and out.[39] The increased openness of the press has also meant a greater range of views being expressed therein, and although it is clear that limits remain, the contrast with the dullness and stereotypes of the past is marked.

The increased diversity of views in the press has had its counterpart in the dissident and cultural spheres. The way in which the Gorbachev administration has handled the dissident issue, at least thus far, suggests a desire to ameliorate the long-running battle between dissidents and state and to recruit the former into the struggle to build a new and better society. The release of Andrei Sakharov and the apparent acceptance that he will not curb his activities is the clearest signal in this regard, but it has been reinforced by the release of a range of lesser known dissidents. In the cultural sphere too there has been significant movement. Some writers who were formally banned, most importantly Boris Pasternak and Evgeni Zamyatin, are to be published in the Soviet Union. T. Abuladze's film "Repentance" (*Pokayanie*) which explicitly deals with the Stalin question has been screened openly and has been reviewed in *Moscow News*. Goskino has been stripped of its censorship functions, which have been passed to the individual film studios.[40] The theatre has become more lively and its role as social critic sharpened. Furthermore there have even been olive branches held out to some leading Soviet emigres, including theatre director Y. Lyubimov and ballet dancer Mikhail Baryshnikov. All of this seems to reflect a willingness to accept the right of different individuals and groups to play a part in public life. Of course, there are still serious restrictions on individual rights and the freedom of participation, but what the Gorbachev leadership appears to be trying to do is to redraw the boundaries of acceptable and unacceptable activity in a way which is more expansive than it has been in the recent past.

Gorbachev's programme also embraces foreign affairs. The most important characteristic of this has been the attempt to make the Soviet strategic environment much more palatable than it has been in the recent past. A major element in this has been the attempt to reach an arms control agreement with the US, most spectacularly in the Geneva summit and the meeting in Reykjavik. With this in mind Gorbachev has put forward a series of imaginative arms control proposals ranging from limited test bans and the removal of medium range nuclear missiles from Europe to the complete elimination of all nuclear weapons by the year 2000. Such proposals have had limited success in evoking a positive American response, and therefore in gaining any concrete movement in the arms control area, but they have been significant Soviet victories on the propaganda front. This is an important factor for the Gorbachev leadership. In the first two years of Gorbachev's tenure, Soviet foreign policy has been much more sophisticated in the way in which it has downgraded military factors and emphasised political-economic ones and has differentiated between the US on the one hand and its allies on the other. Moscow has sought to court Japan and the US allies in Europe, both at the official level and by appealing over the heads of the governments to the populace at large. Significant successes have been achieved in this regard. Attempts have also been made to woo India and to improve relations with China, once again with some success. Increased attention has been devoted to the Pacific region. Finally, Gorbachev has signalled that he wants to withdraw Soviet troops from Afghanistan, although the precise grounds on which he would do this are not yet clear.

Gorbachev's attempt to improve the Soviet strategic environment has been imaginative and has met with some success. But his aim here has not just been to improve Soviet security. Foreign policy is intimately linked to domestic concerns. Stabilisation of the strategic environment and reduction of the perceived threat would enable the redirection of some funds from military purposes in the Soviet budget into assisting the path of reform. It could also make the West more forthcoming as a source of modern technology and investment which could be used to assist domestic reform. The changes made to the organisation of foreign trade in December 1986, including provision for joint ventures,[41] seems designed to facilitate just such a development. The range of resources available for domestic reform is thus dependent in part upon a successful foreign policy.[42]

The programme which Gorbachev has sketched out therefore consists of proposals for structural change in economic and political life and for a change in the thinking of the Soviet populace. Improved economic performance must come about through a combination of structural change and of increased effort and commitment on the part of the workforce. The latter is to be a response both to improved material incentives and the generation of a new sense of commitment to the Soviet future. It is this latter which, in the short term, is the more important. What Gorbachev has sought to do is to engender a new enthusiasm and sense of commitment in the Soviet populace. There is to be a breaking away from the old past characterised by indolence, drift, abuse of power, obsequiousness, empty flattery and corruption. Instead, Gorbachev has projected the image of a society in which all Soviet citizens have a place. Moreover it is not a secondary place, but one whereby they are called upon to play an active part in the public life of society. They are to criticise shortcomings, to exercise an on-going watching brief over their leaders and to choose them through the electoral system. They are to be good citizens, abiding by the mores of socialist society and working hard to develop its economy. Gorbachev's view is one with an integrative conception of society, a society which is animated by the resourcefulness and initiative of its citizens.

However, this view of the future is one to which many individuals and groups in the Soviet Union object. The strength of opposition has already been publicly acknowledged.[43] If all of the proposed changes are implemented, daily life will be much more uncertain for those in responsible positions. Central planners will have to play a new role in which they are far more detached from the day-to-day course of production. Enterprise managers will have to manage their concerns in new semi-market conditions, with which they have no experience and where the ground rules remain uncertain, while within the enterprise they may have to run the gauntlet of regular elections. The power of the state ministries, and perhaps the regional party apparatus (at least in the economic sphere) will be diminished. The new electoral provisions may threaten the control exercised by political officers at many levels and could call the whole substance of the nomenklatura as it currently operates into question. The new working and pay conditions will make life less secure for the urban workers. Ideological hardliners oppose many of these changes in the name of true socialism. Any reductions in defence expenditure will adversely affect the defence industry-military complex. All of these groups wield significant power in Soviet society, and yet it is their partial interests which appear under threat in Gorbachev's programme. Furthermore, the gamble on improved short term economic performance may fail, leaving Gorbachev's promises appearing threadbare and a crucial pillar of his programme in ruins.

But the essence of Gorbachev's appeal is beyond the particular to the general. He is asking all of these groups to forget about their narrow departmental, careerist concerns and to focus upon the broader question of the welfare of the society in which they live. He is appealing to frustrated bureaucrats and economic managers, to those who are fed up with the poor performance of the past and who wish to see significant improvement. He is appealing to those sections of the intelligentsia, both creative and technical, who are disillusioned by the restrictions of a conservative cultural and human rights policy. He is appealing to a populace tired of economic hardship, political cynicism and corruption. In this sense his appeal is ethically based, rejecting notions of material interest in favour of those of social justice and the good of all. It is upon the overall attractiveness or otherwise of the package and the commitment it can arouse, plus short-medium term economic improvement and the absence of significant failures in the international realm, that his quest for authority rests. If sufficient people can be convinced of the worth of his vision and are willing to put their support behind it, if he can stimulate the emergence of a coalition of groups dedicated to renewing Soviet society along the lines that he suggests regardless of the effects on partial interests, then Gorbachev's authority will be consolidated and the chances of success of his programme will be significantly increased. However, if the major power groups of Soviet society take a narrower, departmental focus, then the General Secretary could face a rocky road ahead.

THE VLADIVOSTOK SPEECH

The speech delivered by Mikhail Gorbachev in Vladivostok on 28 July 1986 constitutes an important stage in the unrolling of his authority-building campaign. Many of the themes of the programme outlined above clearly resonate through the speech. The emphasis upon the need for accelerated economic development resting upon both improved technical input and the "human factor" are explicitly discussed with regard to the Soviet Far East. The need for an improved strategic environment is given lengthy consideration, with some significant measures proposed in an attempt to achieve such a result. Furthermore, the linkage between the domestic and international spheres is clearly signalled.

On domestic matters, Gorbachev criticised the tempo of development in the Far East and called for significant improvements to be made in this. What is most interesting about this is perhaps the way he presents the future Soviet profile in this region. The picture he paints is one of an expanded and consolidated Soviet presence on the Pacific littoral. The region is to become increasingly self-sufficient and economically powerful, with a widely developed infrastructure of both industrial development and socio-cultural amenities. Mining and timber industries are to be developed. Manufacturing, particularly catering to local needs, must be built up. Transport and the fuel and energy complex must be improved. Agriculture and fishing must be expanded. Furthermore, the social and cultural facilities that will encourage settlers to stay must be developed. It is to become a thriving community and to contribute to overall Soviet economic development and to the Soviet position in the region.

The development of the Far East can take place, Gorbachev suggested, on the basis of the facilities established in recent years. But Gorbachev also criticised the shortcomings that were evident in the development of those facilities;[44] clearly greater investment and construction of capital goods would be required if the region was to achieve the economic future that Gorbachev has suggested. But the problem here is that in Gorbachev's overall programme, emphasis is placed on the development of existing resources and facilities rather than on the construction of new ones. If the economic base in the Far East is insufficient for the development plans Gorbachev has, and that base does appear to be deficient, then it is difficult to see how those plans can be achieved without some reordering of priorities in the general economic strategy. This problem is not unique to the Far East, but exists in many parts of the country and many sectors of the economy.

It may be that Gorbachev believes that this sort of growth can be achieved through closer integration of the Soviet Far East into the expanding economies of the region. This may be suggested by the way in which he linked the economic development of the region to international factors. He referred explicitly to the need for cooperation with neighbouring countries in the solution of agricultural problems and for the Amur basin to become an arena of major cooperation with the Chinese. He called on the Chinese to cooperate in the implementation of the two countries' respective development plans. The prospect of joint ventures with the Japanese and of cooperation in the investigation of ocean resources was mentioned. Gorbachev also referred to the possibility of Vladivostok becoming a major international centre, including trade and tourism, should military tensions disappear. More generally, while declaring that the tactic of some in the West of seeking to bankrupt the Soviet Union by pressing the arms race is bound to fail, he reaffirmed the commitment to continued pursuit of economic change. In this regard, his reference to exchanging experiences with the Chinese is interesting in the light of the Chinese experiment with the "open door." However, the integration of the Far East into the broader regional economy would involve a loosening of links with the remainder of the Soviet economy based in the west of the country. The dangers of potential regionalism and pressures for autonomism would cause any Soviet leader to hesitate before embarking upon this path.

In the foreign policy sphere, the main thrust of Gorbachev's remarks concerned the need for an easing of tensions in the region. This message was conveyed both in the form of general strictures about the desire for peace and of the possibility of and Soviet desire for improved relations with most of the states of the region, and of a number of specific proposals designed to bring this about. Such proposals referring to the whole Pacific area included the disbanding of military groupings, the renunciation of military bases in Asia and the Pacific (with a promise that American withdrawal from the Philippines would not remain "unanswered"), the withdrawal of troops from other countries, no proliferation of nuclear arms in the region (with a promise not to increase the number of medium range nuclear weapons in the Asian part of the USSR), reduction of fleet activity in the region, the reduction of armed forces and conventional armaments, the non-use of force and the implementation of confidence-building measures. But it is clear that a major aim of the speech was to build bridges to China, and some important initiatives were announced in this regard.

Although Gorbachev did not mention China's "three obstacles" to improved relations with the USSR, he effectively addressed them in the speech. On the question of the Vietnamese invasion of Kampuchea, he declared that the future of Kampuchea should be decided within Kampuchea itself and that no solution could be imposed from without. Furthermore, he emphasised that crucial to this question was the normalisation of Sino-Vietnamese relations. On the question of Afghanistan, he announced the withdrawal by the end of 1986 of six regiments of Soviet forces,[45] and reaffirmed the Soviet desire to withdraw its troops from that country when a political settlement was reached. Finally, on the question of Soviet troops on the Sino-Soviet border, Gorbachev suggested opening discussions with the Chinese about achieving a proportional reduction in the level of land forces and announced that the withdrawal of some Soviet troops from Mongolia was under consideration.[46] In the most significant move, Gorbachev suggested that the disputed border between the Soviet Union and China could follow the main ship channel rather than the Chinese bank as the Soviet position had been up until then. This would transfer to China many of the islands in the Amur which had previously been under dispute, and constitutes a real concession.

Gorbachev's Vladivostok speech was therefore important not just because of the increased priority that it seemed to signal for the Far East in Soviet development plans, nor for the foreign policy announcements it contained; it was important because it showed up the tension within the economic sphere of the authority-building programme that Gorbachev has been constructing, and because it gave added impetus to the foreign policy aspects of that programme. The emphasis upon stability and a lowering of tensions in the region and the positive moves designed to improve the tone of relations with the Chinese were a clear affirmation of one of the fundamental principles behind the authority-building programme: the interrelationship between domestic change and the international situation.

NOTES

1. Since 1966 the party rules have declared that the General Secretary is elected by the CC, but in practice this is merely the means whereby the choice made within the Politburo and Secretariat is ratified.

2. For example, see Thane Gustafson and Dawn Mann, "Gorbachev's First Year: Building Power and Authority," *Problems of Communism* 35(May-June 1986); George W. Breslauer, *Khrushchev and Brezhnev as Leaders: Building Authority in Soviet*

Politics (London: George Allen & Unwin, 1982); T. H. Rigby and Ferenc Feher, eds., *Political Legitimation in Communist States* (London: Macmillan, 1982); T. H. Rigby, "A Conceptual Approach to Authority, Power and Policy in the Soviet Union," in T. H. Rigby, Archie Brown and Peter Reddaway, eds., *Authority, Power and Policy in the USSR: Essays dedicated to Leonard Schapiro* (London: Macmillan, 1979).

3. L. Zaikov, E. Ligachev, N. Ryzhkov, V. Chebrikov and E. Shevardnadze. Chebrikov and Shevardnadze had been candidate members at the time of Gorbachev's election, while Ligachev and Ryzhkov had been CC Secretaries. Four full members of the Politburo which chose Gorbachev had disappeared two years later: G. Romanov, N. Tikhonov, V. Grishin and D. Kunaev. Of course, K. Chernenko had also died. For one discussion, see Ronald J. Hill and Peter Frank, "Gorbachev's Cabinet-Building," *Journal of Communist Studies* 2(June 1986).

4. B. El'tsin, N. Slyun'kov, S. Sokolov, Y. Soloviev, N. Talyzin and A. Yakovlev. Of the six candidates at March 1985, V. Chebrikov and E. Shevardnadze were promoted to full membership while V. Kuznetsov and B. Ponomarev were dropped. Only V. Dolgikh and P. Demichev remain.

5. L. Zaikov, A. Biryukova, A. Dobrynin, V. Medvedev, V. Nikonov, G. Razumovsky, A. Yakovlev, N. Slyun'kov and A. Lukyanov. Of the ten secretaries in March 1985, E. Ligachev and N. Ryzhkov were promoted while I. Kapitonov, K. Rusakov, M. Zimyanin, G. Romanov and B. Ponomarev were dropped and K. Chernenko died. Only Gorbachev, E. Ligachev and V. Dolgikh remain CC Secretaries.

6. In 1981, new members only accounted for 25.7 percent of full members. The rates of re-election of full members of the CC at post-Stalin congresses are as follows: 1956, 62 percent; 1961, 49 percent; 1966, 80 percent; 1971, 80 percent; 1976, 89 percent; and 1981, 87 percent. Gustafson and Mann, "Gorbachev's First Year," p. 4.

7. Georgia (Shevardnadze by D. Patiashvili, July 1985), Kirgizia (T. Usubaliev by A. Masaliev, November 1985), Tajikistan (R. Nabiev by K. Makhkamov, December 1985), Turkmenistan (M. Gapurov by S. Niyazov, December 1985), Kazakhstan D. (Kunaev by G. Kolbin, December 1986) and Byelorussia (N. Slyun'kov by E. Sokolov, February 1987).

8. In the first ten months of Gorbachev's tenure alone, some 30 percent of oblast first secretaries were replaced. *Radio Liberty Research Bulletin* 39/86(22 January 1986).

9. Some 40 percent of ministers and chairmen were replaced in the first ten months of Gorbachev's tenure. *Radio Liberty Research Bulletin* 39/86(22 January 1986).

10. For a discussion of these circumstances, see Graeme Gill, "The Future of the General Secretary," *Political Studies* 34(June 1986).

11. See the discussion in Gustafson and Mann, "Gorbachev's First Year," pp. 7-8..

12. T. H. Rigby, "The Soviet Regional Leadership: the Brezhnev Generation," *Slavic Review* 37(March 1978), p. 23.

13. This is not meant to suggest that from the outset Gorbachev had a clearly-defined programme of changes which he wished to implement. However, the party Programme adopted at the 27th Congress in February-March 1986 is interesting in this regard; *Pravda*, 7 March 1986. Also see the legislative programme foreshadowed in

September 1986;*Vedomosti Verkhovnogo Soveta Soiuza Sovetskikh Sotsialisticheskikh Respublik* No. 37(10 September 1986), pp. 729-736.

14. *Pravda*, 7 March 1986.

15. *Pravda*, 19 December 1986. In his address to the 27th Congress, Gorbachev referred to the problems emerging in the recent past and declared: "The situation called for change, but a peculiar psychology - how to improve things without changing anything - took the upper hand ...."; *Pravda*, 26 February 1986.

16. There have also been suggestions that the real source of the problems lies in the Stalin era. For example, see Gorbachev's speech at the January 1987 CC plenum; *Pravda*, 28 January 1987.

17. *Pravda*, 26 February 1986. This was Gorbachev's address to the 27th Congress.

18. Although the pressures for decentralisation that this has involved have not been unalloyed by obverse pressures for centralisation. For example, see footnote 19.

19. Although the establishment of so-called "super-ministries" through the consolidation of a number of different individual ministries is an important development which appears to strengthen the ministerial role in these areas of the economy. Gosagroprom is one of these.

20. For example, see Gorbachev's speech to the June 1986 CC plenum; *Pravda*, 17 June 1986.

21. Although there has been little real movement in this direction, it was foreshadowed in Gorbachev's speech to the 27th Congress; *Pravda*, 26 February 1986. Also, in November 1986, deputy head of the USA and Canada Institute, Georgii Skorov, declared that the aim was to make prices reflect production costs and consumption value; *Radio Liberty Research Bulletin* 427/86(7 November 1986).

22. *Pravda*, 4 August 1985.

23. This follows the success of the Shchekino experiment, which began in 1967, and the more recent experience of the Byelorussian railway. On the latter, see *Radio Liberty Research Bulletin* 318/86(20 August 1986).

24. The Politburo adopted a decision on the restructuring of wages and bonuses in August 1986; *Pravda*, 29 August 1986.

25. For Politburo attention to private food production, see *Pravda*, 7 May 1985.

26. Gorbachev's speech to the 27th Congress; *Pravda*, 26 February 1986. This could have significant effects on prices in the kolkhoz market.

27. *Pravda*, 1 November 1986. It was due to come into effect on 1 May 1987. For the Politburo's discussion of the role of cooperatives in the provision of consumer goods, services and catering, see *Pravda*, 6 February 1987.

28. "Complex Programme for the Development of Consumer Goods Production and Services in the Period 1986-2000," *Pravda*, 9 October 1985.

29. Walter D. Connor, "Social Policy Under Gorbachev," *Problems of Communism* 35(July-August 1986), p. 32. The effects of the privatisation measures in this sphere of the economy may necessitate qualification of this judgment.

30. For one study, see Elizabeth Teague, "Labor Discipline and Legislation in the USSR: 1979-85," *Radio Liberty Research Bulletin Supplement* 2/85 (16 October 1985).

31. See "On Measures to Overcome Drunkenness and Alcoholism," *Pravda*, 17 May 1985. These measures have since been modified.

32. For example, the Politburo meeting on 29 March 1986 approved a strengthening of the struggle against unearned incomes; *Pravda*, 29 March 1986.

33. See the letter in *Pravda*, 13 February 1986. Also see the article by Prosecutor General A. Rekunkov in *Pravda*, 18 January 1986.

34. The party Programme refers to the party "acting within the framework of the Constitution ...."; *Pravda*, 7 March 1986. Also *Pravda* , 18 January 1986.

35. See the CC resolution in *Pravda*, 30 November 1986; and Gorbachev's speech to the January 1987 CC plenum in *Pravda*, 28 January 1987.

36. *Pravda*, 8 January 1987.

37. *Pravda*, 28 January 1987.

38. See the reports of Komsomol elections in Noyabrsk and Alma Ata, in both of which three candidates participated; *Radio Liberty Research Bulletin* 476/86 (19 December 1986) and 28/87 (16 January 1987). The rejection of official candidates in the elections to leadership positions in the writers' and film workers' unions are also relevant here. The first contested election resolved by secret ballot in the party occurred in February 1987 in Imzhorsky district committee, Kemerovo oblast; *Radio Liberty Research Bulletin* 64/87 (13 February 1987).

39. See the comments of *Guardian* correspondent Martin Walker, "Paper Chase in Moscow," *Guardian Weekly* , 4 January 1987.

40. *Radio Liberty Research Bulletin* 36/87(23 January 1987).

41. Even if the conditions under which these can be set up are unlikely to be very attractive to potential Western investors.

42. For a similar argument applied to the Brezhnev period, see Valerie Bunce, "The Political Economy of the Brezhnev Era: The Rise and Fall of Corporatism," *British Journal of Political Science* 13(April 1983).

43. For example, an editorial in the party newspaper berated the persistence of apathy, bureaucratism and inertia among officials and the population, the continued existence of "parasitic attitudes" and those who paid lip service to change but really opposed it; *Pravda*, 12 April 1986. At the June 1986 CC plenum, Gorbachev criticised those who clung to old ways and prevented the introduction of change; *Pravda*, 17 June 1986.

44. Later in the year Gosplan came under criticism for paying insufficient attention to the development needs of the Far East; *Radio Liberty Research Bulletin* 449/86(1 December 1986).

45. The withdrawal of some Soviet forces did take place at the end of that year.

46. The beginning of a withdrawal was announced in April; *Pravda*, 11 April 1987.

4

Gorbachev's China Diplomacy

Gary Klintworth

The state of Sino-Soviet relations has been and remains one of the most important influences on world politics. Sino-Soviet relations impact directly on regional peace and stability in the Korean peninsula, Japan, and Indochina. The Sino-Soviet alliance and the subsequent Sino-Soviet split had profound consequences for the balance of power between the US and the USSR. Clashes on the Sino-Soviet border in 1969 led to US-China *rapprochement* in 1972, a development that Richard Nixon called one of the most significant geopolitical events since the Second World War.[1]

By the early 1980s another equally significant trend began to unfold as China reassessed its strategic outlook and abandoned an anti-Soviet united front policy.[2] This fundamental shift in Chinese foreign policy, prompted in part by Ronald Reagan's presidency, was endorsed at the 12th Congress of the CCP in September 1982. Defining it as China's independent foreign policy, the then Party Secretary General, Hu Yaobang said that China "would never attach itself to any big power or group of powers, and would never yield to pressure from any big power."[3] China had prepared the ground for the process of Sino-Soviet *rapprochement* while preserving a Washington connection. After the Li Peng-Gorbachev exchanges at Konstantin Chernenko's funeral in Moscow in March 1985, Sino-Soviet relations approached their "best atmosphere" ever, according to Foreign Minister Wu Xueqian,[4] a view endorsed by Soviet Foreign Minister Eduard Shevardnadze who announced that "the period of tense Soviet relations with China was now over."[5]

Brezhnev, Andropov, Chernenko

It was against this backdrop that Gorbachev made his remarkable Vladivostok speech of 28 July 1986. He had been preceded by Leonid Brezhnev's Tashkent speech of March 1982. Brezhnev said that the USSR recognised China as a socialist state; that the USSR was opposed to the two Chinas approach (of the US); that the USSR would never threaten China; and that it was willing to discuss the border issue.[6] But, he said, while Moscow was prepared to come to terms with China, it would certainly not do so to the detriment of third countries.[7] Brezhnev made a similar speech at Baku in September 1982. Statements by Yuri Andropov in November 1982,[8] by Chernenko in February 1984,[9] and by Gorbachev himself at the 27th CPSU Congress in February 1986 restated Soviet interest in normalisation with China but repeated that the Soviet Union would not disadvantage third countries.[10] Meanwhile, during the last year or so of Brezhnev's life, and throughout the Andropov-Chernenko interregnum up until the present, a transformation of the bilateral Sino-Soviet relationship across a very broad spectrum took place.

FBIS transcriptions of Chinese and Soviet press reporting since 1980 show a decline in mutual propaganda attacks and a progressive expansion of friendly exchanges on literature, health, education, student exchanges, banking, aviation, wrestling, officials' talks, trade, cross-border trade, science, technology, tourism, historic anniversaries, and nostalgia for the good old days of Sino-Soviet friendship. China also actively explored economic and political relationships with the East European countries (apart from Albania). In October 1982 China began normalisation talks that have since been held twice yearly despite earlier Chinese insistence that talks could not be resumed whilst Soviet forces occupied Afghanistan.[11] For the ninth round last October, Moscow appointed a new negotiator, Deputy Foreign Minister Igor Rogachev, who conceded that the Soviet Union was ready to discuss Kampuchea and Afghanistan in the context of Sino-Soviet normalisation talks. This was the first time that the USSR had publicly said that it was willing to discuss third-country issues with China.[12]

The Arkhipov-Yao Yilin Exchanges

One of the most important milestones in the post-1980 Sino-Soviet *rapprochement* process was the Ivan Arkhipov visit to Beijing in December 1984. First Deputy Premier Arkhipov was the most senior Soviet leader to visit China in fifteen years and he went despite Soviet reservations about

China's Vietnam policy at that particular time. Arkhipov was the chief adviser to the Soviet aid programme in China in the 1950s, when he befriended several of China's current elder statesmen (though not, apparently, Deng Xiaoping). He is regarded as a comrade and old friend of the Chinese people,[13] an indication that China has not forgotten the experience that it shared with the USSR in the 1950s.

The Arkhipov-Yao Yilin meetings in December 1984 and March 1986 in Beijing, and in July 1985 in Moscow, created the basic institutional framework for a resumption of long-term Sino-Soviet scientific, economic and technical cooperation. Agreements were also reached on possible Soviet nuclear power technology assistance,[14] on Soviet modernisation of 17 industrial plants in China's northeast that were built with Soviet aid in the 1950s; and the construction of another seven completely new complexes.[15] Arkhipov and Yao Yilin also agreed to expand trade over the period 1986-1990 in accordance with the Five Year Plan requirements of their two countries, thus allowing long-term synchronisation of economic plans. Trade, already growing rapidly and worth US $2 billion in 1985, is to rise to US $5-6 billion by 1990.[16] The Soviet Union accounted for 2.5 percent of China's total foreign trade in 1985 and ranked as its sixth largest trade partner. Prospects for continued growth look good.[17]

Other useful indicators of an increasingly practical and routine relationship include agreement to open consulates in Shanghai and Leningrad;[18] a booming regional border trade across sensitive frontier areas in Xinjiang and Heilongjiang;[19] and the construction of a fourth railway line to the USSR through China's far northwest.[20] Sino-Soviet border talks resumed in February 1987 after a nine-year suspension.

GORBACHEV'S VLADIVOSTOK SPEECH

The Soviet vision of the Pacific sketched by Gorbachev in his Vladivostok speech of 28 July 1986 was refreshing and important in several respects apart from China. In relation to China, Gorbachev pointed to the interests shared by both countries: they were neighbours, and Pacific powers; both were socialist states; both had pledged no-first-use of nuclear weapons; and both had similar economic priorities. Gorbachev added that the USSR was prepared to discuss any measure aimed at creating "an atmosphere of goodneighbourliness in a most serious way." We take pleasure, he said, in noting the positive changes that had taken place in Sino-Soviet economic relations.[21]

Most importantly, Gorbachev's speech offered concessions on issues at the very heart of the Sino-Soviet dispute. These were:

a. the official Sino-Soviet border on the Amur River could pass along the main channel (rather than follow the south bank, to China's disadvantage);
b. the Soviet Union was examining the question of withdrawing "a considerable number of Soviet troops from Mongolia" in consultation with the leadership of that country;
c. the Soviet Union would start to withdraw from Afghanistan;
d. the USSR was prepared to discuss with China specific steps aimed at a balanced reduction in the level of land forces on the Sino-Soviet border.

Issues (c) and (d) had been mentioned previously by one Soviet spokesman or another but not by the CPSU Secretary General. Concessions on issues (a) and (b) have never been raised publicly before. On the key obstacle of Vietnam's occupation of Kampuchea, Gorbachev said only that a resolution depended on the normalisation of Sino-Vietnamese relations and that this was the sovereign affair of China and Vietnam.[22]

China's Response

Publicly, the Chinese response was equivocal. Privately they must have been impressed. As Foreign Minister Wu commented, Gorbachev's remarks were "very significant" and China "welcomed them."[23] Deng Xiaoping, however, said on 8 September 1986 in an American television interview that while the Gorbachev speech contained "something new and positive," the Soviet Union "had to take a firm step" towards the removal of the most important obstacle to normalised Sino-Soviet relations, namely Vietnam's occupation of Kampuchea. Deng claimed that Gorbachev had evaded this question altogether but that if he ended Soviet support for Vietnam in Kampuchea then he - Deng - would meet Gorbachev anywhere in the USSR.[24]

Deng's cautious response was predictable. It would not do for China's top leader to appear enthusiastic about the Soviet Union on American prime time television. China cannot afford to jeopardise its access to advanced Western technology or the strategic relationship it has developed with the US, one manifested no better perhaps than in the joint Sino-US facilities in

Xinjiang that monitor Soviet missile tests at Leninsk and Sary-Shagan.[25] On the other hand, China does not wish to upset the momentum it has allowed to build up in the process of Sino-Soviet *rapprochement*. Hence, in a signal to Moscow, Deng balanced his response by referring to the Taiwan issue as *the* obstacle in Sino-US relations. And Taiwan is, in many respects, much more important as an obstacle because it relates to China's internal political affairs.[26]

Nuances, angry words, deceptive manoeuvres and timely retreat are used by clever states to play off rivals against each other. China is no exception.[27] It has been balancing its position between the superpowers since 1981-1982. It has reassured the USSR that it will not enter into an anti-Soviet alliance with the US,[28] while insisting to sundry Japanese and American delegations that there are these three dreadful obstacles to normalised Sino-Soviet relations and that Sino-Soviet relations can never be like they were in the 1950s. In September 1986, Soviet First Deputy Premier Nikolay Talyzin followed up Arkhipov's initiatives in Beijing, while October 1986 saw the US Secretary of Defense Caspar Weinberger hold talks in Beijing and the announcement of a long-awaited US naval ship visit to Qingdao.[29]

Sometimes however there are errors of judgment which appear to favour one superpower over another. Former Secretary General Hu Yaobang, for example, confessed on 9 April 1985, prior to his Australian tour, that he could not remember exactly what the obstacles were to normalised Sino-Soviet relations. Eight days later Deng Xiaoping personally put the matter straight and said there were precisely three obstacles, that they existed and that they were as important as ever.[30]

China is clearly avoiding alignment with one superpower against the other while at the same time using their mutual antagonism as a fulcrum to Chinese advantage. The China-USSR-US triangle has long fascinated strategic analysts in Washington, Moscow and more recently Beijing. China can trace a history in the practice of intrigues amongst warring states going back to the period of that name in 402-221 BC.[31] But it is only in the 1980s that China has been placed to manipulate the middle ground. In the 1950s China was tied to the USSR against the US; in the 1960s it was at odds with both superpowers; and in the 1970s it appeared to be moving towards alliance with the US against the USSR. In the 1980s China moved to improve its relations with the USSR while simultaneously keeping the US at a little distance.

China occupies for the first time what Lowell Dittmer and others[32] have called the pivot position in the triangle. It hopes to consolidate its leverage and extend its advantages through a policy of what might be described as balanced ambiguity. It is against this policy objective that we should measure the likely impact of Gorbachev's China diplomacy.

Gorbachev Tries to Solve "A Bit of the Problem"

What the Soviet Union is seeking, said Soviet First Deputy Prime Minister Nikolay Talyzin, was "a drastic improvement in relations with China."[33] What Gorbachev offered China was something fairly substantial. No previous Soviet leader had been prepared to meet persistent Chinese demands that the USSR take some tangible step on the basic issues blocking normalised Sino-Soviet relations. As Zhou Enlai said in 1975, China wanted the Soviet leadership "to do something to solve a bit of the problem."[34] Zhou had in mind Soviet recognition that there were disputed territorial areas along the Sino-Soviet border; or reductions in the level of Soviet forces on the border; or acknowledgment that the border was the result of unequal treaties. By 1979 Afghanistan and Kampuchea were added to China's list of problems, replacing the ideological dispute that faded with China's post-Mao revisionism.

"Deeds not words were important," reiterated former Secretary General Hu Yaobang at the 12th Party Congress of the CCP in September 1982. Hu said that "if the Soviet authorities really had a sincere desire to improve their relations with China, and *took practical steps*, it would be possible for Sino-Soviet relations to move towards normalisation."[35] Deng Xiaoping subsequently explained that if it was too difficult for the Soviet Union to come to an agreement on all the obstacles then at least it should try settling one.[36]

Until Gorbachev's Vladivostok speech, the Soviet position was clear and inflexible. The USSR would not withdraw forces from disputed border areas - indeed it did not accept that there were any areas along the border in dispute. And Gorbachev had said as recently as February 1986 that the USSR would not negotiate with China on issues involving the interests of third countries.[37]

The USSR had previously also stuck immovably to its view that the boundary with China in the east followed the southern bank of the Amur river, and the west bank of the Ussuri River, as, it claimed, was settled in an 1861 protocol to the 1860 Treaty of Peking. According to Moscow the boundary did not run down the middle of the river on the thalweg principle, a delimitation issue that contributed to the bloody clashes over Zhenbao/Damanski island in the Ussuri River in March 1969. Gorbachev specified the Amur River in his Vladivostok speech but Vice Foreign

Minister Mikhail Kapitsa explained that the Soviet Union was prepared to recognise that the Sino-Soviet border passed along the main channel of the Ussuri River as well. This meant, said Kapitsa, that islands lost by China to Tsarist Russia would now be considered as part of China.[38] The effect of this concession is that Zhenbao/Damanski island and perhaps 600 or so other islands totalling about one thousand square kilometres would become Chinese territory because they lie on the Chinese side of the main channel of the Amur and Ussuri rivers.[39] This would be a most remarkable gesture from a country which hitherto insisted that no border issue existed whatsoever.

Gorbachev's Vladivostok speech therefore suggests a new Soviet flexibility on China and a willingness to move on at least two of the three so-called obstacles, that is:

a. the Sino-Soviet border - a reduction in border troop levels, withdrawal from Mongolia, and acceptance of the middle channel rule for border river delimitations; and
b. the Afghan question.

As Afghanistan and Mongolia were not mentioned directly in connection with China, Gorbachev was able to preserve the fiction of not dealing with China on third country issues. So too with Vietnam. The Soviet Union has said that it will not jeopardise Vietnam's interests as it pursues normalisation of Sino-Soviet relations. Nevertheless, there have been suggestions that Moscow wants Vietnam to withdraw from Kampuchea after a "decent interval."[40]

OBSTACLES, IMPEDIMENTS, IRRITANTS

Both China and the USSR want to normalise their relationship. China however is intent on controlling the speed of its *rapprochement* with the USSR and not leaving the US too far behind. So Deng Xiaoping reverted to a demand for resolution of all three obstacles, in particular an end to Soviet support for Vietnam's occupation of Kampuchea. Even if the Soviet Union were prepared to state publicly that it would like to see Vietnam out of Kampuchea, Deng no doubt would have found some other "obstacle" such as SS-20 missile deployments in the Far East, or perhaps Soviet naval access and overflights in North Korea. Besides, there has yet to be any substantive movement on the obstacles: a Chinese Foreign Ministry spokesman said, for example, that a partial withdrawal from Afghanistan was devoid of practical significance and that the Soviet Union should present a timetable for complete withdrawal.[41]

China's "obstacles" are irritants in the Sino-Soviet relationship but they are not big impediments. They have been overshadowed by the benefits that accrue from growing economic cooperation and trade. In many respects they are useful devices to control and manipulate the process of Sino-Soviet *rapprochement*. They are not strictly obstacles *per se* so much as convenient pegs on which to hang reassurances to the US, Japan, Australia, Pakistan, Thailand and others.

Does it really matter for China if, as Caspar Weinberger claims,[42] the Soviet Union is rotating, not withdrawing, troops from Afghanistan, or that the Soviet Union has invested billions of dollars in Vietnam to hold on to Cam Ranh Bay? Both situations tie down Soviet resources and limit Soviet diplomacy in Asia. Afghanistan has demonstrated the efficacy of guerrilla warfare. It is remote from China's strategic interests. Besides, a *mujaheedin* victory in Afghanistan could destabilise China's own Moslem minorities. China in fact no longer regards Afghanistan with the same degree of apprehension about Soviet encirclement as it did in 1979. It forgot to register any condemnation on the anniversary of the Soviet invasion of Afghanistan in December 1984, partly because of the Arkhipov visit and partly because Afghanistan now matters less in Beijing. It wants a Soviet withdrawal from Afghanistan at "an early date," a rather ambiguous formulation.[43]

Meanwhile, Vietnam's occupation of Kampuchea has also given China certain distinct benefits. China has been able to consolidate a new relationship with the ASEAN states and a defence relationship with Thailand. Vietnam has been effectively isolated from the economic and political mainstream of the Asian-Pacific region. Cam Rahn Bay is not a vital security issue for China; it is now seen in Beijing as a symbol of Soviet rivalry with the US in the Pacific and Indian Oceans rather than as part of a Soviet attempt at encirclement of China.

In other words neither Kampuchea nor Afghanistan is as important to China's security interests as the Sino-Soviet border. It is the Sino-Soviet border that occupies Beijing's strategic planners and absorbs most of China's defence effort. In relative terms, Vietnam's occupation of Kampuchea and the war in Afghanistan are sideshows.

The Mongolian Connection

Gorbachev made his most tantalizing remarks on mutual balanced force reductions on the Sino-Soviet border. Of particular interest were Gorbachev's remarks about Mongolia. Control of Mongolia has for many centuries been the key to influence in central Asia. Genghis Khan conquered Peking in 1215 and reached the Crimea by 1223. Russian and Chinese rivalry over the Mongolian region in subsequent centuries was followed by the entry of Japan which regarded control of Mongolia as "a matter of life and death" in the 1920s and 1930s.[44]

Mongolia, once part of the Chinese empire until 1911, fears China more than the USSR. It does not want to be reunified and has thus become dependent on Russian support.[45] Mongolia reacted sharply to Brezhnev's September 1982 Tashkent speech because it suggested how serious the Soviet Union was about *rapprochement* with China. In tactics reminiscent of those used by Vietnam in 1977-1978, Mongolia expelled some 2,500 Chinese in April 1983, probably with the intention of increasing border tension with China and preempting Soviet troop withdrawals.[46] But Soviet pressure on Mongolia and a calm Chinese response helped to defuse the situation. In August 1984 Y. Tsedenbal, Mongolia's leader for 44 years, was replaced "because of his health." His successor Jambyn Batmonh seemed much more flexible on the China question.[47] By July 1986 at Vladivostok, Gorbachev was able to announce that the USSR would, in consultation with Mongolia's leaders, withdraw "considerable numbers" of the 65,000 Soviet troops estimated to be stationed in Mongolia.[48] This offer has not been given the attention it deserves. In terms of signals it respresents an unprecedented shift in the Soviet position, and shows just how earnest the Russians are about *rapprochement* with China. It must have had considerable impact in Beijing and undoubtedly would have been noted in Hanoi.

China's Rationale for Rapprochement

China's priority is economic modernisation. For that it requires a peaceful environment and an easing of its defence expenditure burden. Consolidation of the present stability and low levels of tension on the Sino-Soviet border are mandatory. China has already been able to cut the size of the PLA by 25 percent because, as Deng said in 1985, the danger of war had receded.[49] Defence was important but there was no pressing need for its modernisation. China is confident that its existing conventional and nuclear capabilities are sufficient to deter the USSR in present circumstances.[50] In any event China does not feel particularly threatened by the Soviet Union. There have after all been only one or two very minor incidents on the Sino-Soviet border over the last decade. China now perceives the bulk of Soviet strategic and naval forces as being directed primarily against the US and Japan rather than solely at China.

China's interest in *rapprochement* with the USSR is mainly economic. Both economies face similar development problems. As the *China Daily* remarked, both are "suffering from the same diseases" and it would be useful for the two countries to study the detail of how each is dealing with economic reform.[51] Links with the Soviet Union and East Europe broaden China's trade horizons and make it less dependent on the West. There are the advantages of counter trade between socialist states sharing a common border - it is more sensible for China to swap surplus textiles for Volgas than to pay yen for Toyotas - and the suitability of much of Soviet and East European technology for China's needs. China's foreign exchange shortages, sluggish Western markets for textiles and footwear and large trade deficits with Japan and the US provide additional incentives. Moreover, the Chinese and Soviet economies are complementary in several areas. China can use Soviet power generation expertise, cars, trucks, aircraft, timber, ferrous and non-ferrous metals, energy, cement and fertilizers. China can provide the Soviet bloc with a range of consumer goods, shoes, textiles, knitwear, vacuum bottles, and foodstuffs such as frozen pork, soybeans and fresh fruit.[52] As well as trade, the Soviet Union offers China's inland provinces unique opportunities for economic exchange and cooperation presently enjoyed by China's coastal provinces in trade and special economic zones involving the West. There is also scope for joint cooperation on energy and water conservation projects on the Amur and Ussuri rivers. And Chinese economists believe China's industrial northeast could ease its 20 percent power shortfall by closer integration with Siberian energy sources and joint cooperation on border river hydroelectric projects.[53] The Soviet timber industry is another sector that could use China's willingness to provide contract labour services, a possibility examined in the 1950s and broached in June 1985.[54] Surplus Chinese labour could help meet Soviet manpower shortages in other Siberian projects. The Soviet Union furthermore has technical and scientific expertise that China wants to tap, particularly in the area of power generation and distribution. Other areas discussed include mining, the aviation industry, and water resource management, space exploration and gas processing. According to a protocol signed on 16 October 1986, China and the USSR will commence cooperation in areas including agriculture, fisheries, meteorology, non-ferrous metals, petrochemicals, machine manufacturing, oil and natural gas and railways.[55] The Soviet Union is also well placed to expand its programme of helping to modernise China's industrial infrastructure: renovation is cheaper and in many instances may be more appropriate than turnkey plant replacement. Much of China's iron and steel output for instance comes from Baotou, Anshan and Wuhan, just a few of the many industrial complexes built by the USSR in the 1950s.

The mutual economic interests of China and the USSR were reflected in the Arkhipov-Yao Yilin agreements. The Talyzin visit to Beijing took place in September 1986. Nikolay Talyzin, Soviet Minister for State Planning, was accompanied by representatives from the Soviet State Committee for Foreign Economic Relations; the Ministries for Timber, Pulp, Paper and Woodworking Industry; Power; Foreign Trade; Foreign Affairs; Machine-building and the State Committee of the USSR for Science and Technology.[56] They met Vice Premier Yao Yilin, the Minister in charge of the Chinese State Planning Commission; and senior officials from the Chinese Foreign Ministry; the State Science and Technology Commission; the Ministry of Foreign Economic Relations; Trade; the Ministry of Water Resources and Electric Power; and the Ministry of Forestry.[57] Talyzin said that the USSR wanted to make use of new possibilities on a broader scale of economic cooperation, joint exploration of natural resources, and a more active exchange of achievements in science and technology including the latest developments in space probes.[58]

Paradoxically, China's positive attitude towards *rapprochement* with the USSR also stems in part from ideological considerations. For all the rancour of the 1960s, China sees less risk of spiritual contamination from the socialist USSR than the capitalist West. Several in the Chinese leadership disapprove of China's excessive fascination with Western materialistic values.[59] China and the USSR after all have a common Marxist-Leninist heritage, manifested by China's explicit rejection of Western values and its attacks on bourgeois liberalism. As Li Peng said recently, China wanted the West's technology but not its lifestyle or ideology. Li is a proponent of closer relations with Moscow and represents the Soviet-trained generation in the Chinese leadership hierarchy.[60]

Any pressure on Vietnam as a consequence of improving Sino-Soviet relations seems to be an effect of, rather than a cause behind the improvement.

China is able to contemplate *rapprochement* with the USSR because it has established new ground rules for the conduct of the relationship. The USSR must deal with a China that has established a sound relationship with the US; has a credible nuclear deterrent capability; has become a great socialist power with enormous potential; and has mapped out an independent role in the Asian-Pacific region that the USSR can accept.

Finally, as already discussed, there is the strategic objective of preserving China's pivot position in the triangular US-China-USSR relationship.

Soviet Interests

The significance of the timing of Gorbachev's Vladivostok speech; what it says for Gorbachev's political clout, for Soviet security objectives in the Far East, and for Soviet domestic economic priorities; the message it contains for different Pacific states and the strategic challenges, if any, that are posed to Japan and the US: these are complex issues that have been ably discussed elsewhere.[61]

For the Soviet Union, *rapprochement* with China has been driven by security and economic interests. With China's retreat from an anti-Soviet alignment with the West, the USSR has been able to improve its security in the Soviet Far East. The renewal of an economic relationship with China complements this development and fits in well with Gorbachev's vision of greater Soviet invlvement in the Pacific Basin economy.

PROSPECTS

China and the USSR are well on the way towards a normalised relationship. For all intents and purposes it is normalised already. Each now regards the other as another great power to be reckoned with in the triangular relationship with the US. The Soviet Union, indeed, seems to be reassessing its view of the world socialist community with particular significance for China. *Pravda* recently admitted that it had made errors of "subjectivism and voluntarism" in its handling of relations with Albania (once China's closest ally) in the 1960s, and that the CPSU now respects the independence of other communist parties and the equality of socialist states.[62] The USSR in short no longer views China as a junior partner or as a renegade from the socialist system. China for its part feels unthreatened by the USSR. Both anticipate increased economic cooperation.

Normalisation of party-to-party relations in due course is indicated by the visits to Beijing of East Germany's Erich Honecker, Poland's Wojciech Jaruzelski, and Bulgaria's Todor Zhivkov. Zhao Ziyang made the first high level visit by a Chinese leader to Eastern Europe in June 1987. It does not follow however that the Sino-Soviet relationship will become an intimate one. Both China and the USSR look upon each other as socialist states. They have differences, for example over Vietnam, and they have shared perspectives, for example on weapons in space; the Middle East; Japanese militarism; Central America; Libya; no-first-use of nuclear weapons and other arms control issues; and bourgeois values. They have been almost at war and they have an unmatched record of close cooperation in the 1950s, a period during which, as Chen Yun recently said, they worked *"swimmingly together,"* "something the Chinese Government and people have not forgotten and will never forget."[63] The argument that Sino-Soviet hostility is based on racial, historical, strategic and cultural differences that are too deep for meaningful *rapprochement* is not at all convincing.[64] It is the same simplistic judgment as that made about the Sino-Soviet monolith in the 1950s.

Both China and the USSR are neighbouring great powers and for the moment their economic priorities coincide. Soviet consciousness that it is an incomplete superpower,[65] and that its economy stands in need of respite should add to the Soviet commitment to ease tension with China as far as possible. China has a reciprocal interest.

There are limitations on how far Sino-Soviet *rapprochement* can go or will be allowed to go, just as there are constraints on China's relationship with the United States. China will never duplicate the abnormal alliance relationship it had with the USSR in the 1950s. There is no need - China now has substantial bridges to the rest of the world. But nor will China conspire with other states against the USSR. And in that situation there is still leeway for considerable improvement in the Sino-Soviet relationship.

What are the implications of Gorbachev's Vladivostok speech? This depends on how significant the speech is judged to be, whether more mere Soviet propaganda; or a milestone in Soviet economic and foreign policies. There is also a range of variables that could affect any long-term assessment: China may misplay its moves in trying to preserve a position of balanced ambiguity between the superpowers. Rising Japanese defence expenditure and the Kuranari doctrine could drive Soviet and Chinese interests closer together. The USSR might fumble over North Korea or strive to develop a position in Kampuchea. The US could harden its policy on Taiwan in favour of China. Leaving these aside for the moment, on present trends, Gorbachev's Vladivostok speech, together with Soviet security and economic requirements and China's economic priorities, lead ineluctably to the conclusion that the prospects for much improved Sino-Soviet relations seem to be fairly good.

The message for small states (and even larger ones like India) that have depended on Sino-Soviet rivalry for their sustenance must be increasingly apparent. Mongolia has been the first small state exposed to the vicissitudes of higher Sino-Soviet priorities. North Korea may realise that the Soviets will not go beyond a few squadrons of MiG-23s. Although Kim Il Sung might offer the use of Nampo to the Soviet Pacific Fleet, Gorbachev's Vladivostok speech signals a Soviet interest in not adding another obstacle to improved Sino-Soviet relations.[66] Gorbachev could, of course, aim to get a little from both as he could in Soviet relations with China and Vietnam.

The implications of the Sino-Soviet *rapprochement* process could have profound consequences for Vietnam's occupation of Kampuchea. Vietnam is entering a leadership transition phase. Its options were already limited before 28 July 1986 - the anti-Vietnamese coalition was recovering from earlier setbacks to become a relatively viable guerrilla force. Vietnam's economy is debilitated and it is dependent on the USSR. Diplomatically it is quite isolated. China, for a small outlay on the Sino-Vietnamese border, is reaping all the benefits from being in the mainstream of developments in the Asian-Pacific region. The Soviet economy moreover is such that it can ill-afford the cost of supporting Third World countries for uncertain gains.[67] Vietnam provides useful naval and air base facilities at Cam Ranh Bay and Danang,[68] so that although the USSR may be dissatisfied with the cost of the Kampuchean war, it may consider the strategic returns well worthwhile. Deng Xiaoping however has suggested that China could live with the Soviet facilities in Vietnam.[69] Vietnam therefore will need to work quickly so as not to be outflanked. It has reaffirmed its decision to withdraw from Kampuchea by 1990 and to seek its own process of normalisation with China.

Sino-Soviet relations have always affected the security perceptions of the US and Japan. Both have acknowledged that improved Sino-Soviet relations can ease tension on the Korean peninsula, in Kampuchea and in the Western Pacific generally,[70] even though the Sino-Soviet consensus may not always be to their liking. For example, Chinese agreement with the USSR on a South Pacific Nuclear Free Zone and acceptance of the Soviet Union's legitimate fishing activities in the South Pacific[71] contrasts with Japan's Kuranari doctrine and US suspicions of Soviet intentions.

Both Japan and the US would be concerned that one of the consequences of reduced tension on the Sino-Soviet border would be to free Soviet resources for redeployment further east towards Japan or west towards Europe. This would complicate US and Japanese security planning. While the likelihood of such a consequence is remote, the perception of its possibility will subtly influence the security outlook of the US and Japan towards Northeast Asia and the global balance. Indeed, a few hours after the text of Gorbachev's speech was received in Tokyo, Japanese defence officials advised Prime Minister Yasuhiro Nakasone that Sino-Soviet *rapprochement* would require Japan to accelerate its own military build-up.[72] China is sensitive to these fears and wishes to preserve a balance of world power and its access to Western technology. Hence the importance of China's continued ability to juggle its relationship between the superpowers.

CONCLUSIONS

The long held view that the Soviet Union lacks finesse and flexibility in the practice of diplomacy and prefers to intimidate may be in need of a review as far as China is concerned. The obstacles in Sino-Soviet relations should not disguise the broad long-term trend in Sino-Soviet relations. To quote Chinese Vice Premier Yao Yilin in his welcoming speech for Soviet First Vice Premier Nikolay Talyzin: "China and the USSR are neighbours. Now it is the 1980s and neither of us can return to the past. Our two countries have reason to become and should become neighbours living in good neighbourliness."[73] For China the USSR is no longer the most dangerous superpower intent on encircling China as it was perceived in the late 1970s. In China's view the expansionary zenith of the USSR has passed. China sees the USSR as "essentially passive" and more cautious whereas the US "had gone on the offensive."[74] The USSR is now regarded as a neighbouring socialist empire which has much in common with China and much to offer China's modernisation. There are threat perceptions and problems as there are between all big neighbouring states; but the last few years have seen the two countries create the framework for the management of a new working relationship. China may not trust Gorbachev. That would be expecting too much and China has yet to see Gorbachev carry out any concrete deeds in Mongolia or Afghanistan, or on the Sino-Soviet border. But unquestionably, Gorbachev is the most positive and forthcoming Soviet leader China has had to deal with since the days of Stalin. The results could presage one of the most important new strategic developments in the Western Pacific region for the remainder of this century.

In summary, the USSR feels somewhat more secure in Northeast Asia in not having to face a combined Beijing-Tokyo-Washington axis. Second, the US has been unable to enmesh China into an anti-Soviet strategy.

Third, both superpowers have in consequence made Japan the subject of increased strategic attention, thus contributing to the momentum that is making Japan the main new factor in East Asian politics. Fourth, and perhaps most importantly, China has reached a stage secure from external threat for the first time in more than a century. It feels confident that it is a rising power in East Asia.[75] This reality of China as an ascending power has been acknowledged already by Thailand. Vietnam is struggling with the concept, but changes at its sixth party congress suggest that it too will accept the need to accommodate Chinese interests in the region.

NOTES

1. Richard Nixon, *Real Peace* (London: Sidgwick & Jackson, 1983), p. 72.

2. Revealed in a frank article by Edmund Lee (A PRC writer), "Beijing's Balancing Act," *Foreign Policy* No. 51 (Summer 1983), p. 27.

3. *The 12th National Congress of the CCP (Documents)* (Beijing: Foreign Languages Press , 1982), p. 55.

4. *Kyodo* (Beijing), 28 March 1985.

5. *Tass* (Ulaan Baator), 24 January 1986.

6. Pi Ying-hsien, "The Normalisation of Peiping-Moscow Relations, Pace & Prospects" *Issues & Studies* (June 1983), p. 84.

7. Donald Zagoria, "The Moscow-Beijing Detente," *Foreign Affairs* 61 (Spring 1983), p. 857.

8. China Daily Report, *Foreign Broadcasting Information Service (FBIS),* 23 November 1982, p. C2.

9. Soviet Union Daily Report, *FBIS,* 21 February 1984, p. B1.

10. China Daily Report, *FBIS,* 29 August 1983, p. Cl; *Christian Science Monitor,* 13 March 1984, p. 11.

11. Pi, "Normalisation of Peiping-Moscow Relations", pp. 87-88.

12. *South China Morning Post,* 17 October 1986, although *Far Eastern Economic Review (FEER)* of 31 March 1983 cites Chinese Foreign Minister Wu Xueqian as saying then that the Kampuchean question was discussed in Sino-Soviet talks.

13. *Xinhua,* 21 December 1984.

14. *AFP* (Beijing), 26 March 1986.

15. *Tass* (Beijing), 10 July 1986.

16. *Xinhua,* 10 July 1986. China's trade with Japan in 1985 by comparison was worth $21.5 bn, and with the US $7.5 bn.

17. *JETRO China Newsletter*, No. 60 (January-February 1986); China Soviet Trade, pp. 16-17.

18. *The Australian*, 7 July 1986.

19. China Daily Report, *FBIS*, 2 September 1986, p. C4.

20. Soviet Union Daily Report, *FBIS*, 29 July 1986, p. R14.

21. *Ibid.*

22. *Ibid.*, pp. R14, R17, R18.

23. *Mainichi Daily News*, 15 August 1986, p. 1.

24. China Daily Report, *FBIS*, 8 September 1986, pp. B1-B2.

25. China Daily Report, *FBIS*, 1 November 1983, Annex, p. 4, quoting Sankei Shimbun; and "US, China sharing missile spy station," *The Canberra Times*, 19 January 1981.

26. Denis Warner, *Pacific Defence Reporter* (September 1986), p. 31.

27. Lucian Pye and Nathan Leites, "Nuances in Chinese Political Culture," *Asian Survey* 22 (December 1982).

28. *AFP* (Beijing), 10 October 1984.

29. *The Canberra Times*, 7 October 1986; *Asiaweek*, 12 October 1986, p. 28.

30. *AFP* (Beijing), 20 April 1985. This may have been one of the mistakes that eventually contributed to Hu's replacement as Party Secretary General.

31. J. I. Crump, *Intrigues: Studies of the Chan-Kuo ts'e* (San Francisco: Chinese Materials Center, 1979).

32. Lowell Dittmer, "The Strategic Triangle: An Elementary Game-Theoretical Analysis," *World Politics* 33 (July 1981), p. 485; Carol Hamrin, "China Reassesses the Superpowers," *Pacific Affairs* 56 (Summer 1983), p. 209; Robert S. Ross, "International Bargaining and Domestic Politics: US-China Relations since 1972," *World Politics* 38 (January 1986), p. 267.

33. Reported in *South China Morning Post*, 22 September 1986.

34. *Report on the Work of the Government 4th NPC (Documents)*, (Peking: FLP, 1975), p. 62.

35. *12th National Congress of the CCP*, p. 58; emphasis added.

36. *Kyodo* (Tokyo), 1 August 1985; William E. Griffith, "Sino-Soviet Relations and the Asian Quadrangle 1984," *Issues & Studies* (January 1985), p. 115.

37. Mikhail Gorbachev, "Political Report of the CPSU Central Committee to the 27th Congress of the CPSU," Soviet Union Daily Report, *FBIS*, 26 February 1986, p. 033.

38. "Soviets concede border issue," *South China Morning Post*, 1 August 1986.

39. Tai Sung An, *The Sino-Soviet Territorial Dispute* (Philadelphia: Westminster Press, 1973), pp. 115-116.

40. To use Frank Snepp's title *Decent Interval* (New York: Random House, 1977). On Soviet pressure on Vietnam see *Asiaweek*, 14 December 1986, p. 41 and *The Bangkok Post*, 23 December 1986, p. 4.

41. *South China Morning Post*, 17 October 1986 and 4 November 1986.

42. *The Canberra Times*, 10 October 1986.

43. China Daily Report, *FBIS*, 9 September 1986, p. C2.

44. Morinosuke Kajima, *The Emergence of Japan as a World Power in 1895-1925* (Tokyo: Tuttle, 1968), p. 385.

45. Griffith, "Sino-Soviet Relations," p. 119.

46. W. R. Heaton, "Mongolia in 1983," *Asian Survey* 24 (January 1984); and "Mongolia in 1985," *Asian Survey* 26 (January 1986).

47. Alan J. K. Sanders, "Mongolia in 1984," *Asian Survey* 25 (January 1985), p. 122; *The Australian*, 7 August 1986.

48. *The Military Balance 1986-1987* (London: International Institute for Strategic Studies, 1986), p. 46.

49. China Daily Report, *FBIS*, 17 June 1985, p. K6.

50. Monte R. Bullard, *China's Political-Military Evolution: The Party and Military in the PRC 1960-1984* (Boulder: Westview, 1985), p. 21.

51. Quoted in *South China Morning Post*, 4 November 1986, p. 8.

52. David Bonavia, *FEER*, 21 August 1986, pp. 38-39; *Xinhua*, 10 July 1986; Soviet Union Daily Report, *FBIS*, 3 September 1986, p. B5; China Daily Report, *FBIS*, 6 March 1987, p. C1.

53. Louise do Rosario, *FEER*, 4 September 1986, pp. 72-73, and 1 January 1987, p. 46.

54. Soviet Union Daily Report, *FBIS*, 12 June 1985, p. B1; and Allen Whiting, *Siberian Development and East Asia, Threat or Promise* (Stanford: Stanford University Press, 1981).

55. China Daily Report, *FBIS*, 17 October 1986, p. C2.

56. *Ibid.*, 10 September 1986, p. C2.

57. *Ibid.*

58. Soviet Union Daily Report, *FBIS*, 9 September 1986, p. B2.

59. *Asiaweek*, 13 April 1986, p. 35.

60. *Asiaweek*, 1 March 1987 p. 11; *Asian Wall Street Journal*, 5 February 1987, p. 4.

61. For a useful analysis of the Soviet position see Richard Nations, "Moscow's New Tack," *FEER*, 14 August 1986, p. 30.

62. In *Ta Kung Pao* (Hong Kong), 4 December 1986, p. 12.

63. *Xinhua*, 24 December 1984; emphasis added.

64. The following is representative: "The Sino-Soviet conflict is not only genuine but rooted deeply in geographic political and cultural bedrock. This conflict is likely to become more intense . . . the ground is . . . barren." Paul H. Borsuk, "Soviet Foreign and Security Problems and Policies," in H. J. Ellison, ed., *The Sino-Soviet Conflict, a Global Perspective* (Seattle: University of Washington Press), 1982, p. 89.

65. Paul Dibb, *The Soviet Union: The Incomplete Superpower* (London: Macmillan, 1986). The suggestion that Gorbachev's Vladivostok speech represents an attempt to rise above Brezhnev's legacy of an over-extended empire is made by Richard Nations, "Moscow's New Tack," *FEER*, 14 August 1986, p. 30.

66. For a discussion see Gary Klintworth, "Kim Il Sung's North Korea: At the Crossroads," (Canberra: Australian National University, Strategic and Defence Studies Centre, Working Paper No. 114).

67. Francis Fukuyama, "Gorbachev and the Third World," *Foreign Affairs* 64 (Spring 1986), p. 716.

68. See Derek Martin da Cunha, *FEER*, 4 September 1986 for a useful analysis of Cam Ranh Bay's strategic value. A comprehensive analysis of the alleged Moscow-Hanoi axis stressing the value of Vietnam and Cam Ranh Bay to the USSR is contained in Thai Quang Trung, "The Moscow-Hanoi Axis and the Soviet Military Build-up in South East Asia," *Indochina Report* 8(October 1986).

69. China Daily Report, *FBIS*, 24 June 1985, pp. W1-6.

70. *The Australian*, 4 September 1986.

71. Lui Tingkang, Chinese Charge d'Affaires, Suva, in *Asiaweek*, 26 September 1986, p. 26; *The Canberra Times*, 6 August 1986.

72. *The Sunday Times* (London), quoted in *The Australian*, 19 August 1986.

73. China Daily Report, *FBIS*, 9 September 1986, p. C1.

74. *Beijing Review*, No. 45 (10 November 1986), p. 15.

75. For an analysis of this development see the author's research paper, "China's Modernisation and the Strategic Implications for the Western Pacific," (Canberra: ANU, Strategic and Defence Studies Centre; *forthcoming*).

5

Implications for Northeast Asia

Paul Keal

Northeast Asia is comprised of Japan, China, Mongolia, most of Siberia and the Sino-Soviet border regions of the USSR, Taiwan, and the two Koreas. It is vital to the Asian-Pacific Basin which is widely regarded as central to the future of the world economy. Admiral James Lyons, Commander of the US Pacific Fleet, highlighted that earlier this year when he said that "the pendulum of history has swung from the Mediterranean to the Atlantic and ... it is now pointing in the Pacific." He added that he fully shared Ambassador Mike Mansfield's view that "the next 100 years are going to be the century of the Pacific."[1] Expectations such as these concerning the future role of the Asian-Pacific Basin are essential to interpreting the Vladivostok speech.

The first half of Gorbachev's speech dealt with domestic affairs, particularly the economic development of the Soviet Far East; the second was aimed at Soviet relations with states in the Asian-Pacific region. Geoffrey Jukes argues that the two halves are related by "the future prosperity of the Soviet Far East [being seen] as linked to development of its economic relations with areas in its vicinity, the most prominent of which are China and Japan."[2] In other words, the Soviet Union seeks to create, in Northeast Asia and the Asian-Pacific Basin, the conditions conducive to the development of its Far Eastern region which it wants to pay its way instead of being a drain on the Soviet economy as a whole. In pursuit of this the Soviets would undoubtedly like to be able to participate in and benefit from the much vaunted economic dynamism and potential of the Asian-Pacific Basin.

What is remarkable about the latter part of Gorbachev's speech is the prominence given to arms control both with respect to Korea and Japan. This chapter focuses first on Gorbachev's references to arms control and then Japan. As Gary Klintworth deals with Sino-Soviet relations, further discussion of either China or Mongolia is not included.

NORTHEAST ASIA AND ARMS CONTROL

Strategic Factors in the Region

Northeast Asia and the adjacent areas of the North Pacific have become the focus of an arms race. The Soviet Union has been building up its armed forces in the region. The United States argues that this represents a challenge which needs to be met. In any case Northeast Asia is now central to US strategy. US strategic policy in the region is probably as provocative to the Soviet Union as the Soviet build-up is to the US.

Since the mid-1960s the Soviet Union has progressively reinforced and modernised its forces in the East Asian-Pacific region. It has built up its strategic nuclear forces; increased the number of intermediate-range nuclear arms in the region; expanded its ground and air forces; considerably enlarged its Pacific fleet; built up its forces on the Northern Territories claimed by Japan; and finally, it has established a maritime theatre-level command (MTV) for the Far East. Japan as well as the US has increasingly perceived these Soviet actions as a threat.

In the East Asian-Pacific region the Soviet Union stations over one-third of its land and submarine based strategic nuclear forces. At least 135 SS-20 Intermediate Range Ballistic Missiles (IRBMs), each with a range of 5,000 km, are deployed in the Far East. A major submarine base from which SSBN submarines operate is located at Petropavlovsk on the Kamchatka peninsula. From there ballistic missile-firing submarines are deployed into the Sea of Okhotsk, "which is shielded from hostile Western penetration by the Kurile Island Chain,"[3] the Sea of Japan and off the peninsula itself. About 40 strategic TU-22M Backfire bombers are located in the Far East.

Vladivostok is the headquarters of the Soviet Pacific Fleet, which is the largest of the four Soviet Fleets. It is supported by the presence in the region of more than 30 naval aviation Backfire bombers equipped with long range anti-ship missiles. Ships travelling to and from Vladivostok are obliged to pass through straits controlled by US allies: South Korea and Japan. These chokepoints are a potential menace to Soviet naval movements - the geographical circumstances of Japan are such that it is uniquely placed for blocking Soviet movements in the Pacific Ocean and the East China Sea. For the United States it would have the additional role of serving as a forward base for an attack on the Soviet Far East.

On the Kunashiri, Etorofu and Shikotan islands, or so-called "Northern Territories," claimed by Japan, the Soviet Union deploys the equivalent of a division. Also deployed are long-range canons and MIG-23 Flogger fighters. The presence of these forces underlines the importance of the Northern Territories in dividing the Pacific Ocean from the Sea of Okhotsk with its strategic value for Soviet SSBN (ballistic missile nuclear submarine) activities. They also have the political function of leaving no doubt in Japanese minds about the fact of Soviet occupation.[4]

The build-up of Soviet forces in the Asian-Pacific region is often cited as evidence of aggressive intent. And while it has been on a scale which is cause for concern, Soviet preparations for war do not, as Andrew Mack argues, "necessarily imply any aggressive Soviet intentions, any more than similar US preparations indicate aggressive US intentions towards the Soviets .... [Rather] the available evidence strongly suggests that the primary Soviet strategic concerns are defensive."[5]

This is supported by Paul Dibb's assessment of the major missions of Soviet forces in the region. The first is to deter the United States and China from attacking Soviet territory. The second is, in the event of war to launch nuclear strikes on the United States, its allies in East Asia and Oceania, as well as on China, so as to prevent the successful prosecution of a separate theatre of war against the Soviet Union in the Pacific. The third mission is to launch conventional attacks against China and against US and allied naval and air forces in the northern and mid-Pacific, including the conventional phase preceding global nuclear war. In addition to these "the primary operational mission of the Pacific Fleet is to protect the ballistic missile submarine force, based at Petropavlovsk ... and to ensure its effective deployment in wartime."[6] In fact the foremost interest of the Soviet Union in the region probably is maintaining the security of its SLBM (submarine launched ballistic misiles) force.

The United States on the other hand has adopted a strategy of offensive defence which necessarily puts this SLBM force at risk. In 1983 Secretary of the Navy John F. Lehman enunciated the principles of a Maritime Strategy which has since been refined on several occasions. The Maritime Strategy is now the blueprint of US planning for the contingency of war in the Asian-Pacific region as well as other parts of the globe. Its key concepts are "forward defence" and "horizontal escalation."

The US Navy's forward offensive strategy has three aspects which would be put into operation in the event of war. First, the US would launch an anti-submarine warfare campaign against Soviet SSBNs designed to force Soviet attack submarines to retreat into defensive bastions to protect their ballistic missile submarines. The purpose of this would be (1) to attack Soviet SSBNs to shift the balance of nuclear weapons and render the option of using the remaining nuclear weapons less attractive; and (2) to protect the Sea Lanes of Communication (SLOCs) in the North Pacific by destroying the threat to them at its base.

Soviet attack submarines protecting Soviet SSBNs could not attack US and allied surface ships. To help bottle-up Soviet submarines in this way, US forces would establish barriers at key chokepoints by using maritime patrol aircraft, mines, attack submarines and sonar buoys.

In the context of Northeast Asia this means forcing Soviet submarines into the Seas of Okhotsk and Japan and establishing control over the chokepoints at the Tsushima, Tsugaru and Soya Straits. Japan would have a crucial role in this "as a springboard from which the United States can launch attacks against the Soviet homeland [and] ... a shield behind which the US Navy can fight Pacific battles."[7]

A third and crucial aspect of the forward offensive maritime strategy is the aim of adversely affecting Soviet perceptions of the nuclear "correlation of forces." It aims to do this by seeking to destroy Soviet SSBNs, in the way just suggested, and by the US improving its own nuclear posture. It proposes to achieve the latter principally through the "deployment of Tomahawk platforms around the periphery of the Soviet Union."[8] The Tomahawk sea-launched cruise missile (SLCM), is a dual-capable system with both conventional and nuclear versions. Soviet forces do not know which is which, and the rationale for deploying them is that this will complicate Soviet planning by greatly increasing the number of strategic targets at sea. Instead of being able to concentrate on aircraft carriers and ballistic missile submarines, the Soviets will have to concern themselves with all US vessels in the Pacific. Whether this will complicate Soviet planning is questionable, as it is likely that the Soviets would in any case probably target US SSNs (nuclear submarines), carriers and battleships.

Nevertheless, current US planning proposes the deployment of some 4,068 SLCMs, of which between 750 and 1,000 will be nuclear-armed.[9] About half of these will be deployed in the Pacific. SLCMs are not subject to any arms control negotiations or agreements and will be matched by similar Soviet systems currently under development.

Horizontal escalation involves striking Soviet forces where they are relatively weak. For example, if the US were fighting a war with the Soviets in the Persian Gulf, where geography favoured the Soviets, the US could escalate "horizontally" by attacking the Soviets where they were weak, the purpose being to draw reinforcements from areas of relative strength, particularly central Europe, so as to render those areas more vulnerable. The aim of the Maritime Strategy in Northeast Asia is "to threaten the Soviets' Achilles heel, their eastern flank, in order to direct their attention from conflicts that may arise in other parts of the world."[10] Threatened with defeat in the Far East, the Soviets would either have to give in or direct forces from other theatres.

While the Maritime Strategy need not necessarily involve the use of nuclear weapons, nuclear escalation is a high risk. The Maritime Strategy involves many of the dangers which Desmond Ball has spelt out in connection with the prospect of nuclear war breaking out at sea.[11] They include the following:

- Aircraft carriers at the head of carrier battle groups crucial to forward offensive strategy are attractive targets for limited nuclear strikes and hard to stop with conventional weapons.
- Dual-capable missiles could raise the risk of nuclear war in the North Pacific. Tomahawk blurs the distinctions between conventional and nuclear war and between tactical and strategic weapons. Because it is deployed at sea where damage would be limited, there could be a temptation to try to preempt its use by striking first. This would be certain to escalate the use of nuclear weapons.
- The anti-submarine warfare (ASW) proposed by the Maritime Strategy is also fraught with the danger of escalation. Since Soviet attack submarines cannot be distinguished from Soviet missile-firing submarines, even ASW operations against the former would risk destroying the latter. Such operations would threaten to destroy part of the Soviet deterrent. In response, the Soviet Union may well react with similarly escalatory actions.

The offensive operations in forward areas called for by the Maritime Strategy "contains the seeds of extremely rapid escalation."[12] These operations call not only for the ASW just mentioned but also strikes against the airbases from which Backfire bombers fly and the submarine bases from which nuclear-powered submarines operate. Forward offensive strategy would aim at catching Backfires on the ground before they could be used against US and allied targets. The Soviet Union may perceive this as a serious threat to its nuclear theatre deterrent and be tempted, in a crisis, to use nuclear weapons first.

For reasons such as these Ball suggests that "the danger of escalation" recommends a policy of directing the Navy "to exempt certain targets from these operations. In addition to SSBNs at sea, Soviet SSBN bases and land-based forces such as Backfire bombers should be exempted from attack for as long as possible."[13]

The Maritime Strategy is oriented to offense with the purpose of convincing the Soviet Union that it would lose any war it started. In fact both superpowers have offensively oriented strategies and force postures designed to deter aggression and prevail on the battlefield should deterrence fail. Essentially the underlying idea is that to be able to deter effectively, armed forces must also be able to engage in offensive actions to fight wars successfully.

The problem about this is that offensively oriented strategies "may... have the effect of increasing the risks of unintended war."[14] This is especially relevant to the situation in Northeast Asia.

The build-up of arms and the strategic doctrines sketched above are crucial to both the general thrust of Gorbachev's speech and its specific proposals.

Arms Control and the Asian-Pacific Region

At the 27th Communist Party Congress in February 1986, and other venues prior to Vladivostok, Gorbachev has articulated foreign policy perspectives which suggest a significant difference from those of his predecessors.[15] He has emphasised the non-military aspects of security and expounded the idea that "ensuring national security ... [is] increasingly becoming a political task."[16]

In February 1987, for instance, he said that "new approaches and methods are required for solving international problems in today's complex world." The Soviet leadership, he said, had come "to conclusions that made us review something which once seemed axiomatic. Since Hiroshima and Nagasaki, war has ceased to be a continuation of politics by other means." And the *Guardian's* apt comment on this was that "[i]f Marxist ideology is redefined to say that there are no objectives worth the risk of a nuclear war, this could have profound implications for the future of Soviet foreign policy."[17]

Geoffrey Jukes has summarised the changes in Soviet foreign and security policies by saying that:

> ... the Party and Society are being told that the Soviet relationship with the outside world is not solely nor primarily adversarial; that while there is a danger of war, and the United States in particular remains hostile, there is also scope and need for cooperation with the major centres of capitalism, and purely military solutions

> for security problems are no longer possible for any country. Parity has been achieved; the Soviet Union does not need more security than it now has, and would be safer with fewer armaments than more; provided its adversaries also reduce their levels.[18]

Evidence for this is found in Gorbachev's policy initiatives in arms control, "where he has recast Soviet positions on intermediate-range nuclear forces (INFs), on deep reductions in strategic offensive nuclear forces, on verification, and on testing."[19]

The need to avoid nuclear war is one reason for Gorbachev's arms control policy. Another is clearly the impediment that military spending creates for economic growth. Paul Dibb points out that the Soviet Union is able to balance the US in armaments only by devoting roughly twice as large a proportion of its GNP to defence.[20] The Soviet Union's relatively weak economic base would benefit substantially from reduced defence outlays. From this point of view it is understandable that Gorbachev seeks to confine the Strategic Defense Initiative (SDI) to laboratory research. Matching the US SDI effort would be a significant drain on scarce Soviet resources. In particular the development of Siberia will be retarded by the present levels of defence spending.

At Vladivostok Gorbachev expressed concern over the immense potentialities for militarisation of the Pacific region and the extremely dangerous consequences which would follow.[21] He cited a large-scale build-up of US forces in the Pacific.[22] "The Pacific Ocean is turning into an arena of military and political confrontation .... This is alarming ... for us from all points of view, including for considerations of security in the Asian part of our country," he said.[23]

At the same time, Gorbachev acknowledged "that the United States is a great Pacific power" and that it "undoubtedly, has important and legitimate economic and political interests in the region. Without the United States and its participation, it is not possible to resolve the problem of security and cooperation in the Pacific Ocean to the satisfaction of all nations in the region."[24]

Concerning the Soviet military build-up in the Far East, Gorbachev said that the Soviet Union had not done, and would not do, more than to meet "the minimal requirements of [its] ... own defence" and that of its friends and allies.[25] In connection with this he mentioned medium-range missiles and the fear that the Soviet Union would redeploy SS-20 missiles from the West to the East. The Soviet aim, he said, was rather to eliminate them. He added that the Soviet Union advocates disbanding "military groupings, renouncing the possession of military bases in Asia and the

Pacific Ocean and withdrawing troops from the territories of other countries."[26]

Finally, Gorbachev stated that the Soviet Union would like to see the Asian-Pacific region incorporated into a comprehensive system of international security as proposed at the 27th Congress of the CPSU.[27] He identified several steps which could be taken to achieve this goal. On arms control and the reduction of forces these included:

- arresting the proliferation of nuclear weapons in Asia and the Pacific Ocean and supporting a nuclear-free zone in the Pacific;
- reducing "the activity of naval forces in the Pacific, in particular, nuclear armed ships." Also, restricting "rivalry in the sphere of anti-submarine weapons, specifically, the arrangement to refrain from anti-submarine activity in certain zones of the Pacific ... [to] help strengthen stability. This could become a substantial confidence building measure";[28]
- "the radical reduction of conventional armaments in Asia to limits of reasonable sufficiency";
- the initiation of confidence-building measures and discussion of "the non-use of force in [the] ... region."[29]

The Pacific Ocean is, as Gorbachev says, increasingly becoming an area of confrontation, with both the Soviet Union and the United States engaged in a build-up of their forces. The Maritime Strategy makes it clear that there are grounds for the Soviet Union to be concerned about the security of its Far Eastern regions equally as much as there are for the US and Japan to be concerned about the Soviet build-up.

At an earlier time a Soviet leader might have described the United States as an imperialist power with no legitimate role in the Asian-Pacific region. Gorbachev's acknowledgment of the US as a great Pacific power which had a legitimate role to play in solving the problems of security and cooperation suggests a maturing of the Soviet Union itself as a great power. It also suggests that the Soviet Union would itself like an acknowledged role in the Pacific which it cannot have without the imprimatur of the United States. If this is what it wants then there is hope for serious negotiation.

Although Gorbachev mentioned summit meetings as essential to the reduction of arms generally, such meetings clearly have a bearing on Northeast Asia. The agenda of future meetings needs to include problems specific to Northeast Asia if arms control is to be achieved on a global scale. In any case, agreements about INFs reached at future summit meetings or ongoing negotiations will be crucial in resolving the questions of whether or not SS-20 missiles will be moved from the West to the East.

The advocacy of disbanding military groupings and renouncing the possession of military bases in Asia and the Pacific Ocean is difficult to take seriously. This is because the Soviet Union would benefit more than the United States. The Soviet Union has, for instance, proposed that it would shut down its operations in Cam Ranh Bay in return for the closure of US bases in the Philippines. The indignant US refusal underscores the obvious point that Subic Bay and Clark Field are of far more strategic importance than Cam Ranh Bay.

Similarly, the proposal for a comprehensive security system harks back to earlier ones. The first, aimed at Asian collective security, was aired by Leonid Brezhnev in a speech to the June 1969 International Conference of Communist and Workers' Parties. It did not specify how such a system would be structured or operate, and neither does Gorbachev's proposal. To engage the interest of non-socialist states the Soviet Union would have to offer the prospect of an arrangement which was not self-serving and genuinely sought to promote common interests. It would have to satisfy non-socialist states that it was not simply seeking to either subject them to Soviet influence or displace Western powers.

Gorbachev's claim that the Soviet Union had not done and would not do more than to meet the minimal requirements of its own defence and that of its allies, raises the question of what constitutes such requirements. Underlying this is a debate about what is necessary for deterrence and stability, and it involves the United States equally as much as the Soviet Union. Essentially it is the problem of whether instead of enhancing deterrence, offensive defence might actually "serve to increase the risk of war by inadvertence."[30]

A strategy of "prevailing" in a nuclear war, to which the US Maritime Strategy would contribute should deterrence fail, is antithetical to the goal of arms reductions apparently cherished by Gorbachev. A strategy of prevailing relies on "destroying the opponent's weapons systems before they can be used - in other words on striking first." This in turn requires building more weapons in order to be able to strike first with some assurance of success in a crisis. The aim of prevailing involves strategies "bound to be perceived as threatening by the Soviets - just as Washington sees Soviet war-fighting/winning strategies and Soviet 'first strike' weapons systems such as the SS-18 and 19 as threatening to the US."[31]

To pursue this point further would require entering a complex theoretical debate about the requirements for and nature of deterrence which is beyond the scope of this paper. Regardless of such a debate, both the

Soviet Union and the United States would, at this juncture, be unlikely to revise their strategies for deterrence radically. What is important in the present context is measures which could be taken to reduce the likelihood of nuclear war through inadvertence or mutual suspicion.

Are the specific steps proposed by Gorbachev feasible ways of achieving this?

<u>1. Arresting the proliferation of nuclear weapons and support for a nuclear-free zone.</u> It was previously pointed out that the US plans to deploy cruise missiles in the Pacific and that the Soviet Union will deploy similar systems in response. These weapons as well as IRBMs could be made the subject of arms control negotiations specific to the Asian-Pacific region. At present there are no North Pacific arms control forums which approximate to the INF talks in Geneva. The initiation of such talks between Asian-Pacific states could advance their common interests and deserve to be considered for that reason.

Nuclear-free zones may also be an effective arms control measure, but agreement about them is difficult to achieve. The Soviet Union's support for the South Pacific Nuclear Free Zone (it has signed the protocols of the Treaty of Raratonga) is regarded with suspicion. The Reagan administration sees the zone as "undermining alliance solidarity and sending signals of weakness and lack of resolve to the Soviets."[32] The United States is concerned that were the attitudes that it perceives as underpinning the zone to spread, it could have its military effectiveness impaired. It is far from enthusiastic about nuclear-free zones. Further, while the South Pacific Nuclear Free Zone did not pose real advantages for either side, additional zones might not avoid being seen as conferring advantage one side at the expense of the other. There is, for instance, unlikely to be a Korean Nuclear-Free Zone, since that would only involve the removal of US nuclear weapons. The Soviet Union would thus gain from a loss to the US.

<u>2. Naval activities and anti-submarine warfare.</u> There are reasons for reconsidering the threat to Soviet SSBNs prescribed by the Maritime Strategy. The practice of sending US SSNs into Soviet SSBN bastions is a provocative one. John Mearsheimer argues that it "would almost certainly be interpreted by the Soviets as an offensive move signalling offensive American intentions, even if Americans meant it as a defensive measure that would buttress deterrence."[33]

The strategy is one in which it might appear to the Soviets that the US purpose was the ability to engage in a damage-limiting first strike.

Focusing "on attacking SSBNs - the most survivable delivery system in the Soviet nuclear arsenal - must surely suggest to Soviet worst case analysts that the US is seeking a total disarming first strike capability."[34]

Negotiations on ASW, possibly aimed at establishing SSBN sanctuaries, may be sensible. But they would have to address these issues, and they may prove intractable. The biggest stumbling block would be that unlike the Soviet Union, the US does not rely on sanctuaries. From the US perspective it would be the Soviet Union that would benefit from ASW-Free Zones.

3. Radical reduction of conventional armaments. In the context of Northeast Asia this is mainly applicable to the Korean peninsula and the concentration of forces along the Sino-Soviet border. Like nuclear-free zones, proposals for the reduction of conventional armaments would have to be ones which did not confer advantages on one side. Gorbachev offered no specific suggestions; but as an area which could be discussed, the reduction of arms is entirely sensible. So would be the prior notification of military exercises, the exchange of observers and the adoption of other proposals negotiated at the Stockholm Conference.

4. Confidence-building measures. Many confidence-building measures have been proposed for Korea but the difficulty there, and for the region generally, is in identifying measures over which some agreement could be successfully negotiated. Alternatively, confidence-building measures might be achieved through unilateral acts. For advances to be made the Soviet Union needs to devise proposals which are not too self-serving. At the same time "the United States should be more willing to exploit the momentum created by the Soviet proposals and offer incentives for more serious Soviet proposals."[35]

The Korean Peninsula

The Korean peninsula is "the greatest potential powder keg of the region." It contains a strong concentration of military forces with at least 150 US nuclear weapons sited in South Korea. In the last few years North Korea has moved closer to the Soviet Union. Partly as a response to the US supplying F-4, F-5 and F-16 aircraft to South Korea, the Soviet Union has begun to supply MIG-23 Flogger aircraft and SA-3 surface-to-air missiles to the North. Soviet aircraft have been overflying North Korean airspace and Soviet warships have been visiting ports in North Korea. In conjunction with these have been suggestions that the Soviets might acquire bases in North Korea similar to that at Cam Ranh Bay.

Rights to overfly airspace would shorten "the route from Siberia to the South China Sea and Soviet bases in Vietnam, making reconnaissance flights of the Chinese coast easier and making detection more difficult."[36] The development of naval facilities combined with aircraft basing rights, Gary Klintworth points out, "would enable the Soviet Union to circumvent US and Japanese defence networks covering the Sea of Japan."[37]

Here, as much if not more than anywhere else in the region, confidence-building measures are urgently required. Since the early 1970s the United States has made proposals for turning the DMZ into a genuinely demilitarised zone. Its proposals have gone unanswered. The United States has also made various overtures to have North Korean observers at military manœuvres in the South. In keeping with these, in April 1984 Secretary of State George Shultz proposed:

- restoration of the non-military character of the DMZ by pulling forces back and removing heavy weapons from the area;
- regular inspection by teams composed of neutral nations to ensure the non-military character of the DMZ;
- prior notification by the North as well as the South of military exercises;
- mutual assignment of observers to such exercises.[38]

Precisely because of the danger of being drawn into direct confrontation with each other, both the US and the USSR have an interest in reducing tension on the Korean peninsula.

In his Vladivostok speech Gorbachev said that there is the "possibility for ... relieving tensions" and that "there are no sensible reasons for evading a serious dialogue."[39] In relation to nuclear weapons he suggested that implementing a North Korean proposal to create "a nuclear-free zone in the Korean peninsula would be a significant contribution." This statement, with the nuclear-free zone as its main idea, was the extent of his explicit reference to the Korean peninsula.

What significance can be attached to the suggestion of making the peninsula a nuclear-free zone? It is sensible but problematic. To begin with, what is meant by nuclear-free? Does it mean only the stationing of weapons or is it also meant to include visits by ships carrying nuclear weapons and the transit of weapons in aircraft? More importantly, the proposal for a nuclear-free peninsula is self-serving. It would require a unilateral act of disarmament from the United States. At present the Soviet Union has no nuclear weapons in North Korea which it might withdraw as a reciprocal act. It is not clear what inducement the Soviet Union could offer to bring about the peaceful withdrawal of nuclear weapons from South Korea. Thus while there are reasons for the Soviets to engage in arms control and confidence-building measures with respect to the Korean peninsula, Gorbachev's proposals at Vladivostok do not lead anywhere concrete in this direction.

JAPAN

Compared with the discussion of militarisation and arms control, Japan received only limited explicit discussion. In recognition of Japan's economic preeminence, Gorbachev said that it had "turned into a power of foremost importance." Japan's success, he said, was due in part to its three non-nuclear principles, though these "as well as the peaceful provisions of Japan's Constitution are being circumvented ever more openly."[40] This was undoubtedly meant as a veiled warning that it would not continue to prosper if it strayed towards militarism or became more firmly embedded in the military planning of the United States.

In relation to this Gorbachev depicted Japan as being pressured by the United States into a US-Japan-South Korean "militarised triangle."[41] As a consequence it now had nuclear-weapons delivery vehicles on its territory.

Turning to Soviet-Japanese relations, Gorbachev intimated that they had been at a low ebb and needed to be improved. He stressed the desirability of establishing joint enterprises to develop the resources "in adjacent and nearby regions of the USSR and Japan." Included in this were the possibility of joint ventures connected with ocean resources and "the peaceful study and use of outer space."[42]

Finally, Gorbachev proposed Hiroshima as the venue for "a conference, in the mold of the Helsinki conference, to be attended by all countries gravitating towards the [Pacific] Ocean."[43]

Although brief and not entirely explicit, these remarks touched upon the three main issues affecting the state of Soviet-Japan relations. The first two are divisive, while the third may be seen as an impetus to settle differences. They are:

- the disputed Northern Territories and the consequent anomaly of there remaining no peace treaty between Japan and the Soviet Union more than forty years after the end of World War II;

- fears of a resurgence of Japanese militarism combined with concern over Japan's role in US strategy; and
- the prospect of Japanese involvement in the development of Siberia and other ventures.

The Northern Territories

A major impediment to improving Soviet-Japanese relations is the dispute between the two countries over the so-called Northern Territories which are part of the Soviet-occupied Kurile Island chain. At the San Francisco Peace Conference, Japan renounced all claim to the Kuriles. It now argues that Habomi and Shikotan, the two southernmost Kuriles, are an integral part of Japan and that they have never been part of the Kurile archipelago. The Soviet Union does not accept this, and as long as there is no agreement there can be no formal post-war settlement between the two powers. The Northern Territories will remain a source of discord and dispute in Soviet-Japanese relations.

It is highly unlikely that there can be a satisfactory solution to the Northern Territories dispute. It has already been pointed out that the Kuriles divide the Pacific Ocean from the Sea of Okhotsk, which is a Soviet SSBN bastion. The Kuriles "are not only a base for confronting American Forces stationed in and around Japan: they are also a shield for Soviet submarines that target the continental United States."[44] Because of this it is difficult to conceive of the Soviet Union being willing to meet Japanese claims.

There is an ominous link between the Northern Territories and Gorbachev's suggestion of "a conference in the mold of the Helsinki conference." In important respects the Helsinki accords represented a post-war settlement which recognised Soviet hegemony over Eastern Europe. They proclaimed the "inviolability of frontiers." At one level this means the boundaries of states, at another it means the line which demarcates the influence of one power from that of another. In the context of Europe the inviolability of frontiers means that the United States will not challenge Soviet influence in Eastern Europe. With regard to Northeast Asia the reference to Helsinki suggests a Soviet attempt to have Japan formally drop its claim to the Northern Territories. Evidence of this is Gorbachev telling Foreign Minister Shintaro Abe, when Abe visited Moscow in May 1986, that progress in Soviet-Japanese relations required "the understanding that no one will be encroaching on the results of the Second World War and the inviolability of the frontiers."[45]

A tactic that the Soviet Union could conceivably adopt in future would be to offer to withdraw from Habomi and Shikotan in return for Japan agreeing to something calculated to weaken its ties with the United States. This could put Japan into a difficult situation but it would be unlikely to succeed.

Without a solution to the Northern Territories problem, the scope for improving Soviet-Japanese relations will be necessarily limited. At present it is difficult to see how this issue can be satisfactorily resolved, and there is nothing in Gorbachev's speech that suggests a way of doing so.

A possible future solution, which would need the cooperation of the Soviet Union, Japan and the United States, would be an agreement to make the Northern Territories a demilitarised zone.

Militarism and Japan's Strategic Role

Since the beginning of the 1980s Japan Defence Agency White Papers have expressed increasing concern about the Soviet military presence in the region. At the same time the United States has pressed Japan to spend more on defence and to take responsibility for specific missions, namely, the mining and blockading of the Tsushima, Tsugaru and Soya Straits; the provision of an air defence screen over Japan; and protection of the sea lanes of communication out to 1,000 nautical miles from Honshu. The involvement of Japanese forces in joint exercises with the United States has become more frequent, and the weapons systems of the two countries have become increasingly compatible.

Japanese intentions and US attempts to have Japan assume increased responsibility are viewed with deep suspicion by the Soviet Union. Moscow sees the White Papers as evidence of an expanding Japanese-American military alliance that is assuming an even more aggressive character. As far as it is concerned the United States is seeking to turn Japan into the Far Eastern flank of NATO. It accuses the United States of attempting to forge an anti-Soviet Sino-US-Japanese alliance. The deployment of F-16s at Misawa is regarded as a threat to Soviet forces in the Far East. Japanese involvement in the SDI is decried as an ill-considered act with potentially serious repercussions. Japan's promulgation of the Pacific Community concept is described as at best a tool to further US and Japanese interests and at worst simply an attempt to establish a latter-day Greater Co-Prosperity Sphere.

Gorbachev's reference at Vladivostok to Japan's three non-nuclear principles and their circumvention echoes a number of earlier comments about Japan's relationship with the United States. According to the Soviet Press the United States is "attempting to turn Japan into a nuclear missile launching base";[46] but there is no evidence to support this claim. The US is charged also with increasing Japan's "military role, both in the system of the alliance with the USA and in the present-day world in general."[47] And this, Gorbachev told the Japanese Council of Organisations of Victims of Atomic Bombings, was a violation of Japan's non-nuclear status.[48]

The Soviet Press warns that Japanese hawks are seeking to revise the three non-nuclear principles and lock Japan even more securely into US nuclear strategy.[49] The Soviet Union is concerned that there may be stores of nuclear weapons for American F-15, A-4 and A-6 carrier aircraft at the Kadena airfield in Okinawa and at Iwakuni airfield on Honshu. Also that F-16 fighter-bombers based at Misawa can carry nuclear weapons aimed at the Soviet Far East and that US aircraft carriers, nuclear submarines and surface ships "full of nuclear ammunition" operate from Yokosuka.[50]

Whatever the truth of these claims, the fact is that Japan stands in the firing line of any US-Soviet conflict. Its geostrategic location is such that it could not avoid being involved in a US-Soviet conflict. Japan would have the crucial role of being "a springboard from which the United States can launch attacks against the Soviet homeland [and] ... a shield behind which the US Navy can fight Pacific battles."[51]

Japan has a vital role in the Maritime Strategy discussed previously, not only as a forward base and a shield for US forces, but because it hosts US "communications facilities, refuelling and repair facilities, stopover airstrips, storage depots and ... military bases."[52] These include:

- US army headquarters at Camp Zama near Tokyo;
- The headquarters of the US Seventh Fleet at Yokosuka which would direct aircraft carrier, surface ships, amphibious and submarine attacks on the Soviet Union;
- The ASW and naval surveillance centre at Kamiseya;
- Yokota Air Base, headquarters of the 5th Air Force, which commands squadrons of nuclear-capable tactical aircraft in Korea and Japan.

All of these US bases and facilities would be subject to Soviet attack in the event of war. The missions, previously mentioned, which the United States wants Japan to fulfil, would lock Japan deeply into US strategic operations and make it hostage to any US-Soviet conflict in the region.

It should be abundantly clear why an important Soviet objective is to detach Japan from the United States and to neutralise it as much as possible. Through veiled warnings, naval movements and the penetration of Japanese air defence zones, the Soviet Union has sought to turn Japanese opinion to its favour. Instead it has influenced Japanese opinion negatively.

Gorbachev's speech contained no specific proposals concerning either Japanese armaments or Japan's involvement with the US. Short of openly threatening Japan in counterproductive ways, there is not much that the Soviet Union can do to change the situation. The emphasis, in the speech, on the development of Siberia suggests that the Soviet Union may adopt a more conciliatory attitude. It cannot hope to involve Japan in the development of Siberia and other joint enterprises at the same time as engaging in intimidating actions and strident accusations. But what prospect is there of greater Japanese involvement in the development of Siberia?

Siberia and Economic Cooperation

At Vladivostok Gorbachev cited a spectrum of areas including fisheries, minerals, timber, energy production, industrial infrastructure, technological innovation, and trade and tourism, which all require development if the potential of the Soviet Far East is to be realised. In most of these areas there is considerable scope for joint enterprises with other countries including, especially, Japan. Furthermore, the development of joint enterprises is regarded as something which would help create more stable relations in Northeast Asia.

The most important implications of Gorbachev's speech for the development of Soviet-Japanese economic cooperation are those it proffered for improved Sino-Soviet and Soviet-Japanese relations. Foremost of these is the prospect that the speech offered of a lessening of tension in Sino-Soviet relations. Tadashi Saito argues that less tension in Sino-Soviet relations is needed for increased cooperation.[53] The reason is that Japan is loathe to help develop an industrial base and infrastructure in Siberia which could threaten China and cause friction in Sino-Japanese relations.

Second to this, Gorbachev admitted the need to improve Soviet-Japanese relations. Improvement in the political aspects of these relations would also promote better economic relations.

The impetus to expanded cooperation with Japan comes from the imperative of social and economic reform in the Soviet Far East and from the need to deal with the non-socialist nations of the Asian-Pacific region to achieve it. The problem is whether Japan will want to become involved to any significant extent. "With the drop in oil prices and the gradual restructuring of the Japanese economy away from imported natural resource-based industries, the Siberian development is becoming less attractive to the Japanese."[54] Ultimately, Siberia simply may not hold a lot of interest for Japanese enterprises.

CONCLUSION

The general implication of Gorbachev's initiative for Northeast Asia is that the Soviet Union does want to improve its relations in the region. Gorbachev wants both the development of Siberia and the opportunity to participate in and benefit from economic growth in the Asian-Pacific region. At the same time he appears to want to reduce defence spending in order to release funds in aid of domestic growth, especially in the Far East. He has recognised the danger of using force in the nuclear age and consequently that national security is better pursued through political means as far as possible. Furthermore, without taking steps to allay the suspicions which have been aroused by its military build-up and attempts to influence Japan, the Soviet Union may find it difficult to extend its economic relations with other countries.

These are some of the reasons why Gorbachev is keen to engage in arms control negotiations. The question is whether it will be possible to go beyond aspirations. Improved relations and arms control agreements specific to the region will be difficult to achieve.

The proposal that the Korean peninsula become a nuclear-free zone is unlikely to be an acceptable starting point for unravelling the problems related to North and South Korea. Without an end to the Northern Territories dispute on terms acceptable to Japan, improvements in Soviet-Japanese relations will be limited, as will Japanese enthusiasm for joint ventures. The Soviet Union will in any case remain hostile to Japan's military involvement with the US. There is nothing in Gorbachev's speech that indicates that the Soviet Union will willingly give up its longstanding aim of loosening Japan's ties with the United States.

The obstacles to Gorbachev's specific proposals on arms control measures in the region will be no less difficult to surmount. Talks aimed at limiting arms; measures to prevent ASW operations causing war by inadvertence; the reduction of conventional arms; the introduction of nuclear-free zones as genuine anti-proliferation measures; and the search for appropriate confidence-building measures: all deserve serious dialogue between adversaries. Arriving at mutually satisfactory agreements on them is obviously another, very complex, matter.

None of this means that Gorbachev's initiative should be written off. Northeast Asia is a region containing a number of intractable conflicts which could flare up into a major confrontation. One way of attempting to lessen the danger of this happening is to take Gorbachev's more specific proposals as the starting point for a dialogue about the problems of the region.

NOTES

The author wishes to thank Mr Andrew Mack for his comments on an earlier draft.

1. Conversation with Admiral James Lyons, reported in the *St Louis Post-Dispatch*, 22 January 1987.

2. Geoffrey Jukes, "Gorbachev on Foreign Policy and Defence,1986," Seminar Paper, Australian National University, 20 November 1986, p. 16.

3. Paul Dibb, "The Soviet Union as a Pacific Military Power," *Pacific Defence Reporter* (November 1984), p. 19.

4. *Defence of Japan 1985* (Tokyo: Defence Agency of Japan), p. 32.

5. Andrew Mack, "The Soviet-American Conflict in the Pacific," paper presented to First Asia Pacific Roundtable on Confidence Building and Conflict Reduction in the Pacific, 10-11 January 1987, Kuala Lumpur.

6. Dibb, "Soviet Union as a Pacific Power," pp. 20-21.

7. W. M. Arkin and D. Chappell, "Forward Offensive Strategy: Raising the Stakes in the Pacific," *World Policy Journal* 11(Summer 1985), p. 482.

8. Admiral James D. Watkins, "The Maritime Strategy," in *Maritime Strategy* (US Naval Institute, 1986), p. 14.

9. Desmond Ball, "Nuclear War at Sea," *International Security* 10(Winter 1985-86), p.12. See also W. M. Arkin and R. W. Fieldhouse, *Nuclear Battlefields: Global Links in the Arms Race* (Cambridge: Ballinger, 1985), p. 125.

10. Arkin and Chappell, "Forward Offensive Strategy," p. 484.

11. Ball, "Nuclear War at Sea," *passim*.

12. *Ibid.*, p. 28.

13. *Ibid.*, p. 36.

14. Mack, "Soviet-American Conflict," p. 16.

15. F. Stephen Larrabee and Allen Lynch, "Gorbachev: The Road to Reykjavik," *Foreign Policy* 65(Winter 1986-87), p. 3.

16. *Ibid.*, p. 6.

17. *Guardian Weekly,* 22 February 1987, p. 1.

18. Jukes, "Gorbachev on Foreign Policy," p. 14.

19. Larrabee and Lynch, "Road to Reykjavik," p. 3.

20. Paul Dibb, *The Soviet Union: The Incomplete Superpower* (London: Macmillan, 1986), p. 260.

21. *Speech by Mikhail Gorbachev in Vladivostok, 28 July 1986* (Moscow: Novosti Press Agency Publishing House, 1986), p. 27.

22. *Ibid.*

23. *Ibid.*, p. 28.

24. *Ibid.*, p. 31.

25. *Ibid.*, p. 33.

26. *Ibid.*, p. 33.

27. *Ibid.*, p. 35.

28. *Ibid.*, p. 36.

29. *Ibid.*, p. 37.

30. Mack, "Soviet-American Conflict," p. 2.

31. Andrew Mack, in Desmond Ball and Andrew Mack, eds., *The Future of Arms Control* (Canberra: ANU, 1987), p. 310.

32. *Ibid.*, p. 323.

33. John J. Mearsheimer, "A Strategic Misstep: The Maritime Strategy and Deterrence in Europe," *International Security* 11(Fall 1986), p. 46; cited by Mack, "Soviet-American Conflict."

34. Mack, "Soviet-American Conflict," p. 21.

35. Reinhard Drifte, "Arms Control and the Superpower Balance in East Asia," unpublished paper presented in Bristol, 1985, p. 17.

36. *Strategic Survey 1985-1986* (London: IISS, 1986), p. 166.

37. Gary Klintworth, "Kim Il Sung's North Korea: At the Crossroads," (Canberra: Strategic and Defence Studies Centre, ANU, Working Paper No.114), p.18.

38. Drifte, "Superpower Balance in East Asia," p. 13.

39. *Speech by Gorbachev,* p. 35.

40. *Ibid.*, p. 25.

41. *Ibid.*, p. 27.

42. *Ibid.*, p. 31.

43. *Ibid.*, p. 34.

44. Peter Berton, "Soviet-Japanese Relations: Perceptions, Goal, Interactions," *Asian Survey* 26(December 1986), p. 1263.

45. Cited by Berton, *ibid.*, p. 1279.

46. BBC, *Summary of World Broadcasts,* SU/7995/A3/3, 5 July 1985.

47. *Ibid.*, SU/8023/A3/2, 7 August 1985.

48. *Ibid.*, A3/1.

49. *Ibid.*, SU/7430/A3/7, 5 September 1983.

50. *Ibid.*, SU/7452, A3/4,5, 30 September 1983.

51. Arkin and Chappell, "Forward Offensive Strategy," p. 482.

52. W. M. Arkin and D. Chappell, "Bonzo's Banzai, Japan as the Finger on the Jugular," unpublished manuscript, Chap. 2, p. 6.

53. In a paper on Gorbachev's Speech in Vladivostok and the Economic Cooperation between Japan and the USSR, submitted in partial fulfilment of the requirements for a Master's degree. Mr Saito was a former member of the Staff of the Japan-Soviet Business Cooperation Committee.

54. Berton, "Soviet-Japanese Relations," p. 1282.

6

Implications for Southeast Asia

Robyn Lim

For Southeast Asia, the potentially most significant reference in the Vladivostok speech was the statement that "if the USA were to renounce a military presence, say on the Philippines, we should not be found wanting in a response." Earlier in the speech, the General Secretary said that "the Soviet Union is a convinced advocate of disbanding military groups, renouncing foreign bases in Asia and in the Pacific Ocean and withdrawing troops from others' territory." By these statements, Gorbachev sought to plug the Soviet Union into the anti-nuclear movement in the Philippines. It is not universally appreciated in the Philippines that, in Zbigniew Brzezinski's terminology, America's status as the "dominant transoceanic power" in competition with the "dominant power on the central landmass" of Eurasia means that the maintenance of strategic mobility in the Asian-Pacific region is far more important to the US than to the USSR.[1] It is in the Soviet interest to hint at a possible "trade off" between Subic Bay Naval Base in the Philippines and the Soviet "facility" at Cam Ranh Bay in Vietnam.

Gorbachev's reference to the discussion of "confidence-building measures and the non-use of force" in the Asian-Pacific region is certain to attract increasing attention in ASEAN (Association of Southeast Asian Nations), which has begun to move towards serious discussion of a regional arms control regime in the form of a South East Asian Nuclear-Weapons-Free Zone (SEANWFZ). This chapter argues that while the ASEAN countries are prepared to concede Soviet claims to "legitimacy" as an Asian-Pacific power, they will be reluctant to devise a regional arms control regime which threatens American strategic mobility in the region. At the same time, however, Gorbachev's taking of the moral high ground on regional arms control presents a formidable challenge to the United States.

This will be even more so if the superpowers reach an arms control agreement in Europe.

SEARCH FOR LEGITIMACY

The Vladivostok speech was followed by an intense round of high level Soviet visits to ASEAN countries. Foreign minister Eduard Shevardnadze's visit to Indonesia in March 1987, for example, was the most high level Soviet official visit to Indonesia since Anastas Mikoyan's in 1964. The Soviets have also launched a diplomatic offensive on economic organisations in the Asian-Pacific region. ESCAP (the Economic and Social Commission for Asia and the Pacific) has been a venue for Moscow's advocacy of a regional conference on peace and security. The USSR has also shown considerable interest in the PECC (Pacific Economic Cooperation Conference); at the PECC meeting in Vancouver in November 1986, the USSR was accorded observer status despite the disapproval of the American and Japanese (non-official) delegations. The Soviet Union's request for "dialogue partner" status with ASEAN is also an interesting new development, not least because all the other dialogue partners (US, Canada, Japan, the European Community, Australia and New Zealand) are market economies.

Soviet success in Vancouver, however, does not mean that the Soviet diplomatic offensive will be positively received in ASEAN. Moscow's relations with non-communist Southeast Asia are an object lesson in the limitations of Soviet power under Leonid Brezhnev. In few regions of the world did the growth of Soviet military power in the 1970s contrast so strongly with the decline in the USSR's political influence. Soviet trade with the region, which is about 4 percent of ASEAN's trade with the US, also attests to Moscow's inability to take advantage of ASEAN's rapid growth in the 1970s.

As a result of the increase in superpower rivalry in the region, and of the Soviet 'lodgement' in Vietnam, all of the ASEAN states tilt towards the US. Two of them, Thailand and the Philippines, are allies of the US.[2] Malaysia and Singapore retain an indirect security link with Washington via the Five Power Defence Arrangement of which Australia, a US ally under ANZUS, is also a member. Brunei also retains defence links with the UK.

Little more than a decade ago, it was common for the Soviet media to portray ASEAN as a *de facto* SEATO. As in other parts of the world, Gorbachev has altered the style of Soviet diplomacy. He has continued the recent trend of a more conciliatory Soviet approach to ASEAN, and indicated recognition of the respectable growth rates which the ASEAN countries (except for the Philippines) are still achieving despite the current economic downturn. In his Vladivostok speech, the Secretary General noted that "there is much of positive value in the activity of ASEAN and in bilateral contacts."

The ASEAN response to the Vladivostok Initiative has been interested but politely negative. It is likely to remain so as long as there is no change in the single most important obstacle to improved ASEAN-USSR relations - Moscow's support for the Vietnamese occupation of Kampuchea. Although Gorbachev stated at Vladivostok that "in our opinion there are no insurmountable obstacles to the establishment of mutually acceptable relations between the countries of Indochina and ASEAN," Egor Ligachev's speech at the Vietnamese Sixth Party Congress in December 1986 reiterated Soviet support for Vietnam, recited the usual formula that improvement of relations with China would not be sought at the expense of third parties, and announced a significant increase in Soviet aid to Vietnam. Sino-Soviet relations and the Kampuchea issue are subjects of separate chapters; suffice it to say here that ASEAN's response to Soviet policy on Kampuchea will remain one of "show us." Whether the USSR can "de-link" its relations with ASEAN from its support for Vietnam in Kampuchea remains to be seen.

The USSR has long sought to exploit "contradictions" between ASEAN development strategies and the dependence of those states on Western and Japanese markets. In the current situation, it has attempted to benefit from ASEAN dissatisfaction with Western protectionism, particularly Thai complaints that the US Farm Bill will have a serious impact on Thai rice exports. Anatoly Zaitsev, Director General of the Soviet Southeast Asia department, visited Bangkok shortly after the Vladivostok speech. He reportedly "promised to expand Soviet trade with Thailand by buying practically every item which Thailand is having problems with the United States."[3] While the Thais are critical of US agricultural protectionism, they have also made it clear that they draw a distinction between improving their economic relations with Moscow and anticipating any change in Thai-Soviet political relations as long as Moscow continues to support Vietnam in Kampuchea.

The recent US agreement to station a Weapons Reserve Stockpile in Thailand is also, among other things, a symbol of continuing US endorsement for Thailand's position *vis-a-vis* Vietnam. A similar message was conveyed by the holding of the annual Thai-US "Cobra Gold" military exercise in northeastern Thailand in 1986 instead of in the south as in the past. These actions are also designed to reassure the other ASEAN states that the US is aware of their concern at the degree of Thai-Chinese military cooperation.

Gorbachev's proposal for an "Asian Helsinki," which received a cool reception even from Rajiv Gandhi during the Secretary General's visit to India in December 1986, is unlikely to be favourably received in ASEAN. Nor is the USSR's suggestion that it should become a "dialogue partner" of ASEAN. The one area in which ASEAN might be receptive to the Vladivostok Initiative is that of arms control, but even here ASEAN is likely to proceed cautiously.

NUCLEAR-WEAPONS-FREE ZONE

Gorbachev's reference at Vladivostok to the "principles of Pancasila and Bandung" which "have not sunk into oblivion," although hardly novel in Soviet statements, was a particularly flattering reference to Indonesia. The rest of the sentence referred to the "positive examples" of the truce in Korea, the 1954 Geneva conference on Indochina, and the 1966 Indo-Pakistan agreement in Tashkent which "live on in diplomatic experience." Geneva and Tashkent were agreements in which the USSR played a major role. The reference to Bandung was also a subtle reminder that the Soviet Union considers itself an Asian power every bit as "legitimate" as China. Whereas Zhou Enlai was prominent at Bandung, the Soviets were not invited; they were therefore excluded from the 1985 thirtieth anniversary celebrations, which provided a venue for the agreement to resume Indonesian-Chinese trade relationships. The USSR can be expected to push for membership of every regional organisation which includes China. The stance of their delegations to the PECC Vancouver meeting suggests that Indonesia and Malaysia, which have always insisted that membership of PECC should not compromise their nonaligned status, are willing to recognise the Soviet Union as a "legitimate" Asian-Pacific power which has the right to join regional organisations that include China .

In his speech at Vladivostok, Gorbachev followed up his reference to Pancasila and Bandung by noting that the idea of creating a "nuclear free zone" in Southeast Asia "has attracted the attention it deserves." In Southeast Asia, the NWFZ concept is seen as a logical extension of the Zone of Peace, Freedom and Neutrality (ZOPFAN) idea. ZOPFAN's key concept is that one of the "lessons of Vietnam" was that the great powers should be discouraged from fighting their "proxy wars" in Southeast Asia. In theory at least, the small countries of Southeast Asia seek to keep themselves "equidistant" from the major powers. The emphasis on

ZOPFAN is on neutralisation as a means of curtailing foreign political and military influence in the region.

In their original Declaration at Bangkok in 1967, the ASEAN states committed themselves to the eventual abolition of foreign bases in the region; this was Indonesia's price for entry. Alone of the ASEAN states, Indonesia has never had foreign military bases on its territory. The 1971 Kuala Lumpur ZOPFAN Declaration had a preambular statement that the signatories were "cognizant of the significant trend towards establishing nuclear-free zones, as in the 'Treaty for the Prohibition of Nuclear Weapons in Latin America' and the Lusaka Declaration proclaiming Africa a nuclear-free zone."

It was not until New Zealand decided to ban nuclear-capable ships from its ports that this reference in the ZOPFAN Declaration was given much attention by ASEAN. The growing "nuclearisation" of the navies of the superpowers was also a matter which could not be ignored by states such as Indonesia and Malaysia which had long wished to exercise greater national control over their straits and archipelagic waters. The New Zealand Prime Minister's visit to Indonesia in March 1986 caused Dr Mochtar Kusumaatmadja, the Indonesian Foreign Minister, to speculate publically about the applicability to Southeast Asia of the South Pacific Nuclear Free Zone (SPNFZ) which had been concluded at Rarotonga on 6 August 1985. In July 1986, the ASEAN foreign ministers' meeting in Manila noted "with special interest" the conclusion of the Treaty of Rarotonga, and instructed an ASEAN Working Group to work towards the drafting "as soon as possible" of a treaty on a Southeast Asia Nuclear-Weapons-Free Zone.

US Secretary of State George Shultz made it plain in Manila that the Reagan administration is actively discouraging the idea of a NWFZ in Southeast Asia. Such a zone is viewed in Washington as a serious impediment to the strategic mobility which the US requires for its "forward posture" in the Asian-Pacific region. It was partly the fear that such zones would proliferate which led the Reagan administration to refuse to ratify the Protocols of the Treaty of Rarotonga. Of the five nuclear-weapons states, it appears that only the USSR and China will sign the Protocols. The Soviet statement when it signed Protocols II and III in December 1986, the first country to do so, was not designed to alleviate American concerns. In similar language to that used when it signed the Protocols of the Treaty of Tlatelolco, the Soviet Union stated that it "reaffirms its position that the admission or transit of nuclear weapons or other nuclear explosive devices by any means, as well as of visits by foreign military ships and aircraft with nuclear explosive devices on board to the ports and airfields within the

Nuclear Free Zone would contradict the aims of the Treaty and would be inconsistent with the nuclear free status of the zone."

Despite US disapproval, however, the NWFZ idea serves a number of foreign and domestic foreign policy functions for Malaysia and Indonesia. Both are active members of the Non-Aligned Movement (NAM). Aware of the degree to which the East Timor issue damaged its standing in NAM, Indonesia has been polishing its nonaligned credentials. It has opened an embassy in Harare, site of the 1986 NAM summit, and may bid for the next chairmanship of the movement. ZOPFAN and the NWFZ idea are also a way for Indonesia and Malaysia, both states with large Muslim populations, to indicate their dissatisfaction with US policy towards Israel and specific actions such as the bombing of Libya.

Both have domestic reasons for rejecting a too-close association with the West. Malaysia is under considerable pressure from "fundamentalist" Islamic elements. For Indonesia, emphasis on NAM credentials is a way of rejecting "prosletysing" liberal democracy, whether it comes from Washington or Canberra. Reference to ZOPFAN also allowed the Indonesian government to draw a line of continuity from Sukarno to Suharto during the April 1987 elections.

In the ASEAN context, ZOPFAN is Indonesia's and Malaysia's way of signalling that they are frustrated by the degree to which the Kampuchea issue has allowed Thailand to draw the parameters of ASEAN's relationship with Vietnam. Nor is Indonesia pleased by the deepening of superpower rivalry in Southeast Asia. Such rivalry exacerbates Indonesia's sense of "maritime vulnerability,"[4] and further postpones the day when Indonesia can aspire to be the major power in offshore Southeast Asia. Indonesia and Malaysia are also concerned lest the elimination of "foreign bases" increase the power and influence in the region of China. It has always been an assumption inherent in the ZOPFAN concept that China be defined as an extra-regional power. Malaysia and Indonesia are also acutely aware of the way in which its support for the Khmer Rouge has given China an "armed proxy" in the heart of mainland Southeast Asia.[5] A NWFZ, especially if linked with "Law of the Sea" issues,[6] would also be a way for Indonesia to exert greater control over its archipelagic waters once China has acquired a "blue water" naval capacity.

Although ZOPFAN is useful to Indonesia and Malaysia for these reasons, Moscow's ability to benefit from ZOPFAN and the NWFZ concept is subject to constraints. In its original formulation in 1971, ZOPFAN was designed to "freeze" superpower competition at a level at which the US was preponderant. It was also a way in which the ASEAN states, afraid that the USSR would inherit the British role East of Suez, could politely reject the USSR's collective security arrangement proposal which was first made in June 1969. Dr Mochtar's outspoken diplomacy notwithstanding, the military and not the foreign ministry run Indonesia. The military are more suspicious of China than of the USSR, but remain hostile to all communist influence. They also have strong institutional links with Washington, the source of most of their arms purchases. Nor has the "Madiun affair" of 1948, in which the USSR was accused of trying to destabilise the embattled Indonesian Republic, been entirely forgotten. In contrast with the late 1950s and early 1960s, there is no anti-colonial issue such as West Irian which Moscow can exploit. Indonesia also has the largest Muslim population in the world, and unless the USSR can arrive at a political settlement in Kabul, the Afghanistan issue will remain a significant impediment to the improvement of Soviet relations with both Indonesia and Malaysia.

US BASES IN THE PHILIPPINES

While it serves a number of functions for Jakarta and Kuala Lumpur, the ZOPFAN concept has the inherent difficulty that sooner or later the ASEAN countries will have to define what they mean by a "nuclear-weapons-free zone." The Treaty of Rarotonga was carefully crafted to contain anti-nuclear sentiment in the South Pacific (a product mainly of French testing) in ways which did not threaten Western security interests. Although the treaty forbids the "stationing" of nuclear weapons on the territory of its member states (stationing being defined as implantation, emplacement, transportation on land or inland waters, stockpiling, storage, installation and deployment), each signatory is free to decide its own policy on such issues as port access by nuclear-capable ships, or passage of such ships through territorial waters.

The American presence in the Philippines makes such a formulation inconsistent with the perceived security interests of the ASEAN states. While the US probably no longer "stations" nuclear weapons in the Philippines,[7] it discourages public speculation on the issue, particularly since approximately 80 percent of the ships which use Subic Bay are nuclear-capable. They include aircraft carriers "loaded down with nuclear-capable aircraft."[8] An increasing number of American ships which use Subic are also equipped with the new long-range "Tomahawk" SLCM (Sea Launched Cruise Missiles). Since these weapons blur the distinction between conventional and nuclear weapons, as well as between tactical, theatre and strategic weapons, their presence in Subic serves to integrate the

Philippines more closely into American nuclear strategy. In addition, nuclear-capable P-3C Orion ASW (Anti Submarine Warfare) aircraft operate out of Cubi Point Naval Air Station, and there are nuclear-capable F4s based at Clark Air Base.[9]

The USSR has been doing its best to promote *glasnost* about what nuclear activities go on in the Philippines. There is little doubt that anti-nuclear sentiment in the Philippines is growing. The campaign against the nuclear reactor in Bataan was one of the most successful during the Marcos era. There are also growing links between the peace movement in the Philippines and those in Western countries, particularly New Zealand. Shortly before she visited Indonesia in August 1986, Mrs Corazon Aquino said that "I can sense a growing feeling among our people for a nuclear free zone in the region."[10] During his visit to the Philippines in September 1986, Zaitsev further encouraged the linking of the Soviet presence in Vietnam with that of the Americans in the Philippines.[11]

The new Philippine constitution, ratified in February 1987, states that "the Philippines, consistent with the national interest, adopts and pursues a policy of freedom from nuclear weapons in its territory." It further states that after the expiration of the bases agreement with the US in 1991, foreign military bases, troops or facilities shall not be allowed in the Philippines "except under a treaty duly concurred in by the Senate and, when the Congress so requires, ratified by a majority of the votes cast by the people in a national referendum held for that purpose, and recognized as a treaty by the other contracting state."

It remains to be seen whether Gorbachev's attempt to take the moral high ground on regional arms control issues will give the USSR much leverage in the Philippines. Judging by its performance in February 1986, Moscow's ability to understand the mysteries of Philippine political culture is doubtful. Perhaps unduly influenced by Mrs Imelda Marcos' frequent visits, the USSR badly misjudged support for President Ferdinand Marcos and was the only foreign government to congratulate him on his "re-election." In contrast, the coming to power of the Aquino administration has been claimed, with some justification, as one of the few foreign policy successes of the Reagan administration.

There will be a good deal of rhetoric on both sides during the US Philippine bases renegotiation, which is due to begin in 1988. Such negotiations are always difficult between allies of such disparate power; they are even more difficult when one is the former colonial ruler of the other. One of the difficulties for the United States is that, although the Catholic church is strongly anti-communist, few of the Philippine intelligentsia have a perception of foreign threat. Nationalists such as the late Jose Diokno have always argued that the greatest threat to Philippine security is the presence of American bases on Philippine soil. While the new constitution enshrines the "archipelago principle," there seems to be no Philippine equivalent of what Michael Leifer has aptly termed the Indonesian sense of "maritime vulnerability".

There may be some temptation for the Aquino administration to try to "play the Russian card" in the bases renegotiation. Marcos certainly tried to do this, usually by sending Mrs Marcos to Moscow. Although such actions impressed some ultraconservative members of the US congress, and the occasional academic, they were not taken seriously by US administrations. Marcos did not even maintain an ambassador in Moscow for the last four years of his regime.

Mrs Aquino has appointed a former key technocrat, Alejandro Melchor, as ambassador to Moscow. While Melchor can be expected to pursue vigorously any trade opportunities with the USSR, there will be strict limits to the degree to which the Philippine government can try to play the "Russian card," even if it is tempted towards displays of independence from Washington; such displays may be deemed even more necessary if Mrs Aquino continues to shift towards the right in domestic policy. Apart from the conservatism of the institutional Church, the parlous state of the economy has made the Philippine government heavily reliant on American and Japanese aid and investment. Presumably under US pressure, in January 1987 it reversed a previous decision to allow Soviet merchant ships to be repaired in shipyards close to Subic. Although the offer was attractive on economic grounds, the government apparently decided that the security risk was too great.

In her first year in office, Mrs Aquino visited Indonesia, Singapore, the US and Japan, but is yet to take up an invitation to visit the Soviet Union. The then deputy foreign minister, Mrs Leticia Ramos Shahani, visited Moscow in November 1986, and was assured that Moscow does not have links with the Communist Party of the Philippines (CPP) or its military wing the New Peoples' Army (NPA). The NPA, which has a membership of around 23,000, is by far the largest communist insurgency in ASEAN. Yet, despite some alarmist talk , there is little evidence of Soviet influence in or arms shipments to the CPP/NPA. While the CPP no longer describes itself as Maoist, it does not favour the Soviet model either, but is increasingly eclectic. Moscow is also encumbered by continuing links with the "old party," the PKP, which reached a "political settlement" with Marcos after martial law was declared in 1972.

The NPA's major problem is shortage of arms. While it is difficult for the Philippines and its major ally to prevent arms coming into the Philippine archipelago, Moscow is unlikely to challenge Washington in a country which is so closely linked with the US. Gorbachev's main foreign policy task is to consolidate the gains of the 1970s, and make the USSR technologically and economically competitive with the West, not to risk a crisis with Washington in a country well within the US sphere of influence. In his Vladivostok speech, Gorbachev referred to American "interference" in the Philippines, a charge which Indonesia has also made. He is unlikely to antagonise ASEAN by making himself vulnerable to the same accusation.

While the USSR faces formidable obstacles to any significant increase in its influence in the Philippines, the fact remains that the Philippines occupies an important strategic position in the Asian-Pacific region. There is a fear of a "vacuum" in the centre of the region should the US be forced to withdraw from the bases. Although the bases may no longer be "vital" for American strategy,[12] their main function as perceived by regional and extra-regional states is a symbolic one, as tangible evidence of America's "will" to remain an Asian-Pacific power. The ASEAN countries are committed to the eventual elimination of foreign bases from the region, but for the foreseeable future they will continue to value the "over the horizon" American presence afforded by the Pentagon's access to bases in the Philippines.

Yet the Vladivostok speech has thrown down a serious challenge for the US. The dilemma for Washington is that the asymmetries of power between the superpowers in the Asian-Pacific region are such that a NWFZ has the potential to handicap the US *vis-a-vis* its strategic adversary. At the same time, however, the US cannot afford to let Gorbachev occupy the moral high ground on regional arms control. Particularly if there is an arms control agreement in Europe, the political costs to the US of maintaining a negative attitude to regional arms control are likely to increase. Nor can the "non-fungibility"[13] of Soviet military power in Southeast Asia be assumed as a permanent feature of the strategic landscape if the USSR manages to "de-link" its policy towards ASEAN from its support for Vietnam in Kampuchea. In Southeast Asia as elsewhere in the Asian-Pacific region, the Vladivostok Initiative poses a formidable challenge for the next American administration.

NOTES

1. Zbigniew Brzezinski, *Game Plan* (Boston: Atlantic Monthly Press, 1986), p. 31, quoted by Douglas T. Stuart, "The International Context of Arms Control," in Gerald Segal, ed., *Asian Arms Control* (London: Macmillan, forthcoming).

2. US commitments to Thailand are multilateral under the 1954 Manila Treaty, and unilateral under the 1962 Thanat-Rusk agreement. The chances of the US "returning" to mainland Southeast Asia, however, are extremely remote.

3. *Bangkok Post*, 10 September 1986.

4. See Michael Leifer, *International Straits of the World: Malacca, Singapore and Indonesia* (Alphen aan den Rijn: Sijthoff & Noordhoff, 1978).

5. M. R. Sukhumband Paribatra, "Can ASEAN Break the Stalemate?" *World Policy* 3(Winter 1986), p. 96

6. J. Soedjati Djiwandono, *Southeast Asia as a Nuclear Weapons Free Zone* (Kuala Lumpur: Institute for Strategic and International Studies, 1986), p. 4

7. William M. Arkin and Richard W. Fieldhouse, *Nuclear Battlefields: Global Links in the Arms Race* (Cambridge: Ballinger, for Institute for Policy Studies, 1986), p. 146

8. Rear Admiral Gene. R. La Roque, US Navy (ret), Director, Center for Defense Information, Hearings before the Subcommittee on Foreign Affairs, House of Representatives, 98th Congress, 1st Session, 17 June 1983, p. 185.

9. *Ibid.*

10. BBC, *Summary of World Broadcasts,* 23 August 1986.

11. *Asiaweek,* 14 September 1986.

12. See Richard J. Kessler, "The Philippines: a US Policy Dilemma," *Bulletin of the Atomic Scientists* (January 1985), and David Chappell, "US Security and the Philippines: an Exchange," *Bulletin of the Atomic Scientists* (May 1985).

13. By "non-fungibility" is meant the inability of the USSR to translate military power into political power.

7

Implications for South Asia

Ramesh Thakur

Writing in 1985, a British commentator noted that "President [Ronald] Reagan has wrought an astonishing change in the public perception of the [NATO] alliance .... the President has persuaded millions of Europeans that America is a greater, or at least as great a threat to world peace as the Soviet Union."[1] During the course of events in 1986, General Secretary Mikhail Gorbachev of the Soviet Union rapidly challenged and overtook Ronald Reagan as the great communicator in international affairs. On 28 July 1986, in a major foreign policy speech at Vladivostok, Gorbachev located the Soviet Union firmly as an Asian-Pacific power, tried to define a new Soviet role in the region, and launched a fresh approach to the problems of regional security and the Soviet Union's bilateral relations with its Asian neighbours. An Asian observer noted that "the advent of Gorbachev signals a new touch of finesse in foreign policy and diplomatic activities .... Western leaders and political commentators seem to be ill-prepared for and surprised at the spectre of a potentially successful communist drive for leadership in international and regional affairs."[2]

My purpose in this chapter is to assess the implications of the Vladivostok Initiative for South Asia. The South Asian region in common usage refers to the countries of Afghanistan, Bangladesh, Bhutan, India, Nepal, Pakistan and Sri Lanka. Even a broad-brush survey of all these countries is precluded by the confines of space and time. In any case, all the major regional implications of the Vladivostok Initiative are embraced by Soviet relations with Afghanistan and India. Consequently, I propose to limit myself to these two critical Soviet relationships. However, since Afghanistan is the subject of another chapter, and also since Afghanistan is on the edges of South Asia anyway, I shall concentrate principally upon India.

South Asia is important to the superpowers for a number of reasons. To the west and east, it straddles and links two other areas that are of vital interest to the superpowers, namely the Middle East and Southeast Asia. To the north it borders the two communist giants, one of which shares a long and troubled frontier with India, while the other has more than a hundred thousand troops in Afghanistan as an invading force within striking distance of the Gulf. To the south the region juts out athwart important sea lanes of communication and supply in the Indian Ocean. Internally, the countries of South Asia are wracked by domestic challenges of varying intensity and gravity, as well as by deep-seated inter-state conflicts with the potential for erupting into wars at short notice. Internationally, South Asia continues to be a prominent focus of attention: for the continuing trauma and tragedy of the Soviet occupation of Afghanistan; for the possibility of nuclear proliferation with India and/or Pakistan acquiring 'the bomb'; for the trans-regional repercussions of another India-Pakistan war; for the presence of extensive debilitating poverty and efforts to alleviate it; for India's importance as the leading third world and most populous worldwide democracy; for India's leadership role as spokesman for the nonaligned and LDC (less developed countries) groupings in world affairs; and for Pakistan's central role in the Muslim world and as a geographical conduit to Afghanistan.

AFGHANISTAN

The above paragraph should help to explain why South Asia has been the scene of a striking interplay of the national interests of five major and middle powers: China, India, Pakistan, the USA, and the USSR. Afghanistan's geopolitical importance stems from its historic location between empires which at times impinged upon one another. In more modern times it has existed as a political vacuum between rival imperial systems suspicious of each other's intentions across the no-man's land: Persia and Mughal India from the 16th to 18th centuries, and Russia and Britain in the 19th and 20th centuries.

Soviet troops intervened directly in Afghanistan in late December 1979. Explanations for the Soviet invasion seven years ago remain speculative. We do not know the military cost that the Soviet leaders expected to pay for their Afghan venture. We do know that they seriously miscalculated both the military and political repercussions of the invasion upon the US political system, the political price that they have had to bear internationally, and the military casualties that they are continuing to take in

Afghanistan. The Soviet Union has been forced painfully to relearn the lessons of British follies in Afghanistan of the last century: the maintenance of an imperially-appointed ruler in Kabul requires a permanent occupation which which takes its toll upon financial and human resources.[3] Like the British, the Soviets are learning that a puppet cannot be maintained in Kabul without occupation; invasion of Afghanistan is easier than its conquest and subjugation; and national security may be served better by a friendly but independent ruler in Kabul.

At Vladivostok, Gorbachev announced that six Soviet regiments would be withdrawn from Afghanistan by the year's end. All Soviet troops could be withdrawn at the request of the Afghan government. But if external intervention against the Kabul government continued, Moscow would not simply abandon its neighbour: "Our internationalist solidarity with the Afghan people, *as well as the Soviet Union's security interests,* absolutely exclude this."[4] Gorbachev waved a carrot as well, saying that he supported efforts to broaden the political base of the government in Kabul by including political elements which were presently outside Afghanistan but wanted to participate in a process of national reconciliation and reconstruction.

The war in Afghanistan has been stalemated for some time. Several rounds of indirect talks between the Kabul and Islamabad governments under UN auspices at Geneva have proven inconclusive. The chief stumbling block is Soviet opposition to the international demand that their forces be withdrawn on a definite and short-term timetable. The Afghan government announced a unilateral, but qualified, ceasefire for six months from 15 January 1987. Offers to begin a process of national reconciliation which would include amnesty, incorporation of exiled elements in a virtual coalition government, and an Islamicisation of the political system, have been interpreted in the West as temptations aimed at dividing the seven groups of the resistance. The Soviet price for the deal included an end to "outside interference" in Afghanistan.

Geographical contiguity makes it difficult to envisage a total reversal of Soviet advances in Afghanistan. During his Indian visit in November 1986, Gorbachev was reported to have conveyed his keenness to pull out of Afghanistan, but not at the cost of dismantling the political structure that has been built up there in recent years.[5] It is true that the USSR gains some military lessons from the war in Afghanistan.[6] A Soviet military victory may be possible with the injection of a million troops and the extension of the war to Pakistan, but it cannot be presumed. The consequences of such a widening of the war would be momentous, perilous, and uncontrollable. Success by the Kabul government against the *mujaheedin* will depend both on a generation of popular support and on massive Soviet military backing: except that the latter undermines the former.

The staying power of the guerrillas is greater than that of the invading forces, but not their ability to translate isolated military successes into durable territorial gains against superior firepower. Pakistan has proved willing to act as the conduit for Saudi and US-financed and US-supplied aid to the resistance, but dare not escalate its involvement for fear of matching escalation by the Soviets. Moscow could increase the level of intimidation through intensified violations of Pakistani airspace and by means of encouraging the relatively dormant Baluch and Pushtun separatist movements. Cross-border raids and blasts may also increase questioning by local Pakistanis of the wisdom of confrontation rather than accommodation.

For these reasons, the most likely "solution" to the Afghanistan problem is the establishment and maintenance of a "special relationship" between Moscow and Kabul which, in return for the withdrawal of Soviet troops, proscribes external aid to anti-Kabul resistance and precludes Afghan opposition to the Soviet Union on the international scene. This is not unlike the solution that the British settled upon in the days of the Raj, and it would not be looked at unfavourably by the nonaligned. To Westerners, nonalignment seems to imply political neutrality, a foreign policy posture of equidistance from both blocs. To the nonaligned themselves, however, the policy has not precluded closer relations with one bloc at the expense of the other in principle or practice.

INDIA

The conspicuous treatment accorded to Rajiv Gandhi at the funeral of President Konstantin Chernenko, and his continuing courtship since then, underline the importance that the Soviet Union attaches to its Indian connection. Soviet relations with India are both broader and, in the long term, more important to South Asian international relations than its armed presence in Afghanistan. The Indo-Soviet relationship has proven to be mutually beneficial, generally consistent and perhaps surprisingly durable. It is, however, complex rather than unidimensional. Nor, despite being asymmetric, is it a solely one-way affair.

Survey of Indo-Soviet Relations

India began with mixed feelings about America and the Soviet Union. In Jawaharlal Nehru's view, "All the evils of a purely political democracy are evident in the United States; the evils of the lack of political democracy are present in the USSR."[7] The tilt away from the US began with the latter's single-minded proselytising efforts in the crusade against communism. John Foster Dulles condemned nonalignment as immoral and short-sighted fence-sitting. For its part, India was greatly upset by the US decision in 1953-1954 to arm Pakistan, not the least because the draught of the cold war could now be felt around the subcontinent. By the same token, once the cold war and the India-Pakistan axes intersected in Kashmir, it was natural for India and the USSR to become diplomatic allies on this particular issue.

Relations with the Soviet Union thus started hesitantly, with small, exploratory beginnings in cultural and commercial relations. Politically, however, there were major breakthroughs in 1955 when the Soviets expressed strong support for India on such sensitive subjects as Goa and Kashmir. More important than verbal support has been the consistent Soviet defence of Indian interests at the United Nations.

Indo-Soviet relations grew at a more relaxed pace during the sixties. The Sino-Indian war of 1962 interrupted but did not halt the increasing friendship. A relatively neutral stance by the Soviet Union proved to be a wise investment for future returns. In a different context, the Tashkent agreement of 1966 between India and Pakistan was symbolic of the increasing importance of the Soviet Union in the subcontinent.

Relations between India and the USSR accelerated in the seventies, leading to a rapid consolidation of the Moscow-New Delhi axis. The triangular development of China's split with the USSR, *rapprochement* with the USA, and conflict with India, meant that India and the Soviet Union had acquired a geostrategic community of interest. The announcement in July 1971 of Richard Nixon's impending visit to China shook both Moscow and New Delhi. India concluded that the development would reshape the world's power pattern, but with a detrimental impact on India's position; the Soviet Union discovered that the front line of its diplomacy in South and East Asia had suddenly been rendered very vulnerable.[8]

The Indo-Soviet Friendship Treaty of August 1971 may be seen in this context to have represented a response by two states to a dramatic shift in the international power structure to their mutual disadvantage. It also contained a hint of an alliance during the subcontinental war that followed in December. The Americans found themselves in embarrassing alliance with Beijing in defending the interests of a repressive dictatorship in Pakistan. In outcome, the US managed to alienate India without in fact helping Pakistan. After the war, although there were attempts at righting the Indo-American relationship, it was only the advent of the Janata government in 1977 that lent them some credibility and plausibility.

The 1977-1979 Janata government raised the possibility of shifts in India's external ties. In particular, there were suggestions that Prime Minister Morarji Desai and President Jimmy Carter would work to retrieve Indo-American relations. Carter's visit to India in January 1978 was symbolic of the desire to reestablish friendly relations, but did not go much beyond rhetoric. Both Desai and Foreign Minister Atal Behari Vajpayee were known to have been unhappy with the 1971 Friendship Treaty with the Soviet Union; yet they did not move to abrogate the treaty. Instead, they were more concerned to reverse the drift away from "genuine nonalignment" and thereby extend the range of flexibility in India's foreign relations. Thus India took to diversifying its purchases of armaments in the decision to buy Jaguar and Harrier aircraft from Britain. It was also reported to have investigated the possibility of procuring Western technology for the manufacture of submarines under licence.

There were limits, however, to the degree to which even the Janata government could move Indian foreign policy away from Moscow and towards the West. Andrei Gromyko's visit to India in April 1977, along with the reciprocal visit to the USSR by Desai and Vajpayee in October, reaffirmed the enduring bases of friendship between the two countries. When Premier Alexei Kosygin journeyed to New Delhi in January 1979, the USSR had already agreed to supply India with 200 tons of heavy water under unspecified safeguards. He also agreed to supply 600,000 tons of oil to India at official OPEC prices in exchange for rice.[9] On 7 June 1979, India's second satellite "Bhaskara" was put into orbit from a Soviet cosmodrome.

Indo-Soviet relations during the 1980s have been shaped by the two factors of the Congress Party's return to power and the ramifications of the Soviet invasion of Afghanistan. Moscow could only have been pleased with Indira Gandhi's triumphant return to the Prime Ministership. Reactions to the Soviet intervention in Afghanistan were symptomatic of the differences in emphasis between Gandhi and her predecessors. The Lok Dal and the Janata censured the Soviet action shortly after the scale of the invasion became apparent. By then, however, Indira was back at India's helm, and she seemed to condone or at least accept the need for the Soviet move. Speaking in the *Lok Sabha* on 30 January 1980, the great helmswoman declared that "we do not approve of foreign presence or intervention anywhere in the world. However, we do not believe in one-sided condemnation." She insisted that her government was not "pro any country" but only "pro India."

If it was not prepared to antagonise Moscow needlessly, India also carefully refrained from endorsing the Soviet military presence in Afghanistan. There were several reasons for Indian reticence, including the fact of a large domestic Muslim population, ties with the Arab world, and Afghanistan's membership of the nonaligned movement.[10] After the Soviet invasion of Afghanistan, President Mohammad Zia-ul-Haq of Pakistan rightly noted that his country was a buffer state between India and the Soviet Union, and that this was greatly in India's interests.

India's geopolitical landscape was transformed yet again with the decision by the Reagan administration to rearm Pakistan as a frontline state against Soviet expansionsim. In 1981, the US decided to grant $3.2 billion worth of military and economic assistance to Pakistan. While the beneficent effects of the security package upon Pakistan are debatable,[11] it did succeed in converting the Soviet presence in Afghanistan from being politically undesirable into becoming a strategic option in Indian defence planning. For it enables India to confront Pakistan with the possibility of a two-front nightmare in the event of another India-Pakistan war. The US security programme to Pakistan thus had the unintended, but not entirely unpredictable, side-effect of restoring the strategic basis of Indo-Soviet friendship.[12] Gorbachev was reported to have assured India in November 1986 that the Soviet Union would come to India's aid in the event of a conflict with Pakistan. In return, Rajiv Gandhi endorsed the Soviet position on arms control and disarmament at the Reykjavik non-summit.[13]

The Political Framework of India-USSR Relations

The enduring basis of the Indo-Soviet relationship lies in a convergence of international interests on several issues despite sharp differences in social, economic and political systems. Nevertheless, as is the case in the military and economic spheres as well, there are significant points of divergence between Indian and Soviet political interests in the world arena.

The most important determinants of the shape of Indo-Soviet relations have been the state of India's relations with the United States, Pakistan and China. Where the US has appeared indifferent to Indian nationalist aspirations and hostile to Indian nonalignment, the USSR has commended one and courted the other. At Vladivostok itself, Gorbachev praised nonalignment as an Asian response to the threat of a world divided into nuclear-armed blocs. (He was conveniently overlooking Yugoslavia's role as co-founder of the nonaligned movement.) He added that "[t]he acknowledged leader of this movement is great India, with its moral authority and traditional wisdom, with its unique political experience and its enormous economic possibilities."[14] The US, handicapped by NATO ties, has often been cast as the apologist for dying vestiges of European colonialism. Enthusiastic Soviet championing of anticolonialism has brought particular diplomatic support for India, for example with the military liberation of Goa in 1961. The ramifications of the US-Pakistan military relationship were touched upon above. Pakistan played an intermediary role in the American opening to China in 1971, a development which brought India and the USSR even closer together. Prospects of a Sino-American "strategic relationship" cause grave apprehensions in both Moscow and New Delhi. The two countries share perceptions of a US military presence in the Indian Ocean as a threat to vital interests - hence the speculation about Moscow's readiness to support a conversion of India's navy into a blue water fleet of some potency.[15]

The most tangible demonstration of Soviet diplomatic support has come at the United Nations on the issues of Kashmir, Goa, Bangladesh, etc. Growing political ties have also created substantial pro-Soviet interests in the Indian bureaucratic and business sectors. Individual careers have been affected - favourably as well as adversely - by the development of Indo-Soviet relations, while the increased economic strength of that relationship has in turn created a considerable commercial vested interest in preventing any damage to it. The Indo-Soviet Chamber of Commerce boasts 1,200 members with Manubhai Shah, a former Commerce Minister, as president.

More recent additions to pro-Soviet interest groups include cultural, entertainment and travel industries. The study of the Russian language, society and politics provides opportunities to acquire knowledge about a foreign culture other than the *passé* Anglo-American model, one that is European as well as Asian, rich in its literature, and with claims to offering insights into the rapid transformation of a feudal, primitive society into a modern industrial power. The intimacy of Indo-Soviet relations means too that both Russians and Indians can travel to each other's country without arousing too much controversy. An Indophile in Soviet academia is unlikely to arouse the same official suspicions as an enthusiastic student of America, China or Israel. Indo-Soviet Friendship societies have blossomed. In 1984, Indo-Soviet cooperation reached new heights as the Russians took the first Indian cosmonaut into space with them.

During the November 1986 Gorbachev visit to India, agreements were signed for the holding of cultural festivals, and the opening of two further Indian consulates in the Soviet Union in Tashkent and Nakhodka in addition to the existing consulate at Odessa. A "Festival of India" was organised in the Soviet Union in July 1987 and inaugurated by Rajiv Gandhi; this was to be followed by a Soviet festival in India in November. About 2,300 artistes from each country would be involved. National cuisine festivals were also planned.

Yet important points of difference remain, some actual, others potential. These are the product of separate origins, divergent goals, and asymmetric capabilities. The massive Soviet military presence in Afghanistan highlighted the clash of interests between the USSR as a superpower with a global reach trying to fashion a world order to its own liking, and India as a regional power trying to keep its neighbourhood free of any superpower intrusion. India has also steadfastly rejected Soviet overtures aimed at forging an Asian collective security system. Just as India in the 1950s resisted Western efforts at isolating it from the Sino-Soviet world, so India will resist any Soviet attempts to restrict India's ties with China and the USA. Obviously, India is not going to jettison a tested and tried Soviet friendship in a fresh courtship of China. Equally, however, the Soviet attachment cannot be allowed to preclude a normalisation of relations with China. A cultivation and maintenance of good relations with everyone is the pragmatic-flexible essence of nonalignment, and is also demonstrably in India's interest in increasing its margin of manouevrability. The concept of an Asian-Pacific security pact, revived by Gorbachev at Vladivostok, has been lukewarmly received by India, being described variously as thought-provoking and a good concept in need of further study.

Interestingly, it was the same worry in reverse that surfaced during Gorbachev's visit to India in 1986. How far will the USSR accommodate Indian sensitivities in its efforts to thaw relations with China? Gorbachev went out of his way at Vladivostok to court China. Noting that a shared border meant that Chinese and Soviet peoples were destined to be neighbours "henceforth and for all time," Gorbachev hoped that the border dividing them at present would soon unite them in a line of peace and friendship. The Soviet Union was prepared to enter into discussions with China "at any time and at any level" to this end.[16] Gorbachev went on to sketch some areas of possible Sino-Soviet cooperation, including a proportionate reduction of troops at the border.[17]

India and the Soviet Union part company also on the subject of nuclear non-proliferation. The Soviet Union is a joint parent of the 1968 Non-Proliferation Treaty; India is a staunch critic and leading non-signatory of the NPT.[18] Moscow has been a longstanding advocate of nuclear-weapon-free zones all around the world; India was one of the chief objectors in a UN study group looking at the value and feasibility of setting up such zones in various regions of the world.[19] Yet the Soviet Union forebore from joining in the chorus of international criticism levelled at India after its "peaceful nuclear explosion" of 1974. There is thus a reciprocity of silence between India and the Soviet Union regarding each other's actions that attract significant international, especially Western, condemnation. This is not the least of the reasons why Indo-Soviet friendship is reinforced by a remarkably benign public image of the Soviet Union in India. In an opinion poll published on the eve of the Gorbachev visit, 93 percent of Indians were found to regard the USSR as India's best friend, compared to only 6 percent who chose the USA.[20]

A final point worth noting is that India's role as a counter to China gives the USSR a vested interest in a strong, united and stable India. By contrast, many US objectives in Asia over the past four decades would have been better served by a weaker and more fragmented India. The implications of this are not lost upon India's political leadership.

Military Ties: 'Not Quite an Alliance' [21]

At the start of the 1960s, a mere 10 percent of India's imported arms came from Soviet sources. By 1971, an overwhelming 90 percent of Indian arms imports were of Soviet origin. Since the late 1970s, the Janata, Indira Gandhi and Rajiv Gandhi governments have consciously followed a policy of trying to reduce dependence on Soviet military supplies by diversifying arms imports. The USSR nevertheless remains India's chief arms supplier, and is likely to retain this position for the foreseeable future. Thus in June 1980, the two countries signed an agreement for the purchase of $1.6 billion worth of Soviet military equipment by India; repayment was spread over 17 years at a highly concessional 2.5 percent rate of interest. This was followed by an equally major arms deal in 1982. Between 1954 and 1983, Indian military purchases from the USSR exceeded $10 billion; India had bought only half that amount from Western sources.[22]

The Janata government's 1979 Jaguar deal with Britain had marked a radical departure from established Soviet dependence. The 1981 Reagan decision to supply advanced arms to Pakistan committed India to a search for weaponry qualitatively superior to that which the USSR was prepared to offer at the time. To evident Soviet dismay, Indira Gandhi continued the Janata trend by buying Sea Harrier planes, Sea King helicopters, and Sea Eagle missiles from Britain; Mirage-2000 fighters from France; and SSK-1500 submarines from West Germany. Rajiv Gandhi continued the diversification process with a purchase of 400 Bofors field howitzer 77Bs from Sweden in 1986. The first batch of the 155mm artillery guns arrived in October 1986; the agreement provides for a factory to be set up in India to manufacture additional units under licence after the initial deliveries.[23]

Shortly after some of the earlier agreements were signed, a high-level Indian military delegation visited Moscow. Led by the Defence Minister, it included the Defence Secretary and the deputy chiefs of the three services. Reports of the visit indicated firstly that Soviet leaders had expressed concern over India's trend at diversification of arms supply, and secondly that they had made an unexpectedly good offer in an effort to woo back Indian custom.[24] They were prepared to provide India with weaponry and technology qualitatively comparable to anything on offer to Pakistan. They were also prepared to buy Rs 5 billion worth of MIG-21 components from Hindustan Aeronautics Ltd (HAL). If accepted, this would ensure that a major portion of HAL production was concentrated on MIG-21 components. It would also ensure an uninterrupted supply of spares to the Warsaw Pact and other Soviet-aided countries equipped with MIG-21s, thus leaving the Soviet industry free to concentrate on advanced systems for home use. The offer was also concrete testimony to Soviet faith in the technical capability and infrastructure of HAL, which has been producing MIGs since 1968.

An agreement for the supply of sophisticated Soviet military equipment to India was signed in March 1984.[25] A senior Indian delegation visited Moscow a few months later to finalise the deal for the purchase and delivery schedules of "frontline equipment."[26] For example, India was the first country outside the USSR to be offered MIG-29s, thus receiving preferential treatment even in comparison to Warsaw Pact allies. Also in the pipeline were plans to manufacture under licence the even more advanced MIG-31/FOXHOUND, an aircraft reputedly more sophisticated than the Mirage-2000 or the F-16. The offensive capabilities of the Indian Navy were enhanced with the agreement to supply advanced versions of *Foxtrot* class diesel-electric attack submarines, *Nanucka-II* guided missile corvettes, and *Kashin-II* class guided missile destroyers equipped with modern weapons systems. Nor was the Indian Army ignored. To enhance the survivability of its T-72 Main Battle Tanks (MBTs), which are licence-manufactured in India as well, the USSR had agreed to transfer the highly classified tank-armour technology to India. One estimate put the figure of $20 billion on the military hardware involved in the 1984 agreement - the largest single arms transfer between the two countries. One Western news report even pointed to a Soviet offer to supply India with a nuclear-powered submarine as part of the deal.[27]

An opinion poll published before the 1986 Gorbachev visit showed 68 percent of Indians in favour of putting most of the defence eggs in the Soviet basket.[28] The offer of an AWACS system, broached during the 1984 deal, was repeated during Gorbachev's visit. (In fact Moscow offered the TU-124 MOSS, which is less sophisticated than the American AWACS; India wants the MAINSTAY, which Moscow claims is not yet perfected.) India's then Foreign Secretary A. P. Venkateshwaran explained in a 1987 US interview that India would seriously consider taking up the offer if the US supplied such a system to Pakistan. He argued that bolstering Pakistan with an AWACS system would be militarily meaningless against Afghanistan because of the mountainous terrain on Pakistan's northern border. But it would be an excellent force-multiplier for Pakistan in the context of its conflict with India, allowing it to peep into the plains of India. Since India could not sit idly by if Pakistan acquired such capability, the net result would be a spiralling arms race on the subcontinent.[29]

The 1986 Gorbachev visit marked a return by India to a position of dependence on Soviet arms. The consensus in India seems to be that the chief reason for this was Defense Secretary Caspar Weinberger's earlier trip to India and Pakistan.[30] In India, Weinberger appeared sympathetic to Indian concerns. Yet immediately afterwards, in Pakistan he announced willingness to supply AWACS, the M1 Abrams tanks, and the improved version of F-16s. While the USSR flatters India by giving it the status of a world power, the USA insults it by treating it "like an impoverished tinpot nation." The influential Indian defence 'think tanker' K. Subrahmanyam commented that the US "has done a commendable job of reminding us of" the 1971 Friendship Treaty with the USSR, the 15th anniversary of which had passed barely unnoticed in India in August.[31]

The Gorbachev visit saw deleivery of the MIG-29s advanced by four months. The navy was offered more *Kilo* and *Tango* class submarines and TU-142 Bear maritime reconnaissance aircraft; the last can reportedly fly right down to South Africa and back without refuelling. Both the air force and the army's aviation corps were offered more Mi-24 helicopter gunships and Mi-26, (also known as the HALO), the world's biggest transport helicopter. (Both have been used in increasing numbers in Afghanistan by the Soviet Union since 1986.) The political significance of the deal lies in the fact that "Even more than the Soviet willingness to sell, what marked a change from the recent past was the Indian inclination to buy."[32] The Indian inclination was certainly eased by such considerations as rupee repayments, the price competitiveness of Soviet equipment, the Soviet acceptance of India's indigenisation programmes, and Soviet purchases of defence componentry produced under licence in India.

The Soviet profile has been more sharply etched than the American in South Asia in part because of the relatively greater salience of the region to the Soviet strategic landscape. The USSR is as much an Asian as a European power, and geographical imperatives impart a measure of permanence to the Soviet presence in the minds of India's military planners. India cannot realistically hope to escape the repercussions of any major transformation of power relations in Central Asia.

For all the range and volume of Soviet military sales to India, nevertheless, the Moscow-New Delhi military relationship is a limited association rather than an alliance or a protector-client relationship. To begin with, the very size, professionalism and modernisation of the Indian defence services makes it impossible to envisage India as a mere client of any external power. Since independence, India has refused to countenance foreign military bases or advisers on its territory. India's strategic doctrines are indigenous, focusing upon perceptions of threats to Indian political-security interests rather than global quarrels. This is reinforced by the fact that Indian military commanders are by and large home-grown and Indian-trained. The size of India's armed forces has also enabled the country to procure defence equipment from overseas under licence to manufacture after an initial delivery. The components used in the manufacture of Indian weapon systems under foreign collaboration are largely indigenous. The bulk of the defence forces' equipment - clothing, transport and armaments - is produced in Indian ordnance factories. The fact that India has one of the largest reservoirs of scientific-technical manpower means that the country's defence forces can confidently hope to maintain their largely indigenous character for the future as well.

The intimacy of the Indo-Soviet military relationship is dampened then by the regional emphasis in India's defence outlook, training and needs in contrast to global Soviet perspectives. There is also appreciation in India's military as well as civilian leadership that the social and political contexts are different in the two countries. The undoubted respect for Soviet military accomplishments and gratitude for Soviet military assistance are tempered by a recognition of the harsher aspects of Soviet life. The Indian military assesses its needs and Soviet equipment using professional criteria; the final decisions on purchases and sales are made by political leaders in a wider context than just the military calculations. This has not generated any noticeably serious restiveness in the Indian forces.

The goal of self-reliant defence - which is essentially a political, not a military, objective - is underscored by an awareness of the hidden or delayed costs of defence procurement from the USSR. Many of the Soviet systems develop teething symptoms in India. Commerically attractive rates inevitably point up the political price that will be exacted in due time. Indian negotiators have also concluded that the low unit prices of Soviet equipment can conceal high subsequent prices of spares and ancillaries.[33] Nor has India's quest for self-reliance been always helped in the past by the Soviet predilection for technical secrecy and reluctance to share the latest expertise and knowledge.

Training tours to the USSR by Indian officers have been limited to the narrow tasks of familiarisation with Soviet equipment and weapon systems. Not only are Indian officers spared any Soviet political indoctrination; in fact Indian officers do not even attend staff college courses in the USSR comparable to those in Commonwealth countries (e.g. Britain and Canada) which still attract a few Indians every year. Similarly, the number and duration of Soviet military instructors in India is strictly controlled. Soviet officers do not attend Indian staff colleges; there are no Soviet military advisers in India; there is no Soviet military or naval base in India, although Indian facilities are available for Soviet use upon specific requests; and there does not appear to be any regular exchange of military intelligence.

Economic Relations

According to an Indian government economist, "The Soviets may be getting money for jam from us. But at the same time they are giving us guns for butter. It all balances out, more or less."[34] This just about sums up the trade relationship. The origins of Indo-Soviet commercial links date back to a trade agreement signed in New Delhi on 2 December 1953. The Soviet Union is a socialist society with a centrally planned economy. India has officially been limping towards a "socialististic pattern of society" by means of a mixed economy, where a substantial planned public sector coexists alongside a vigorous if semi-autonomous private sector. This combination has provided the basis both for Indo-Soviet economic cooperation and occasional irritation.

From an Indian perspective, the Soviet economic link was critical in facilitating the evolution of India's chosen path of development. The public sector orientation of Soviet aid was more crucial than the amount, especially in the early, formative years. Even in the 1970s, Indian official statistics ascribed an 11-12 percent share of domestic product to the public sector. For its part, the Soviet Union, in entering into economic links with India, was seeking to attain the multiple objectives of eroding Western influence, exporting the socialist/Soviet model of development to a leading third world country, and securing an outlet for its own expanding economy.

Public sector industrial ventures between India and the USSR began with a steel plant at Bhilai. They multiplied rapidly in the 1960s, and included: steel mills; coal mining; heavy electrical and heavy machinery plants; electric power stations, etc. At times Soviet economic help was significant in breaking the stranglehold of Western multinationals, e.g. in the petroleum and pharmaceuticals-medical supplies industries.

Soviet loans are characterised by low interest rates, e.g. 2.5 percent over a 12-year repayment period. Credits are generally repayable in rupees or goods; barter trade agreements are frequently negotiated between India, the USSR and Eastern European countries. The rupee-rouble clearinghouse arrangements have had three attractions for India: development finance, trade diversification and hard currency conservation. The volume of trade between India and the USSR jumped from Rs 15 million in 1951, to Rs 1.8 billion in 1965, Rs 8 billion in 1975, and Rs 14 billion in 1980.[35] For the 1955-75 period cumulatively, India ranked second in Soviet trade with developing countries.

Somewhat less important than, but still an appreciated aspect of, the public sector orientation of Soviet economic aid has been its predictablity. The USSR has accepted long term, five year, comprehensive commitments without worrying about legislative bottlenecks in the appropriations procedure. Soviet credit is typically for industrial complexes, not just individual plants, and stimulates the development of ancillary industries. The aid is for whole programmes, from the initial blueprints to training, supply of raw materials and plant machinery, and final marketing. There is also an emphasis upon a progressive utilisation of Indian componentry and personnel as the programme nears completion.

For all these advantages, Soviet trade with India appeared to have plateaued by 1986. Financial credits extended during Leonid Brezhnev's 1980 Indian visit were still not exhausted. The emerging sectors of industrial growth in India, e.g. automobiles and electronics, were teaming up with Western and Japanese firms. Even Soviet-aided public sector companies like Bharat Heavy Electricals and the Oil and Natural Gas Commission were looking to Western technology for the future. In the first half of 1986, West Germany, the USA, Britain, Japan, Italy, Sweden and France ranked ahead of the USSR in the number of foreign collaboration agreements.[36] The trade gap between India and the USSR widened even further with the collapse of the international oil prices in the mid-1980s, since oil comprised more than 75 percent of Soviet exports to India.

Gorbachev tried to change all this and give new momentum to flagging Indo-Soviet trade. On 27 November 1986, Gandhi and Gorbachev signed an important economic and technical agreement about certain specific projects for which the USSR pledged substantial aid. Bilateral trade is now targeted to quadruple by 1992 to Rs130 billion. The projects include the construction of a 2,400 MW hydroelectric complex in Tehri in Himachal Pradesh, modernisation of the Bokaro steel plant, the construction of four underground coal mines in Jharia in Bihar, and oil exploration facilities in West Bengal. The Soviet Union offered a credit of 1.5 billion roubles (about Rs20 billion or US $1.6 billion) to cover the package. This was on top of the Rs10 billion credit offered during Gandhi's May 1985 visit to the USSR,[37] and just about doubles the amount offered over the previous three decades. The two countries were also reported to be finalising a memorandum of understanding to cover the transfer of nuclear power technology.[38] The offer to build a giant nuclear power plant was made by Kosygin to Morarji Desai in 1979, and repeated by Brezhnev to Indira Gandhi in 1982.[39]

This is not to say that Indo-Soviet economic ventures have been bereft of significant problems. The difficulty seems to have arisen essentially from differences in levels of development and contrasting socioeconomic systems. Unlike its Soviet counterpart, the Indian government cannot compel labour or management to sacrifice private expectations at the altar of the public interest. Assumptions of economic efficiency and productivity have proven fragile when transplanted from a rigidly controlled economy to a more competitive environment. Public sector undertakings, with some notable exceptions, have not fared particularly well in India in comparison to private enterprises. Soviet and Indian experts differ over the causes of the poor performance of Soviet-aided industries. The Soviets point to inexperienced and incompetent management and undisciplined labour; Indians complain about the poor quality of Soviet equipment, supply delays, and designs inappropriate to Indian conditions. But both sides are agreed on the fact of unsatisfactory performance as testified to by recurring idle capacity and excessive production costs.

Another cause of Indian unhappiness is the so-called 'switch trade', that is, the Soviet tendency to import traditional Indian products, such as cashew nuts and textile and leather goods, and then re-export these goods to West European markets. Indian officials have begun to wake up to the fact that, by cutting out the Soviet middleman, they could have sold the goods directly to the hard-currency markets at greater profit margins.[40] But cutting back on Indian exports to the USSR would exacerbate the problem of trade surpluses in India's favour. Caused by a widening lack of complementarity between the Indian and Soviet economies, and held in nonconvertible rupees, they are in effect an interest-free loan to the USSR. In the 1980s, Soviet leaders have urged Indian counterparts to buy Soviet machinery and arms with the surplus balance.[41] But it is Western credit, investment, technology and entrepreneurship that India has been more interested in in recent years.

CONCLUSION

It seems clear from the above survey of Soviet relations with Afghanistan and India that there has been no fundamental change in Moscow's policy towards South Asia as a result of the Vladivostok Initiative. Gorbachev's Vladivostok description of Indo-Soviet friendship as "a stabilizing factor on an international scale" was transparent political hyperbole.[42] The substance of Soviet interests and policies remain unaltered. What has changed is the style. Vladivostok was instrumental in repackaging Gorbachev for a more attractive worldwide and regional marketing of the long-pursued Soviet policy of peaceful coexistence. The Vladivostok Initiative will bear fruit in South Asia, therefore, to the extent - but only to the extent - that the medium is the message. In part this is because the Indo-Soviet relationship is already fairly fruitful. India's relations with the US are generally cool, with the occasional hints of warmth. The relationship between Moscow and New Delhi is normally close, with the odd hiccup now and again. The Weinberger visit to Pakistan and the Gorbachev visit to India in 1986 will have done more to consolidate this underlying pattern of South Asian international relationships than the Vladivostok Initiative *per se*.

Yet the Vladivostok Initiative could turn out to have a profound *derivative* effect on the Soviet role in South Asia. As I have argued, Soviet relations with India are affected prismatically by Sino-Soviet-US triangular diplomacy. The principal targets of Gorbachev's marketing diplomacy at Vladivostok were these major powers. If the triangular relationships should undergo significant realignments, then the Vladivostok Initiative will indeed prove to have been an important determinant of Soviet policies towards

South Asia. But this is so speculative as to render worthless any further analysis of the scenario at present.

Alternatively, the Soviet role in South Asia could be dramatically altered with a fundamental reappraisal by Washington of its relationship with India and Pakistan. Rajiv Gandhi is neither committed to the USSR nor antagonistic towards the USA; he is not in favour of importing communist ideology from the USSR ; he is desirous of importing capitalist technology frm the West. But India would require a minimal US acceptance of vital security and political interests in the region for this to be feasible.[43] So far, there has been no suggestion of such a reconsideration by the US.

NOTES

1. Ian Aitken, "With Mr Reagan's help Mr Kinnock could win," *Guardian Weekly*, 21 July 1985, p. 10.

2. Zara Dian, "The Vladivostok Challenge," *Asian Defence Journal*, October 1986, p. 3.

3. One recent estimate put Soviet fatalities in Afghanistan at between 12,000-40,000; the direct costs of the war at $18-36 billion; Zalmay Khalilzad, "The war in Afghanistan," *International Journal* 41(Spring 1986), p. 271. There is also the additional cost of looking after the Afghan economy.

4. *Current Digest of the Soviet Press* 38(27 August 1986), p. 32; emphasis added.

5. *Statesman Weekly*, 29 November 1986, p. 7.

6. See Martin Walker, "The distant war that keeps the Red Army happy," *Guardian Weekly*, 7 July 1985, p. 9.

7. Jawaharlal Nehru, *The Discovery of India* (London: Meridian, 1960), pp. 562-563.

8. See Alain Jacob, "The Soviet Union is forced to review its world strategy," *Survival* 12(September 1971).

9. *Economist*, 17 March 1979, p. 65.

10. See Ramesh Thakur, "The Reasons for India's Distinctive Approach," *Round Table* 280(October 1980).

11. A US commentator noted that the "dangers to America's own security interests should be evident. The United States has been drawn into a broad security relationship with an opportunistic, vulnerable ally whose arms acquisitions and nuclear weapons programs are directed against a country that America does not consider an enemy." Francine R. Frankel, "Play the India Card," *Foreign Policy* 62(Spring 1986), p. 162.

12. See Ramesh Thakur, "American Policy in South Asia: Regional Fallout of Global Strategy," *Political Science* 36(December 1984).

13. See "Appeal for world without war," *Statesman Weekly*, 6 December 1986, p. 6.

14. *Current Digest of the Soviet Press* 38(27 August 1986), p. 6. This contrasts quite sharply with the offensive and insulting tones adopted by Western commentators. After the seventh nonaligned summit meeting in New Delhi in 1983, an editorial in the *Washington Post* attacked the nonaligned countries for ritually criticising the US: "The same governments then put out hands and ask America for money .... It has long been impossible to know what the Nonaligned Movement stands for, especially when members creep around later to explain that they didn't mean what they said, they just had to go along with the crowd." *Guardian Weekly*, 23 March 1983, p. 16.

15. See Selig Harrison, "Cut a Regional Deal," *Foreign Policy* 62(Spring 1986), for the potentially threatening consequences of such a development to US security interests around the Indian Ocean.

16. *Current Digest of the Soviet Press* 38(27 August 1986), p. 7.

17. *Ibid.*, p. 8.

18. See William C. Potter, "The Strategic Consequences of Nuclear Proliferation in South Asia for the Soviet Union," *Journal of Strategic Studies* 8(December 1985).

19. See the 1986 draft Study on the Question of Nuclear-Weapon-Free Zones, "Review and Supplement of the 1975 Comprehensive Study of the Question of Nuclear-Weapon-Free Zones in All Its Aspects"; unpublished because the study group was disbanded for lack of agreement. In essence, India and Argentina rejected some very few, but key, paragraphs, largely on the political ground that nuclear-weapon-free zones are a side-issue which seek to legitimise and buttress the discriminatory NPT regime.

20. As reported in the *Guardian Weekly*, 30 November 1986, p. 6.

21. Surjit Mansingh uses this as the sub-title for her chapter on India's relations with the Soviet Union in *India's Search for Power: Indira Gandhi's foreign policy 1966-1982* (New Delhi: Sage, 1984), ch. 4.

22. *Soviet Military Power 1984* (Washington, DC: US Department of Defense, 1984), p. 119.

23. *Asian Defence Journal*, December 1986, p. 105.

24. *India Today*, 15 August 1983, p. 50.

25. *Statesman Weekly*, 17 March 1984, p. 5.

26. *Ibid.*, 11 August 1984, p. 5; and *Asian Defence Journal*, December 1984, p. 157.

27. *Sunday Times* (London), as cited in the *New Zealand Times*, 29 April 1984.

28. *India Today*, 15 December 1986, p. 50.

29. As reported in *Statesman Weekly*, 24 January 1987, p. 4.

30. See Bhabani Sen Gupta, "A Different Beginning," *India Today*, 15 December 1986, p. 54.

31. *India Today*, 15 December 1986, p. 49. This is in fact a longstanding Indian complaint. Nayar argued some years ago that there is a basic conflict of interests between Indian aspirations to be a subject of international politics, and the US goal of rendering other countries as objects in the pursuit of American security interests. Baldev Raj Nayar, "Treat India Seriously," *Foreign Policy* 18(Spring 1975).

32. Shekhar Gupta, "A Buyer's Market," *India Today*, 15 December 1986, p. 57.

33. See P. R. Chari, "Indo-Soviet Military Cooperation: A Review," *Asian Survey* 19(March 1979), p. 238.

34. Quoted by Lincoln Kaye, "Moscow's 'temporary' finance deal stays put," *Far Eastern Economic Review*, 5 February 1987, p. 55.

35. Government of India, Ministry of Commerce, *Report 1981-82*, p. 27.

36. *Economist*, 29 November 1986, p. 26.

37. For an analysis of the 1985 deal, see R.G. Gidadhubli, "Economic Diplomacy of the Billion Rouble Credit," *Economic and Political Weekly* 20(25 May 1985).

38. *Statesman Weekly*, 29 November 1986, p. 7.

39. For an account of Indian hesitations over the Soviet offer, see Peter Lyon, "The Soviet Union and South Asia in the 1980s," in Robert Cassen, ed., *Soviet Interests in the Third World* (London: Sage, for the Royal Institute of International Affairs, 1985), pp. 38-40.

40. See Mansoor Ali and R.K. Srivastava, "India's Trade Relations with the Soviet Union: Lessons for the Third World," *Asia Pacific Community* 30(Fall 1985), pp. 64-65.

41. See *Far Eastern Economic Review*, 11 August 1983, p. 30.

42. *Current Digest of the Soviet Press* 38(27 August 1986), p. 6.

43. This argument is developed both by Frankel, "Play the India Card," and by Harrison, "Cut a Regional Deal."

8

Vladivostok and Australian Foreign Policy

Stuart Harris

In this paper I consider three broad questions about Gorbachev's Vladivostok statement. While it is helpful to know what any political statement says, it is more important to know why it was said. This means considering Soviet objectives; Soviet methods; and how Gorbachev perceives these objectives and methods.

Second, I want to consider what Vladivostok implies for other countries in the region, particularly our major allies - the US and Japan. I shall also look at the position of China and the Soviet approach to the Third World where relevant to Asia and the Pacific.

Third, I shall ask what Vladivostok means for Australia's policy framework. Critical to that framework is the fact of great uncertainty, the natural tendency to seek simple, normally single-factor, explanations, and, consequently, blanket policy responses. Such explanations are almost certainly wrong (and the responses thereby flawed). Uncertainty is pervasive here for various reasons.

SOVIET OBJECTIVES AND METHODS

First, ideologies are ever present. Obviously this is so for the Soviets, whether ideology determines the Soviet Union's goals, or simply rationalises what it does. Second, ideological beliefs colour the perceptions of observers on both sides of the East-West confrontation. Third, because intolerance of alternative views is common, debates frequently involve carefully worded - often disguised - arguments. Fourth, the issues are complex, information is incomplete and inconsistent and differences of interests are widespread.

All of these factors can be illustrated from debates in the countries involved. I shall start by looking at how we in the West, and particularly in the US, perceive Soviet objectives and methods.

Much is said about the Soviet aim to achieve long term global hegemony and to spread communism throughout the world. Shorter run Soviet objectives are seen as enhancing Soviet security by creating buffer states on or near its borders, dividing the US and its allies, and increasing Soviet influence over the Third World through subversion and military aid to radical revolutionary movements.

Many observers, however, question whether the Soviets in fact have a master plan or a global strategy. Some argue that Soviet policy in practice is a series of often erratic responses to targets of opportunity. Moreover, many question whether the Soviets now want to export revolution and suggest perhaps that they accept that, through non-military competition, what they see as the superiority of Soviet socialism will be enough to prevail in the long term.

As well as objectives, therefore, Soviet methods are important. Is the Soviet Union seeking influence militarily or through political methods; if the latter, then through acceptable political methods or through subversion? The differences are obviously vital for policy.

For those (like Zbigniew Brzezinski) for whom the USSR is expansionist, adventurous and willing to use nuclear blackmail; for whom the Soviet Union is threatening and opportunistic, using its military strength to destabilise and intimidate; who see all Soviet actions in a global perspective of superpower rivalry and the Soviet Union as an expanding and militarily threatening rival: for all those, resisting the Soviets at every step, including with the threat of military response, may seem appropriate.

Yet for many, the USSR, while becoming under Leonid Brezhnev a nuclear superpower, has a declining political strength internationally and a tired domestic regime, shows little sign of wanting to expand territorially in Western Europe, but is unwilling to relinquish influence particularly where what it sees as its security interests are concerned. Although now less aggressive and militant, they also see it wanting to expand its diplomatic and political influence globally but, nevertheless, doing so cautiously. For those observers the USSR is susceptible to diplomacy, bargaining and compromise. They also suggest that time is not on the Soviet side in Europe, Asia and elsewhere.

Certainly, time is important since significant changes in the perceptions of Soviet goals and methods over time have influenced policy.

Individuals, such as Henry Kissinger, have changed their perceptions. The dominant elites have also varied - and so has the prevailing view.

Both superpowers have, at times, seen the situation as one of two camps struggling for world supremacy, often taking the view that all countries had to belong in one camp or another. At other times a more pluralistic situation was accepted. This has meant that different weight is given from time to time in, for example, the US, to policies of confrontation and rollback, to containment and to cooperation in the policies towards the Soviet Union.

Given these different strands in the debate, what can one conclude? There is little doubt that the Soviet Union is trying to strengthen its international security, to expand its influence, protect its domestic political and economic system and pursue its various national interests; that is normally true of all major countries. Yet in seeking such objectives any country - even a great power - must compromise among competing domestic and international objectives. A master plan involving a consistent strategy is difficult if not impossible to achieve for any country, including the Soviet Union.

With no master plan, no consistency, it is difficult to predict what the Soviet policy might be - and that is itself important in considering policy options. Soviet history can certainly be read as supporting such inconsistency and unpredictability - but then most strands in the debate derive support from Soviet history.

I have noted that fears of aggressive Soviet global ambitions are now seen by some as excessive, given Soviet political and economic weakness relative to Western strength. Fears of the Soviet military threat are also questioned. Who has quantifiably measurable superiority depends on how the count is done - but most accept that the US remains ahead militarily. Moreover, observers such as Henry Kissinger and McGeorge Bundy argue that, given the level of current arms on both sides, superiority is an outmoded concept. In addition, it is argued, undue fears of the Soviet Union ignore the advantage that the US has in its strong allies, the Soviet's logistic problems and its limited political attractiveness.

The regional perception of threat is real, nevertheless, fed in part by the regional build-up of Soviet power. Again, there is debate about its cause and significance. Is this build-up a global enhancement of Soviet military capability or a response to regional factors including the US regional military build-up and Soviet fear of encirclement? Or are the Soviets seeking to take advantage of regional instability through intimidation? How significant quantitatively is the Soviet build-up to the West's global or regional interests or to countries in the region?

The standard Western view is to see regional issues predominantly in terms of the US-Soviet global rivalry, with emphasis on Europe. Yet, in

Asia and the Pacific it is a multipolar world, not everything adverse to US interests is Soviet-motivated, nor is everything that the Soviets do necessarily directed at US global interests.

These questions are of direct regional interest. An important change occurred in perceptions in Japan, as elsewhere, with the Soviet invasion of Afghanistan and the shooting down of the KAL airliner. Until then, the Soviet military capability was increasing and viewed with concern - but mainly in terms of its consequences in the event of a superpower clash. The Japanese accepted that the Soviets wanted to weaken the US-Japan alliance but they were not unduly concerned about a direct threat nor that the Soviet Union could gain political advantage in the region.

Now, out of conviction or for diplomatic reasons, Japan takes the Soviet threat more seriously. Many still see no direct threat to Japan but others, particularly the Defence Agency, argue that a direct threat exists.

In response, what Russell Solomon calls the "military realists" normally stop short of the US stance in their attitude towards confrontation. Responding, however, to what they perceive as a regional as well as a global threat, they see Japan as needing a joint military strategy with the US.

The "poltical realists" in Japan argue that there are severe limits to Soviet military power even with their build-up, and that the Soviets are still on the defensive and vulnerable. They accept, not a military threat, but a Soviet potential to take political advantage of instability in the region.

The Japanese defence build-up is seen by some as unlikely to help, despite the added power that it offers to menace. Japan's political and economic attention to the region is seen as more relevant, although some in Japan are keen, nevertheless, to expand defence expenditure in case the US military effort falters.

Here, as elsewhere, Soviet motivations in dealing with Japan are important - and mixed; the Soviet Union does not like Japan's increased defence spending, or its support for the Strategic Defense Initiative (SDI), and it wants Japan to expand its already sizeable economic interest in the Soviet Far East; but it faces a dilemma over the disputed northern islands. To Japan, China is also important - as it is to the Soviet Union.

We often forget that, until the early 1970s, to many in the US (and to some other Western European opinion) China was more feared than the Soviet Union. Because of concerns that arose from North Korea, from Chinese clashes with Taiwan and in the South China Sea, from Vietnam, from its nuclear capability and from its sheer size, China was seen as the main threat in Asia.

That fear of China has largely gone. The present Chinese governing system, despite recent events, has been accepted as reassuring. Moreover, although we do not know why the Cultural Revolution happened, or indeed how it could have happened, we are reassured that the trauma of that event makes continued stability and moderation likely.

There are different perceptions, however, of relations between the Soviet Union and China. One strand of the debate argues that Soviet strategic concerns over China have a historical continuity from the Mongol invasions, through border clashes in the 1920s and 1930s, to the present day. China certainly became a major security threat to the Soviet Union in the 1960s (reciprocated in China, with Mao Zedong and Zhou Enlai seeing the USSR as their main threat).

The Soviet Union, on this argument, sees China, like Germany, as a historic rival; like the US as a nuclear rival; with an extremely long common border; with a large population; and, in throwing off ideological colonialism, as undermining Soviet ideological authority globally (and more threateningly its domestic legitimacy). Other factors also intrude - "we are Europeans," Brezhnev said.

Some, indeed, argue that the natural state of Soviet-Chinese relations is substantial coolness - with 1953-1956 a brief exception to the historical rule.

Others see this as too stark. They suggest that there are many common interests, that a reconciliation is taking place and that it is for real. This is how I would interpret, I hope correctly, Gary Klintworth. [See Chapter 4.] Certainly both countries are looking for a peaceful international environment to pursue domestic reform. Nevertheless, while the Soviets may now have a more benign view of China than before, the strategic and geopolitical realities remain.

For those who see the Soviet's major potential strategic threat in the region as a US-China-Japan triangle, the rivalries in North Korea and Vietnam have major significance. If the Soviet Union wanted an alliance with Vietnam as a strategic counterpoint to China, a perceived need accentuated by China's increasingly close links in the late 1970s with the US, then they achieved it. Vietnam was not only a military defeat for the US, but created in addition a strategic (and psychological) problem for China.

This influences attitudes on Kampuchea. Some accept that without Vietnam's involvement in Kampuchea, Vietnam would see the Soviet alliance as unnecessary and Vietnamese nationalism would win out. Others argue that Kampuchea is not in Soviet interests - having high political and economic costs and few benefits - and that without it, Vietnamese dependence on the Soviet Union would remain.

The Gorbachev Approach

Soviet motives reflect both continuity and change in post-war Soviet history. Continuity can be seen not just in a repressive domestic regime and in bureaucratic inertia but also in objectives. Some, indeed, see historical continuity with Tsarist desires either to dominate globally or to protect Russian security, with ideology at any time simply being a legitimising cover.

Others see change in both ideology and objectives. The Gorbachev approach is a new expression of a Soviet world view. Hence it is important that Gorbachev was speaking mainly for domestic consumption, particularly at the 27th CPSU Congress, but also to a degree at Vladivostok, which was essentially a regional extension of that Congress speech. Gorbachev's words accepted the need for cooperation and interdependence with an expanding capitalist society; he asserted that military responses are outdated; and he departed from Marxist orthodoxy - to make global integration (in a "contradictory" world in which both systems survive) the dialectic synthesis rather than socialism (leading ultimately to communism) which would have constituted the orthodox synthesis. These statements are, in one sense, just words. For a domestic Soviet audience, however, words have a special significance.

Even though the Leninist-Stalinist model of global domination persists in much of the popular Western media, it has long passed from most serious Western and Soviet debate. Since Stalin, moreover, there had been substantial shifts in Soviet ideology. While class struggle remained inexorable and socialism was still to dominate, it was to do so peacably. (Perhaps, if Hugh Thomas is right - and George Kennan before him - that Stalin's cold war objectives were primarily to provide an external threat that would facilitate his achieving his domestic objectives, then this was so even during Stalin's time.) Gorbachev's approach, however, is a reinterpretation of both ideology and history. Even before this, it was possible to argue that Soviet ideology was not monolithic but was substantially affected by events. Gorbachev's approach reinforces that view. If ideology is not monolithic, then an important policy consequence is that we can seek to influence ideology.

In analysing policy we look for worst cases. The simple worst-case analysis would argue that there is no change in the Soviet approach, simply old wine in new bottles - even old wine in old bottles; that crude subversion, if avoided, will simply be replaced by more subtle pressures and that confrontation should be the main plank of policy. Yet the West German Foreign Minister Hans-Dietrich Genscher has said of the Gorbachev approach, "worst-case" analysis is necessary, but it must not determine policy.

Moreover, the problem with confrontation is that international relations are seldom a zero-sum game - as the arms race indicates. Response stimulates response; military response stimulates military response.

The Soviet Union has done, in recent years, threatening and unpleasant things. But changes have occurred in their policy. Just as Arthur Conan Doyle's "dog that did not bark" was important, so there are many things the Soviet Union did not do, and might on a strong view, have been expected to do. Although the circumstances are different in each case, this is so in North Korea, Mozambique, even the Philippines - where its links were with President Ferdinand Marcos, not the insurgents.

There are various possible reasons for such Soviet pragmatism, many of which are reflected in the internal Soviet debate. In the published debate between the Soviet Chief of Staff and the Defence Minister, the former saw Western imperialism as aggressive and predatory. He saw a confrontational approach as necessary. This, however, was not the dominant view accepted for Soviet policy purposes.

The internal Soviet debate also explains the situation in the Third World generally where the Soviet dog often has not barked. Some in the West point to the pervasive and corrupting influence of the Soviet Union in the Third World. Others argue that Soviet intervention in the Third World has been grudging, cautious and calculated to avoid or minimise risk.

In the extensive Soviet debate on Third World policy, many Soviet scholars have argued against past policy on the practical grounds that it has not worked. It has not worked, they say, because without the necessary preconditions - Marx's industrial proletariat - ethnic, religious, nationalist and other influences dominate. Some also find it difficult to press the Soviet model internationally while criticising it domestically.

For many Soviet academics, links with India offer a better example to follow than those with poor, radical Third World countries; the Soviet Union, they believe, should concentrate on geopolitically based relationships with (preferably medium-to-large) nonaligned countries.

This background is important in assessing Gorbachev's Vladivostok Initiative. This is because, first, despite strong elements of continuity in the Soviet system, there are clear impulses for change.

Second, although Gorbachev is articulating the rhetoric of change, some of those impulses for change are not totally new. We have seen some of them under Georgy Malenkov, Nikita Khrushchev, Leonid Brezhnev and Yuri Andropov.

Third, as we saw earlier, the motivation of Vladivostok was not only its effect overseas. To some extent it was aimed at a regional domestic audience, indicating a wish to bring the Soviet Far East more effectively into the Soviet economy.

Nevertheless, the foreign policy message was important and not just because Soviet Far East development depends upon Pacific investment and trade as much as domestic links. To assess its regional significance, we need a perspective on the USSR's potential impact on the region.

To acknowledge a global Soviet threat does not require us to give up the idea of a multipolar rather than a bipolar world in Asia and the Pacific. In such a context, there is a role for America's allies beyond merely helping to project US power. Such a role, while sustaining a deterrent capacity, emphasises containment or denial rather than confrontation - and would permit cooperation where it was considered to be in our national interest.

We could accept too that the Soviet Union will only act in its perceived self-interest. We can acknowledge that it may start with fears: nuclear attack and geographic encirclement by the US, China and Japan. That it has contributed to this situation by its own actions does not imply that everything that the West has done has been sensible. Superpower confrontation by itself tends to be cumulative.

Soviet policies, because of contradictions and inconsistencies in the use of power, may be difficult to predict. Even if now less adventurous, energetic, and threatening than the hawkish view suggests, this may be as much because of internal problems and international incapacity as of changes in policy.

It is open to question as to whether the Soviet Union is on the offensive in Asia, or whether it simply has a reactive policy. Again, different conclusions may come from the bipolar as against a multipolar perspective. Increased Soviet submarine strength is presumably to counter what the Soviets see as the US nuclear threat; the strengthened Soviet military position on the border with China, however, was to limit China's strategic gain, although resulting only in giving a military dimension to a political conflict . Gorbachev's offer at Vladivostok of border concessions and a reduction of troop levels in Mongolia may reflect a Soviet-China thaw, since Gorbachev appears to want a new strategic relationship with China - but then so did his predecessors. Or he may simply be wanting to restore the dispute to a more manageable political level.

No major concessions were offered on the other two issues of China's concern. For Afghanistan, despite probably a genuine desire to withdraw troops, the political price may be too high. On Vietnam, although the Vietnamese may have read his remarks as being less supportive than they could have hoped, it offered little to the Chinese.

Other issues covered by Gorbachev at Vladivostok included an offer to reduce the arms build-up in the region if the US would match it; and a less China-oriented version than earlier of the Soviet proposal for a Helsinki-type discussion on security in Asia, associated with confidence building measures. Gorbachev also indicated Soviet interest in participating in the Pacific Economic Cooperation process.

In many respects, however, the importance of the speech may lie in the positive tone and approach rather than in specifics. Before looking at the policy implications, however, let me simply note the initial responses in the region.

The *Economist* newspaper's suggestion that the Chinese have simply pocketed the concessions and asked for more probably understates the cautiously positive Chinese approach. If, however, the objective was to divide the US and its allies,then since Vladivostok the Japanese have in fact increased the proportion of their GNP devoted to defence. The Kuranari initiative is widely interpreted as a counter to Soviet initiatives in the Southwest Pacific.

The ASEAN countries have generally been cautious to cool, given the limited Soviet flexibility so far on Vietnam. The response generally on arms reduction and on collective security discussions has been similarly cool.

On the Soviet objective of strengthening and extending the Soviet presence in the region, there has been a limited response, even by India.

In Kiribati, the Soviets argue that the termination of the fishing contract arrangement offers evidence that their objectives are primarily commercial. In Vanuatu, the Soviets have made gains. It would be unrealistic to suggest, moreover, that some Pacific island nations are not now more inclined to play the Soviet card and to trade off their security concerns for the perceived economic benefits.

AUSTRALIAN POLICY IMPLICATIONS

So what does Gorbachev's speech at Vladivostok mean for Australian policy?

The answer is probably very little in the short run - the policy framework is largely unaffected. The significant factor is that Gorbachev reasserted an already growing interest in the region and a Soviet intention to be involved in Asia and the Pacific; in a sense he was also seeking to legitimise that presence. Many in the region, including Australia, will accept - some more grudgingly than others - that the Soviet Union has legitimate interests as an Asian-Pacific nation. It would not be easy to do otherwise. For various reasons, however, Australia's policy framework needs little change. Let me examine why.

First, I noted earlier that the specific changes Gorbachev is introducing, so far at least, mostly concern the Soviet domestic system. Moreover, while important, they may be concerned less with structure than with style. Gorbachev sees foreign policy as serving domestic policy - as would we - but much of the debate about the extent and nature of Soviet change, while potentially very significant, as yet has little direct bearing on our foreign policy framework.

It is true that, on a number of foreign policy issues - on human rights, at Stockholm on military verification and arms control - the Soviets have been more forthcoming than previously. This is consistent with a Soviet desire for a peaceful international environment to pursue their domestic objectives - and such an environment is consistent with our own interests. And we have welcomed a number of steps that they have taken internationally - including on intermediate nuclear weapons and on chemical weapons. We do not know yet, however, that Soviet long term goals have changed (or, in precise terms, what all of those goals really are). On the other hand, although we know that great powers normally want to expand their political and strategic influence, we also do not know that current Soviet long term goals are necessarily sufficiently incompatible with those of the West to be unmanageable.

From Vladivostok we have then at best a statement of intent that could be very significant, with the possibility that important changes may follow.

But although we do not make policy on a worst-case basis, we need at least to contemplate it. Consideration of a Soviet threat has tended to centre on the security threat in military terms - such as the growth of the Soviet navy in the Pacific and the build-up at Cam Ranh Bay.

Such a threat is probably overstated, as the Minister of Defence Mr Kim Beazley has suggested. Gorbachev may well be sincere - for Soviet national interest reasons - in claiming that he is not aiming at military expansion in the Southwest Pacific. While the conflict scenario from which we start is an important determinant, in general, the practical difficulties in using military measures are large, and the benefits not clear. Which is probably why the Soviets have increasingly used political rather than military means to pursue their foreign policy.

Yet major Australian policy concerns can validly exist, without necessarily implying bad faith on the part of the Soviets. The US and the Soviet Union are engaged in a competitive struggle for power and influence - with the Soviet Union aiming to reduce US influence. This struggle has largely taken place so far outside the Asian-Pacific region.

A bipolar balance has been struck between superpower influence in the main area of competition - Europe. Rules of the game, agreed (if implicit and often incomplete) spheres of influence, and conventions about how the competition is to be played out have developed, often unconsciously, in other areas such as the Middle East and Latin America.

The remaining areas are particularly vulnerable, even fragile, when competition is extended to them or is intensified. This is especially so in the Asian-Pacific region, given the political and economic vulnerability of many countries in the region.

Security is ultimately concerned with protecting values and value systems. Threats to these values and value systems come from many sources - political, ideological, religious and cultural - and not just from military invasion or interdiction. Hence Libyan actions in the Pacific may be as threatening in the short term as any others.

Even taking Soviet Ministers' statements of intent at face value, therefore, the impact of increased Soviet regional involvement may be very significant. This is apart from the consideration that, whatever Ministers say, security agencies often have objectives of their own.

The Soviet aim may be predominantly economic interchange, but evangelisation of Soviet political values will be difficult or impossible to avoid - even if within a context of "peaceful competition." Caution in Australian policies is required for this reason if no other. Caution need not imply total rejection of Soviet approaches - the Chinese experience suggests that Marx and Lenin can be interpreted to be consistent with a non-evangelical approach.

For large, politically stable and economically viable liberal democracies, "peaceful competition" with other value systems may not matter if properly perceived - we would expect liberal values to prevail. Such peaceful competition may be overwhelming and destructive, however, for small states or countries that are otherwise vulnerable.

On balance, the full significance to Australia of Gorbachev's new directions in Asia and the Pacific remains, as yet, unclear. Their pursuit will force Australian policy into finer distinctions of acceptable and unacceptable Soviet policy and behaviour than before. It will also mean applying more, rather than fewer, foreign policy resources to the pursuit of our interests in the region.

In considering Soviet policies, however, we will need to get our perspective right. For example, is the concept of a USSR seeking to dominate the world useful? Probably not, since the Soviet Union could not do it militarily nor economically. Moreover, politically it has discovered that communism does not always overcome nationalism or other influences - as Yugoslavia, China, Albania and Kampuchea have shown. The Soviets, from a national interest viewpoint, may prefer Finlands and Austrias to Polands and Hungarys.

Conflicts of Interests

If the Soviet Union is like other major powers in trying to protect the external and internal security of its political regime while also trying to extend its power and influence, the important policy question is how it tries to do that. What methods will it use and what risks (or costs) is it prepared to incur?

The USSR has, in terms of our interests, got a lot wrong in Asia, particularly in Afghanistan and Kampuchea. Together with Cam Ranh Bay, such events contribute to instability in the immediate region. And we are concerned about Soviet aid to North Korea.

Obviously, therefore, we have important conflicts of interests with the Soviets. But conflicts of interests are what international relations are about. The important question is how we should respond to, and manage, such conflicts of interests.

The West's short run policy options seem to be: to confront at each step; or to contain where interests differ and to cooperate where common interests are served. The long run policy options are to seek to exclude the Soviet Union from world society in order to keep it weak; or to encourage it to join the world in the hope that this will lead to a change in its ways.

Of the short run options, to confront at every step is hardly feasible. The West lacks the resources and the risks are too great. In the Pacific, the US and Japan in particular are responding to growing Soviet military build-up with their own build-ups. We can, to a degree, be responsive to Soviet approaches to Pacific island countries such as Kiribati or Vanuatu; and we can contain in the military field where necessary. Mr Beazley said recently that Soviet naval forces in the Pacific have been contained or "effectively checkmated" by US forces in the North Pacific.

It is doubtful, however, if it is feasible to oppose at all times. Ultimately, the policy does not work unless you are sure of winning - and there can be only a few Grenadas.

Moreover, other costs would be involved. First, Australia, and the West generally, has an interest in influencing Soviet ideology. If, as suggested earlier, it can be influenced by events, confrontation, as the Minister for Foreign Affairs Mr Bill Hayden has said, may influence it adversely.

Second, confrontation ignores the non-zero sum game benefits of avoiding a competitive arms build-up and the related tension. A competitive arms build-up by the superpowers in the region will also probably be seen by many smaller countries as calling for their own arms increases - and perhaps attachment to one or other bloc.

Third, confrontation does not encourage reformers in the internal Soviet debate. If we accept that reformers in Moscow have more influence now than they have had for some time, it may be to Australia's advantage if they can demonstrate that a constructive approach receives a positive response from the West.

Fourth, confrontation is unnecessarily costly and risky. It ignores the natural forces which greatly favour the West; the West's greater economic dynamism; its technological superiority; and the success of Western cultures and institutions.

Fifth, confrontation ignores the logic (as did the domino theory) that fear of a giant leads to counter build-up of suspicion and strength. The natural outcome of growing Soviet involvement will be greater caution towards the Soviets.

Seweryn Bialer argues that democratic nations have no choice but to face the conflict with the Soviet Union, at the same time striving to cooperate in terms of mutual interest. On that proposition, confrontation would not be the option selected. Again, quoting Mr Genscher, the Foreign Minister of a country that knows the Soviet Union well, "let us [the West] not sit back idly and wait for Mr Gorbachev to deliver. Let us rather try to influence, expedite and shape developments from our end." Many have taken issue with what is seen as an over-optimistic approach, particularly that the West should take Mr Gorbachev literally "with all that this implies." Because, as I have suggested, ideology is not a useful guide to Soviet actions, it does not mean that the Soviets can easily ignore what

George Kennan called "a method of looking at the world which is anchored in the experience of centuries."

So where is the mutual interest that might benefit from cooperation? There are many existing areas of cooperation already. Apart from our substantial trade and economic links, we cooperate with the Soviet Union in many technical areas from the distribution of radio bands, the operation of air traffic controls, to actions after nuclear disasters such as Chernobyl, as well as in cultural and academic exchanges. There is value in looking at such issues independently but objectively - in terms of pragmatic Australian national interest, not ideology.

Longer term policy options affect the integration into the world economy which the Soviets see as necessary to improve their economy, and in particular, to develop their technological strength. The Soviet Union has made clear its interest - from wanting to join the General Agreement on Tariffs and Trade (GATT) to wanting to participate in the Pacific Economic Cooperation Conference - and the Australian government has seen advantage, on balance, in supporting such moves.

The case for not responding to these desires is either the wish to confront, or concern at the scope for political disruption that participation might offer. There are technical problems - the non-market nature of their economy - though these also apply to China and some other existing participants. If, however, Gorbachev's reference to Soviet "scientific and political projects on the issue of creating a new world economic order" means bringing a significantly political and ideological approach to such forums, then the case for caution is stronger.

A more fundamental argument against Soviet participation is that the Soviets may only want to buy time to strengthen their economy and improve their global position, and that their long term objectives are not benign. This could be true but even so, it need not affect the policy framework unless we believe that nothing will change those objectives.

The case for cooperating with the Soviets is mainly political. It is based, first, on a judgment that Soviet integration into the world economy will only improve their economy if the Soviet system also moves in political and social terms in the direction of the West, participating generally in the global society. Without this, economic change and improvement from outside will not occur. This indicates an acceptance of some steps in this direction and a judgment of further steps by Soviet actions.

Second, as argued earlier, in Asia mutual tolerance limits, except perhaps for Vietnam, have not been worked out between the superpowers. With both a new area of superpower interaction and new leaders (in the Soviet Union at least) the impact on the exercise of sovereignty by regional nations could be large; the risks of unintended conflict high; and superpower competition, overall, particularly risky. Productive exchanges with the various parties involved may be critical to reducing this risk.

The world is not bipolar but multipolar. Strategic and economic balances in the region are shifting with large - if unpredictable - impacts. The modernisation of China is fundamentally important in itself - as is Japan's rise to financial and investment dominance. In the past both superpowers have underestimated developments in Asia and the Pacific; they have also wrongly read the signs of change in each other. Seeing everything from a Eurocentric and US-Soviet bipolar perspective provides opportunities for Soviet exploitation in the region, stimulating rather than avoiding conflict and ignoring the need to respond to local aspirations. It may also leave the nations of the region highly vulnerable.

CONCLUSION

Let me then answer the three questions with which I started this paper.

What Gorbachev said at Vladivostok reflects a new approach of possibly major significance domestically in the Soviet Union.

It was a positive and significant message addressed to the world but it needs to be interpreted in the broader context of Gorbachev's message to his domestic audience. Whether concerned with style or structure domestically, internationally it formalises, among other things, a greater Soviet interest in the Asian-Pacific region; it also reflects facing up to existing global political realities by the Soviets. It would be unwise to dismiss it as not having a major international significance; it is still far too early, however, to know what it implies for Soviet foreign policy in practice.

Why it was said is still not completely clear. The Soviet interest in the Pacific has many facets - the security challenge facing it; improved relations with China; and the interest in regional economic opportunities, given the disappointing economic performance of the Soviet Far East, are among them. A full understanding of Soviet motivations is still to come, but the speech is consistent with diverse interpretations of their possible objectives.

What it clearly implies is increased US-Soviet competition and a more direct challenge to Western influence generally in the region. In particular contexts, beneficial effects may flow from Gorbachev's new directions, especially if the problems of Kampuchea or Afghanistan should be resolved. The almost inevitable increase in regional tensions, however, will probably be adverse for all in the region, and could be serious. To avoid that would require great sensitivity both by the Soviets and by the US.

For Australian policy, Vladivostok probably means little if any change as yet - which is not to dismiss its possible future importance. While the ANZUS relationship remains of central importance, Mr Hayden said in 1984 that the West "needs to make active efforts to encourage it [the Soviet Union] to overcome the dangerous effects of its own, often self imposed, isolation." Australia, he has also said, was seeking to draw the Soviet Union into productive relationships with the rest of the world rather than shun it or isolate it. That position was based on various assumptions, and Vladivostok did nothing to affect the validity of those assumptions and, consequently, the policy that flowed from them.

From a foreign policy viewpoint, the new Pacific-oriented directions of the Soviet Union may offer much or little, but we will probably not know for some time. Rethinking of basic policy positions in detail - by the Soviets or anyone else - is not something done quickly.

In the meantime, we have to do two things. The first is to remain cautious in case no material change occurs. Arguments for a policy of cooperation, where cooperation is clearly in our national interest, remain unaffected. We should be willing to accept Vladivostok in good faith, until experience suggests otherwise - and changes in Soviet policies towards the NPA in the Philippines, for example, as with any stepping up of aid to North Korea, would be considered to conflict with that good faith. We will want to ensure, however, that the Soviets understand the widespread regional wish that East-West or other tensions should not be introduced into the region, and that Soviet activities do not extend beyond commercial or similar exchanges.

Second, we need to recognise that major risks remain, less in the traditional concept of immediate military threat than through the weight of great power competition, and through the threat to Western values of the potential for evangelising an alternative - and very different - set of values. It is not necessary to postulate malign intentions to see both of these as threatening, particularly among smaller or weaker countries. Of course, if Soviet intentions are malign, then the dangers are that much greater.

There is always a danger that we will see hope of change when the reality is different. There is also a danger that we will resist change from which we could benefit. We need to be questioning and cautious but not negative - we cannot afford to make a mistake in either direction.

9

Defence Implications for Australia

David Charles

Ever since Mr Gorbachev delivered his Vladivostok speech in July last year we have heard loud warnings about the red menace; we have heard about the risk of a Cuba in our backyard; and we have heard comparisons made between the Soviet build-up in the Pacific and Hitler's military build-up in Europe before World War II.

The government's view, expressed by the Minister of Defence on 20 February in his statement on defence initiatives in the South Pacific, is that changes occurring there "carry the potential risk that disputes between the major powers, and influences which could be harmful to our longer term strategic interests, may be introduced to the region." However, as Kim Beazley went on to point out only a couple of days later in the Parliament, developments in the Asian-Pacific region are of great strategic concern to us, and for that reason we do not simply rely on the views or advice which we might receive from others. We have our own intelligence capabilities, and make our own evaluation. So it is on the basis of our own assessment that I am speaking to you this afternoon. I will be emphasising a defence and strategic perspective.

In order to understand the significance of recent activities by the Soviet Union in the Asian-Pacific region, we need to look at the facts. Mr Gorbachev's Vladivostok Initiative offers some key insights into these activities. So let us take a look at what can be learned from the content of the Vladivostok announcements and see whether such alarmist views are justified in the defence area.

Much of Mr Gorbachev's speech was geared to Soviet economic aspirations for the Soviet Far East. These aspirations are perfectly legitimate, and the Australian government has no quibble with them. Indeed, accelerated economic development in the Soviet Union accompanied by rising prosperity for the Soviet people would be a significant contribution to international confidence, thereby easing tensions. But he also dealt with matters which are significant from the defence and strategic perspective. And here he specifically examined the roles of China, Japan and the US as major regional players. He also mentioned less influential countries in his considerations, including the ASEAN countries, the Pacific island states and Australia. But his strategic preoccupation is clearly with China, Japan and the US.

What is behind Mr Gorbachev's preoccupation with China, Japan and the US, and for that matter, his attitude to Southeast Asia and the South Pacific? And what are the defence implications?

The answer to these questions is given by Mr Gorbachev himself. Mr Gorbachev is concerned about the strength and influence of Western alliances. I would like to quote a key sentence in his statement: "The Soviet Union is a convinced advocate of disbanding military groups, renouncing foreign bases in Asia and in the Pacific Ocean and withdrawing troops from others' territory."

Mr Gorbachev acknowledges that the United States is a great Pacific power, and that without US participation it would be impossible to resolve problems of security and cooperation in the Pacific.

But Mr Gorbachev says he is resolutely opposed to what he describes as the USA's attempt to extend NATO's competence over the entire world, including Asia and the Pacific Ocean. What Mr Gorbachev is really saying, then, is this: it is in the USSR's interests to see an end to the ANZUS alliance, the Manila Treaty, the US-Japan alliance and the US-South Korea alliance. The inevitable result is that Mr Gorbachev is opposed to Japan-US defence cooperation. He is against ANZUS and the Five Power Defence Arrangements (linking Australia with the United Kingdom, New Zealand, Malaysia and Singapore). He would like the US bases in the Philippines closed. He wants an end to US assistance to South Korea and he wants the US forces (which in fact remain there subject to a UN resolution) to leave. He would like to see the US remove those features of its strategic deployments which cause the most difficulty for Soviet strategists. He also wants to counter China's growing links with the West.

This is a very significant policy statement. A statement that warrants close analysis because it is here that we find the defence implications of the Vladivostok speech.

The defence White Paper of 1987 describes the fundamental elements of the government's approach to defence as:

- To maintain and develop capabilities for the independent defence of Australia and its interests;

- The promotion of strategic stability and security in our region;
- As a member of the Western strategic community, to work for a reduction in the level of tension between the superpowers, and to limit the spread of influences in our region that may be harmful to Western interests.

Intrinsic to the government's defence policy, therefore, is our alliance with the United States and New Zealand. As the Minister for Foreign Affairs Bill Hayden said when welcoming the Soviet foreign minister to Canberra on 3 March: "Australia is firmly and unequivocally committed to its alliance with the United States as a fundamental of our national interests."

These relationships and our close defence relations with Papua New Guinea and our partners in the Five Power Defence Arrangements enhance our self-reliance in the technological, training and intelligence fields, while at the same time contributing to the stability and security of our own region. Since the White Paper deals with these aspects in considerable detail, I do not propose to go over that area here.

But I should make the following points.

Mr Gorbachev is wary of any alliance or strategic development in the Asian-Pacific region which he sees as threatening to Soviet security. And in particular, Mr Gorbachev is concerned about any developments which might bring Japan, China and the United States - the three powerful regional players - into closer strategic alignment.

But the thrust of Mr Gorbachev's message is clear - he considers that the Soviet Union's strategic and defence interests are threatened by strategic arrangements by and between the United States and its allies in the region.

This is hardly new. But what is new is the apparent willingness of the current Soviet leadership to distinguish between the economic development aims of the Soviet Union and its traditional strategic and military objectives. This is one feature of the Vladivostok speech which the government cautiously welcomes. There is a long way to go, but it gives cause for hope that the Soviet Union may yet come to play a more constructive and positive part in the international system, including the Asian-Pacific region.

The Australian government's consistent position since 1984 has been (to quote Mr Hayden in 1984) that the West "needs to make active efforts to encourage the Soviet Union to overcome the dangerous effects of its own, often self-imposed isolation." Australia, Mr Hayden said in 1984, was seeking to draw the Soviet Union into productive relationships with the rest of the world rather than shun it or isolate it. This remains the Australian government's overall policy approach.

Much of the content of the Vladivostok speech is encouraging in that perspective.

Early indications are that the new policy approaches and presentational style of the Soviet leadership are producing at least some of the effects they are looking for. So we need to ask: does the prospect of an energetic Soviet economic and diplomatic presence in our region give rise to immediate security concerns for Australia? On present indications, the answer to this question is "No." As I have just said, we are dealing with a new leadership and a new approach. For our part, we are not prepared to condemn the Soviet Union out of hand before it is given a chance to 'put its money where its mouth is'. We are willing to test Soviet performance and we have made this clear to the Soviet government. But we are not complacent. Nor are we blind to the lessons which flow from our experience of the Soviet Union's activities in the international arena.

Our chief concern is that the Soviet Union will try to use whatever economic and diplomatic influence it can build up in the region to pursue its political objectives as a superpower opposed to the Western strategic alliance. As a result, our region could become a focus of increasing superpower competition. This would have the potential to upset the strategic stability we now enjoy in our part of the world.

Moreover, we are aware that the development of official bilateral relations does not preclude the cultivation of potentially subversive contacts or attempts to influence the political life of target countries. So a heightened Soviet interest in our region introduces a broad range of factors and issues which could in certain circumstances upset the strategic stability that currently characterises our region.

But there are countervailing factors to be weighed in the balance.

The US, Japan and Australia are contributing to a strong, favourable, Western economic and defence presence in the Southwest Pacific.

The prospects of the Soviets using their "window on the Pacific" for an economic *entrée* into the region will be constrained by the poor performance of the Soviet economy, its difficulties in attracting foreign investment, and the lack of development in the Soviet Far East.

We should not underestimate the cohesive strength of the regional associations - ASEAN and the South Pacific Forum - and the strong Western alliances in our region.

A more active Soviet involvement may bring with it a risk of instability and a diminution of Australia's favourable strategic circumstances. But at this stage Soviet activities have not acquired a significant security dimension.

It is a long way from commercial fishing access to military access, let alone military bases in the South Pacific. And Vladivostok itself, Mr Gorbachev's "window on the Pacific," is still closed to foreigners. Mr Gorbachev may be able to see a brighter world through his partly-opened window, and the winds of change may perhaps be blowing. But he has yet to remove the bars on that window.

Our attitude should be one of sober assessment and vigilance, but we must avoid an alarmist over-reactive response. As the Prime Minister recently characterised it, the government's attitude is one of "wary, cautious optimism."

We believe that the Soviet Union is likely to continue to emphasise diplomatic, fishing and trade interests rather than military ones in its attempt to gain political influence.

In response, the appropriate defence policies for Australia are those presented in the government's White Paper. The government will continue to develop a self-reliant defence force; to maintain sturdy relationships with our friends and allies; and to foster regional cohesion and stability.

10

The Soviet Union in the South Pacific

Richard A. Herr

The central motif of the March 1987 symposium, "Gorbachev's Vladivostok Initiative: New Directions in Asia and the Pacific?" suggests that 28 July 1986 will be recorded as a watershed date in Soviet relations with Asia and the Pacific. As this area is both extensive and varied, however, such a theme may prove historically valid in the round without applying with equal strength to all the components of the region. Will General Secretary Mikhail Gorbachev's Vladivostok speech prove significant specifically in relations between Moscow and the South Pacific? One might be tempted to answer "no" from a narrow historical perspective, given that the major political changes for the Soviet Union occurred nearly a year before the Vladivostok speech. It was in August 1985 that the USSR secured its controversial fisheries access to Kiribati. Yet, despite the important antecedents to a broader Soviet involvement in the South Pacific, Gorbachev's address may well mark the transition from one era to another.[1]

Such an assessment can be sustained on two grounds. The first is that the Vladivostok speech appears to be designed to draw together a number of policy strands to create a coherent and focused Pacific-oriented initiative. And to the extent that the South Pacific is a serious element in this grand strategy, the Soviets' previous reliance on serendipitous opportunism is likely to be replaced by a more directed search for influence. The second basis for regarding Gorbachev's speech as critical to South Pacific affairs stems from its impact on other states. Although, as Geoffrey Jukes observes, "its primary audience was not Western Kremlinologists but the Soviet [Communist] Party and Soviet society as a whole,"[2] the speech has reverberated throughout the Asian-Pacific area and beyond. The prospect of greater Soviet involvement in the South Pacific has elicited only limited and cautious reaction in the island countries themselves; but it has produced something close to alarm in Western states with their own interests in the region. Whether or not Gorbachev's Vladivostok Initiative can be said to have caused it directly, the Western security posture of "strategic denial" is now close to collapse, and there are signs that a more accommodating fallback position is being developed. Such a change would concede, in effect, the policy of a general Pacific economic interaction that was espoused at Vladivostok.

Those who believe that any intercourse with the USSR will pose a threat to the island countries and, through them, to wider Western security interests are concerned at the prospect of an accommodation which could legitimate a continuing Soviet presence in the South Pacific. Countries such as Japan have proferred thinly disguised pleas for Australia to exercise its hegemonic responsibilities in the region by curtailing Moscow's inroads.[3] These anxieties have been echoed by the conservative end of the political spectrum in Australia which openly accuses the Labor government of failing to halt Soviet encroachment in the South Pacific.[4] These reactions have been predicated on a belief both that Gorbachev's address signals serious intent in the Pacific and that strategic denial can still be pursued in the South Pacific. Whether the first premise is true remains to be tested; the second appears to be badly frayed.

This chapter surveys the course of recent Soviet activities in the South Pacific. It will be argued that the Vladivostok initiatives have genuine implications for the island countries both by broadening the opportunities for diplomatic contacts and yet simultaneously escalating significantly the costs of pursuing relationships outside the existing pattern. The confusing calculus of cost/benefit in this changing diplomatic environment appears to be adding to the volatility of foreign policy-making in the island countries. It is also increasing the pressure on Western states seeking to maintain the Western alignment of the region. The bases of the policy of strategic denial are being eroded to an extent which will either require their defence postures to be revised fundamentally or else replaced altogether. These adjustments may already be in train.

STRATEGIC DENIAL

The two principal regional powers in the South Pacific - Australia and New Zealand - have a history of continuous defence cooperation with the United States from World War II onwards. Perhaps more significantly, the two have been formally allied with each other since 1944, and with the United States from 1951 in the ANZUS pact. Their participation in other

Western alliances [the South East Asia Treaty Organisation (SEATO) and the Five Power Defence Arrangement] have served to extend and cement their military commitment to Western security. It was to be expected therefore that the two ANZAC states would seek to maintain a politico-strategic climate in their neighbourhood which would be congenial to Western interests; more specifically that the island countries would be aligned with the West on critical cold war issues.

Early in the decolonisation of the South Pacific this Western political orientation was assumed more than pursued as deliberate policy. The islands' long contact with Western states, the ready transfer of democratic institutions, the extent of deeply entrenched Christian values and the relatively tranquil passage to independence: all this tended to reassure the Western powers, including Australia and New Zealand, that post-colonial South Pacific would have a pronounced Western bent on the question of security. The maintenance of a close and supportive relationship by the former metropoles, buttressed by a special ANZAC involvement with those states not previously under their control, helped to sustain a pro-Western sentiment in the South Pacific.[5]

Even when apparently challenged in 1976, the basic forms for maintaining the Western alignment of the islands scarcely changed, although the logic of this strategy became more explicit. The ANZUS allies recognised that the paramount perceived national interest for the independent states of the South Pacific was (and remains) economic development. Thus, it appeared possible for Western states to promote their aid and trade links with the islands in order to preempt the opportunities for potentially hostile third parties to exploit an economic avenue to influence in the South Pacific. This rather vague strategy took form over a period of years and emerged as a more or less coherent policy of strategic denial.[6] The salient features of strategic denial comprised:

a. A desire to exclude virtually all Soviet (and suspected Soviet surrogate) activity from the South Pacific;
b. The encouragement of regionalism to minimise the likelihood of aberrant behaviour by individual states;
c. The use of informal mechanisms, particularly trade and aid, in preference to treaties to maintain a pro-Western alignment in the region;
d. A reliance on Australia and New Zealand as the hegemonic powers in the area.

Although a policy largely of the ANZUS powers within the Western alliance, strategic denial was tacitly endorsed and encouraged by a variety of extra-regional actors, including China and Japan, who wished to limit Soviet influence in an area that was important to their security interests.

This Western approach to security in the South Pacific has depended, of course, on the willing cooperation of the island countries. Generally such cooperation was forthcoming. The islands, mindful of their own limited diplomatic and defence capacities, were disinclined in their early years of independence to pursue wide ranging foreign policies. Only rare issues such as the United Nations Third Conference on the Law of the Sea (UNCLOS III) could draw the region's microstates willingly onto the world stage. Besides the reticence to seek involvement in global concerns, the islands have quietly accepted the mutual benefits for themselves of a tacit Western alignment. This was perhaps most dramatically evidenced in the months following the Soviet military intervention in Afghanistan in December 1979, when the majority of regional states moved to close their ports to Soviet shipping. Other signs of alignment could be seen in the continuing refusal of island countries to permit a resident Soviet mission to be established despite allegedly repeated Soviet requests for an embassy, or to accept the occasional offers of Soviet aid.

It is an interesting feature of the emergence of strategic denial that, although its aim was to exclude the Soviet Union as completely as possible from South Pacific affairs, it relied substantially on informal mechanisms for implementation. Indeed, the ANZUS allies discouraged enquiries from islands states regarding accession to the defence pact.[7] As Henry Albinski has pointed out, the ANZUS partners were concerned that inclusion of a wider, weaker and more parochial membership would pose unacceptable risks for the alliance.[8] There was also a perception that defence agreements between the Western powers and the island states could provoke a countervailing Soviet response.

This is not to say that explicit defence ties have been totally eschewed. It is true that neither Australia nor New Zealand has defence treaties with the South Pacific's independent states, although Australia does have a joint prime ministerial statement and a status-of-forces agreement with Papua New Guinea (PNG). However, the United States did include defence clauses in its treaties of friendship with Tuvalu and Kiribati. These clauses require the regional party to consult with the United States before making portions of territory available to third party states and, in return, Washington has given qualified assurances of assistance should Tuvalu or Kiribati be the victims of aggression. While these defence provisions were felt to be largely *pro forma* to obtain congressional approval, the clause in the Kiribati treaty may have contributed to Tarawa's decision not to accede to the Soviet request for shore facilities in their 1985 fisheries agreement.

By the early 1980s, the newly found consensus on the general features of strategic denial began to be challenged. In its fundamentals, a policy of excluding nearly all Soviet influence in the South Pacific depended on one of two essential conditions operating. Either the islands would have to be so completely committed to their Western alignment that they would resist any blandishment from the USSR, or the Soviet interest in the region would have to be so low that no serious effort to gain influence would be made. Since the Western authors of the policy were unwilling to rely on the second condition, they worked towards ensuring the continuance of the islands' alignment. And, ironically for the West, it was precisely in this area that most of the politico-strategic changes threatening strategic denial occurred.

One of the more critical developments was the radicalisation of elite attitudes in the region by French resistance to decolonisation. Although moderate by global standards, the foreign policy orientations which emerged from Vanuatu's traumatic transition to independence have created an outspoken voice in the South Pacific for nonalignment.[9] French mishandling of the decolonisation of New Caledonia (Kanaky) seems likely to produce a similar result in a fellow Melanesian country as well as encouraging other South Pacific states to question Western motives in their region.

French nuclear-weapons testing at Moruroa has been a longer running issue for the islands, but only recently has it been linked widely to the value of Western alignment. Here the pivotal event was the linking of opposition to these tests to a regional nuclear free zone (NFZ); abortively in 1975 but successfully a decade later.[10] The 1983 proposal forced the United States to the defensive, since it feared that the NFZ would have adverse consequences both for ANZUS and, in terms of its "demonstration effect," for other parts of the world. The importance of nuclear weapons to American perceptions of Western security in the South Pacific became painfully apparent in the following year, when the New Zealand Labour Party under David Lange won office with a pledge to refuse port access to nuclear-powered and/or nuclear-armed warships.

The continuing ANZUS imbroglio has produced more than just a dramatic insight into asymmetrical treaty relations under stress. The incident revealed to the South Pacific nations how fully their own security was tied to the American nuclear umbrella.[11] In some states the revelation provoked reflection, while in others it served to reinforce commitment to a Western alignment.[12] In the event, sufficient agreement existed for a minimalist NFZ treaty to be drafted, signed and ratified despite the objections of the British, French and American governments. The Treaty of Rarotonga [as the pact establishing the South Pacific Nuclear Free Zone (SPNFZ) is usually called] was not intended to undermine the Western alignment of the region, of course, but it did move the islands away from a critical area of Western defence strategy.

More than any other event, however, it was the American position on marine resources, especially tuna, which engendered the widest and most intense suspicions in the islands regarding the benefits of alignment. The Reagan administration's refusal to accept elements of the new law of the sea regime vital to the South Pacific islands was seen as endangering the economic viability of a number of the poorer states in the region. And for states with marine resources as the principal hope for some form of economic self-sufficiency, this threat was tantamount to undermining national sovereignty. It was almost precisely in these terms that President Ieremia Tabai of Kiribati justified his decision to enter into a fisheries access agreement with the Soviet Union in August 1985.[13]

The wisdom of Tabai's decision was questioned and/or repudiated by island states as well as Western countries. This was despite his claims that the transaction was entirely commercial, and notwithstanding his government's assiduous efforts to prevent Moscow from gaining any non-fishing advantages from the agreement. Nonetheless, Tabai could not control the encouragement that the arrangement would give to the USSR to seek similar access elsewhere in the region, nor the demonstration effects on other South Pacific states of the first major commercial treaty between the USSR and an island government. While it appears likely that the first effect was felt in the Kremlin, there can be even less doubt of the second. Vanuatu reached a similar but more extensive agreement with the USSR in January 1987, a trade mission has visited Fiji, and PNG has been giving thought to a fisheries access arrangement.

Thus, by the mid-1980s, at a time when the new foreign policy initiatives of Gorbachev were being formulated, island countries were already beginning to question aspects of their relationship with the West. It would be an exaggeration to suggest that regional states were moving towards declared nonalignment, as is evidenced by the fact that Vanuatu alone has formally joined the Non-Aligned Movement. Yet there was a more general questioning of the benefits of alignment both in economic terms and in terms of broader security issues, such as the relevance of nuclear deterrence to the South Pacific.

The uncertainties which have surrounded this introspection have divided island countries in a way which appears to be undermining the consensus on security issues that obtained when alignment was tacitly assumed. The erosion of unqualified support for alignment weakened the collective inhibitions on dealings with the USSR, with the result that a growing number of island states have been prepared to give at least some thought to commercial ties, ties that were unthinkable only five years earlier. Thus strategic denial, understood as the absolute bar to the Soviet Union that it seemed to be at the end of the 1970s, has become almost untenable by the end of the 1980s.

OPPORTUNISM

The reduced value attached to alignment may be attributed largely to policy differences between some Western states and the island countries; but is the more receptive climate in the South Pacific today towards the USSR explained primarily by opportunism? It is possible that the shift of opinion in the region has been manufactured not so much by the mistakes of the West as by the machinations of the East. How large does the South Pacific loom in Soviet interests, and is this significance sufficient to account for the Soviet's limited, albeit noteworthy, recent foreign policy successes in the region? The evidence here is mixed, but it suggests opportunism more than conspiracy.

Paul Dibb has argued rather cogently that Soviet interests in the South Pacific are essentially instrumental.[14] The islands are of little intrinsic value to Moscow,[15] and therefore whatever interest the Soviets have shown in this area can be traced back to Australia's role in helping to maintain the central balance between the superpowers. Dibb points out that the joint US/Australian facilities in Australia particularly concern the Kremlin,[16] a point reaffirmed by Foreign Minister Eduard Shevardnadze during his March 1987 visit to Australia. The doubts of the past year over the future of American bases in the Philippines may have increased the strategic returns to the USSR of investing in the Pacific Islands, but here too the involvement would be a means to an extra-regional end rather than a motive for valuing the South Pacific in its own right.

Historically, Soviet attempts at involvement in the islands have been predicated on a quiet acceptance of the region as a Western sphere of influence, as an "ANZUS lake." Even as late as the end of the 1970s Soviet commentaries on the South Pacific acknowledged the Western alignment of the islands, arguing only that areas existed for cooperative interaction which would benefit the islands if taken up.[17] Indeed, until 1980 it was rare for Russian activity in the region to even touch the islands directly. Oceanographic research, missile testing, fishing, transport, and the like tended to be concentrated outside the islands' territorial seas, and only occasionally did vessels engaged in these activities visit regional ports. Perhaps the most prominent exception was the chartered Soviet cruise-ship traffic in the mid-1970s, but political reaction in the region to the Afghanistan invasion constricted this passive commercial intercourse significantly.

Sufficient evidence exists of occasional efforts by the USSR to develop relations with the South Pacific during the 1970s (essentially the decade of decolonisation in the region) to believe that Moscow was anxious to secure some early influence in this corner of the world.[18] However, the obvious lack of results suggests strongly either that Moscow's gestures were largely perfunctory or else that they were badly implemented. A realistic explanation almost certainly includes elements of both - that Soviet interest and effort were both desultory. The asymmetry between the USSR and the South Pacific nonetheless is of such a magnitude that even minor shifts in effort by the USSR could produce vastly disproportionate repercussions in the islands.

Perhaps stung by the widespread condemnation of its intervention in Afghanistan, Moscow has appeared to be willing to devote more resources to creating a niche for itself since 1980. In October of that year, a substantial offer of aid was made through the Committee for Coordination of Joint Prospecting for Mineral Resources in South Pacific Offshore Areas (CCOP/SOPAC). The offer of a five year study of tectonic plate movement was accepted by officials at the meeting but later repudiated by the island governments. The episode was commonly treated in the popular media as another indication of Soviet attempts to gain a foothold in the South Pacific by stealth, although there was nothing special to distinguish this offer from previous gestures, or indeed from similar offers still being made through CCOP/SOPAC.

The lessons of the episode are not so much that such a major aid offer was made; the USSR has had a large interest in South Pacific oceanography for about three decades, and such a project would have been compatible with its other research. Rather it was the ill-grace with which Moscow reacted to the island governments' repudiations of the initial acceptance of the Soviet offer. The matter was referred to a meeting in Bangkok of ESCAP (Economic and Social Commission for Asia and the Pacific), which was then the parent body of CCOP/SOPAC. The Solomon Islands led on the issue for the islands, and the obdurate persistence of the Soviet officials still rankles with the Solomons. While there may have been no mischievousness in the initial offer, Moscow clearly set great value on its acceptance, and thus on access to the region that this would have afforded.

Throughout the early 1980s the Soviet Union continued to seek overt, and allegedly covert, avenues of influence. The most celebrated of the covert attempts was the imputation by the Fiji government in 1982 that Moscow had sought to interfere in the country's general elections.[19] Yet it was not until 1985 and the fisheries access agreement with Kiribati that the USSR reaped any reward from its apparently increased effort. And, as noted above, the breakthrough did not appear to arise from the effectiveness of any covertly supported fifth column. Indeed, despite much media speculation, the effectiveness of Soviet-supported "trade unions, church and peace groups ... being used as part of Moscow's strategy to increase its influence in the region"[20] has been minimal to date, except for the nuclear issue on which the islands have a history of opposition going back two decades and antedating the creation of many of these groups. In the area of trade unionism, for example, the Moscow-backed World Federation of Trade Unions (WFTU) has actually lost membership and now has only one Solomon Islands affiliate.

The declared intentions of the Vladivostok speech will not necessarily improve the Soviet's success rate in the South Pacific. They do point to a resolve, nevertheless, to continue with the initiatives begun before July 1986 which have given the USSR a place in the region that was previously denied to it. Present indications suggest that this resolve will be manifested in additional activity in the islands which, given the shifting regional opinion on the strength of alignment - if not on alignment itself - may be judged increasingly on the economic merits which Moscow would prefer rather than on the strategic risks which the West stresses. If there was any substantive content to Shevardnadze's reassurance during his Australian tour in March 1987 that the Soviet Union would not seek military bases in the South Pacific, it was that Gorbachev's USSR denied that the South Pacific was an ANZUS lake and that the Soviet Union sought some continuing presence in the region.

SIGNIFICANCE OF VLADIVOSTOK

Opportunism may account for much of the Soviet Union's apparent success in the South Pacific, but the consolidation of its relatively modest successes to date will depend on such factors as Soviet diplomatic skill, the resources devoted to the effort and the priority attached to maintaining a regional presence. The rhetoric of the Vladivostok speech displayed both sophistication and resolve. The speech listed all the independent members of the South Pacific Forum (except the Solomon Islands) by name. Gorbachev affirmed a Soviet desire "to expand ties" with these states.[21] He went on to support the SPNFZ and, clearly aiming a barb at the three Western nuclear powers, called on them "to guarantee its status."[22] Rhetoric, however, is not action, and the price that Moscow is prepared to pay for Gorbachev's pronouncements on the South Pacific has not yet been indicated. The first post-Vladivostok indicators, nevertheless, have appeared and their implications are, unfortunately for both the island and Western states, somewhat ambiguous.

In keeping with the Vladivostok speech's emphasis on economic development and international pragmatism, but to the consternation of critics, the Soviet Union failed to renew its fisheries agreement with Kiribati when this expired in mid-1986. This incident has confused the question of Soviet motives in the South Pacific. Speculation was current at the time of its signing that Moscow had paid an uneconomic premium, although it was not clear whether this was for acceptance or to achieve non-economic objectives.[23] The judgment that the USSR paid a premium for access appears to have been validated by the course of the 1986 talks to renew the agreement, albeit without settling the issue of why Moscow paid the uneconomic fee in the first place.

Both Kiribati and the Soviet Union were apparently genuinely willing to renew the agreement, but Moscow wanted amended terms. Tarawa demurred. The Soviet negotiators claimed that the fees for sixteen boats had made the returns uneconomic, and proposed reducing the access to eight boats with a commensurate reduction in the licensing fees. One report holds that the 1985 fee levels cost the Soviets $850 a tonne for fish that was worth only $700 a tonne (all in "hard" currency).[24] Tabai's government, facing general elections in 1987 where the agreement was expected to figure prominently, was unwilling to offer many concessions. This determination may well have been buttressed by reportedly maladroit diplomacy on the Soviet side.[25] The agreement lapsed, although both parties appeared to keep open the prospect of another agreement some time in the future.

It has been alleged that, despite the overtly economic explanation for the failure of the 1986 access talks, the real reason for Soviet resistance to renewing the agreement was Moscow's inability to broaden it to include shore facilities.[26] This may be true but, if so, the USSR was taking a very calculated risk. Although talks were in train with Vanuatu for a similar access arrangement and a trade mission was exploring trade prospects with Fiji, no replacement for Kiribati was definite when the fisheries agreement lapsed in October 1986. The diplomatic risks to the USSR were perhaps further increased in that a major argument in favour of agreements with other regional states was the success of the Kiribati treaty.

On the other hand, if economic considerations are accepted as the sole explanation for Moscow's retreat from Kiribati, then the January 1987 fisheries agreement with Vanuatu raises additional questions about Soviet priorities in the South Pacific. It appears that the USSR has paid roughly the same amount in fees for access to Vanuatu waters as for its previous access to the Kiribati zone (US $1.5 million), but for only half as many boats.[27] The one significant difference between the two access agreements is that the Vanuatu agreement provides for port access whereas the Kiribati agreement did not. (It is also possible that air access will be added but, contrary to expectations, Vanuatu did not concede this initially in its fisheries agreement.) The higher fee per boat might be justified economically if Vanuatu waters were especially more productive than those of Kiribati. But this point is disputed by fisheries authorities who also point out that the Soviets have preferred purse-seining to the longlining methods normally used in Vanuatu waters. Should this opinion be borne out, then the economic viability of the Vanuatu agreement for Soviet fishermen will be even less than that of the Kiribati agreement.

In part, for reasons such as this, the most significant aspect of Soviet actions in the South Pacific since the Vladivostok speech may be the inability of Western states to reassure themselves that Moscow's motives in the region are strictly commercial. Shevardnadze unwittingly fuelled these fears during his 1987 visit to Australia. He was reported to have said that the USSR sought political influence through its fisheries agreements and, in time, through expansion of normal commercial, tourism, cultural and sporting contacts, "but in no case [a] military presence."[28] While addressing what he no doubt believed to be Australia's chief concern - that of a Soviet military presence - he reaffirmed the logic of strategic denial. If the non-military mechanisms could help to prevent the entry of the USSR into the South Pacific (a strategic objective), why then should not the same mechanisms work in favour of the Kremlin once inside the region? Shevardnadze's comment carries the implication that this is the intent of Moscow's post-Vladivostok policy in the South Pacific.

The Australian Labor government has found itself somewhat on the horns of a dilemma as a result of Gorbachev's new-look Pacific policy. It has been unwilling to appear paternalistically domineering within the region in the face of the putative Soviet challenge, and yet a perceived failure to carry out satisfactorily its regional hegemonic role could see other states acting directly to protect their own, and/or Western, interests. The first position is grounded both in a desire to avoid a charge of neocolonialism and in a genuine belief that, within limits, the independent states ought to enjoy the exercise of sovereignty as they see fit. The latter qualm is already being justified by the appearance of a wider range of actors seeking to involve themselves more actively in the South Pacific.

The Australian Foreign Minister, Bill Hayden, has been hard pressed to walk a fine line between the two unpalatable extremes. It has not been easy. In May 1986 he told an audience at the University of the South Pacific that it was possible for the Soviets to have a relationship with the islands where defence implications were absent.[29] This position was put more positively some months later when Hayden was reported as welcoming a constructive participation by Moscow in the region.[30] However, on other occasions he reminded island governments that whether or not a specific relationship had a defence implication depended in large part on the capacity of a small state to monitor a potentially difficult relationship.[31] The subtleties of this advice have been missed sometimes, particularly by Vanuatu, with Prime Minister Walter Lini reacting openly and angrily to Australian calls for prudence. Ultimately, however, Hayden's position marks an acceptance by Australia of a qualified Soviet involvement in the South Pacific.

To ensure that Moscow's involvement remains circumscribed, Australian policy has exhibited elements both of continuity and change. The Labor government has sought to impress upon France and the United States the urgency of improving their relations with the islands. The United States recently removed one major impediment by reaching a US $60 million multilateral fisheries access agreement with the islands (although this treaty has yet to be ratified). France has proved more intractable, regarding Australian advice on the decolonisation of New Caledonia as an intrusion into its exercise of sovereignty. Indeed, rather than perceiving its position on New Caledonia as a threat to the Western alignment of the islands, Paris has argued that support for the Kanaks constitutes aid to the USSR's ambitions in the South Pacific. And, of course, the French government remains unmoved on the question of nuclear testing at Moruroa.

While retaining a preference for the non-formal ties which characterised strategic denial initially, the present Australian government acted early to enshrine one issue-area in a treaty. This was the SPNFZ. It was hoped that that arrangement would reduce the attractiveness of the region to superpower rivalries by removing from it one of the main areas of global contention - nuclear weapons. However, Moscow has sought to turn the tables on the West by becoming the first nuclear power to sign the treaty's protocols in December 1986. As there appear to be few other areas where Canberra can hope to use formal devices to reduce Moscow's interest in the South Pacific, this line of diplomacy may be at an end.

If Australia cannot reduce the level of Soviet interest in the South Pacific (a prospect apparently eliminated by Gorbachev's Vladivostok speech), and if the islands are no longer prepared collectively to exclude the USSR (a situation seemingly forestalled by the Vanuatu agreement), the only posture that Australia can adopt appears to be that which pertains in other areas of the globe where Western allies must deal with a continuing Soviet involvement. It will have to take measures to ensure that Soviet activities remain confined to non-strategic channels. The initiatives announced by Australian Defence Minister, Kim Beazley, in late February 1987 can be interpreted as just such an accommodation to a post-strategic denial defence regime.[32] The emphasis is on surveillance and patrolling in the South Pacific rather than on the exclusion of the Soviet Union.

Another possible development could be along the lines of a recent proposal by the Deputy Prime Minister of PNG, Sir Julius Chan. Sir Julius suggested that Australia enter into a mutual security pact to formalise more effectively *inter alia* this aspect of the two countries' relationship. The specific proposal has been perceived with some embarrassment due to Australian sensitivities to the reaction of Indonesia,[33] but the concept in general is not without some attractive features for an allied hegemonic power in a region where the sentiment of alignment appears to be eroding. And, given that one of the reservations restraining formal defence ties was a fear that this would draw the then absent USSR into the region, region-based defence pacts could appear to have less deleterious consequences in a South Pacific where the Soviet Union is already present.

Whether or not the inevitable formalisation of relations will lead Australia to seek bilateral or multilateral defence agreements within the region, its preeminence (along with New Zealand's) as the hegemonic regional power will be diminished by the appearance of a permanent Soviet interest in the South Pacific. Already there are indications that the United States, Japan and China are preparing to take a more active role in the region in reaction to a perception of growing Soviet influence.[34] Other states such as Israel have begun to take note of the region not so much because of the direct interest of the Soviet Union as of its putative surrogates - Libya, Cuba and Vietnam.[35] The swelling volume of activity is overtaking Australia's diplomatic resources despite the high priority accorded to the South Pacific in Canberra.

The reaction of the islands to this outburst of politico-strategic voyeurism has varied widely both amongst the members of the regional community and within the individual states. Tuvalu has opted out of the fisheries auction, believing that even commercial transaction with the Soviets will have strategic implications.[36] Vanuatu and Kiribati clearly rejected the proposition. Some states have appeared to enjoy the prominence and opportunities offered, in the short term at least, by superpower rivalry.[37] Domestically the reaction has been similarly diverse. The newly formed Fiji Labour Party has included within its policy platform a pledge to move Fiji out of its Western alignment.[38] Yet in Kiribati and Vanuatu political parties have been formed to oppose fishing ties with the USSR.

Although divided on such issues as commercial ties with the USSR and the value of Western alignment, collectively the countries are united in their desire to ensure that they can manage their security at the regional level. Since 1980 this sentiment has given rise to a succession of sporadic calls for regional defence, most recently by the Solomons' then Prime Minister, Sir Peter Kenilorea.[39] The intention has been to ensure that regional disputes do not create pretexts for extra-regional intervention. Such a force has never been envisaged as coping with a major power intrusion, but a greater capacity for collective security regionally may prove a means of constraining the opportunities for superpower rivalry.

CONCLUSION

Gorbachev's Vladivostok speech almost certainly marks the end of an era for the South Pacific. The watershed has occurred not because the Soviet leader proposed sweeping or innovative initiatives for the South Pacific, but rather because he formally declared Moscow's belief that it has a legitimate role in all parts of the Asian-Pacific basin. This assertion has directly challenged any exclusive Western interpretation of a sphere of influence in the South Pacific, such as that upon which the doctrine of strategic denial appeared to rest.

The Vladivostok speech was not aimed at the numerous small states that comprise the South Pacific region, despite being fraught with security implications for them. It is unlikely, for example, that the islands would be included in any of the multilateral consultations proposed in the Vladivostok speech to treat various Asian-Pacific problems identified in the address. It was an unabashed reaffirmation of the interests and prerogatives of a superpower. Its impact would have been much less had it not been delivered at a time when the region's commitment to a Western alignment was being undermined by doubts within some of the countries on the value of their pro-West leanings. Nevertheless, the Soviet Union has seized its opportunity and seems determined to retain the diplomatic advantages achieved through its two fisheries agreements.

There has been no collective decision by the island countries to pursue a course of expanded ties with the USSR. Each decision has been made individually at the national level. Yet, as evidenced by the broadening numbers and increasing depth of extra-regional interest in the South Pacific, the ramifications are being felt across the region. Australia's security interests similarly are forcing the Commonwealth to develop its defence capacity in the region, and it seems likely that the informal intimacy of past years may be replaced, in part, with formality and structure. The island countries too are having to respond to perceptions of increasing superpower rivalry, although a single regional direction has yet to emerge. The problem is recognised as being genuine, nonetheless, for whenever the islands have been the subject of great power rivalry, they have been the ones to pay the price.

NOTES

1. References are taken from *Speech by Mikhail Gorbachev in Vladivostok, 28 July 1986* (Moscow: Novosti Press Agency Publishing House, 1986).

2. Geoffrey Jukes, "Gorbachev on Foreign Policy and Defence, 1986," Department of International Relations Seminar Paper, Australian National University, 20 November 1986, p. 29.

3. Paul Austin, "Japanese warn of Soviet push into Pacific," *Australian*, 9 January 1987.

4. Mary-Louise O'Callaghan, "Govt. blamed over Soviets in Pacific," *Sydney Morning Herald*, 7 August 1986.

5. The issue of alignment is developed in my "The American Impact on Australian Defence Relations with the South Pacific Islands," *Australian Outlook* 38(December 1984).

6. R. A. Herr, "Regionalism, Strategic Denial and South Pacific Security," *Journal of Pacific History* 21(October 1986).

7. Perhaps the first published account of such interest in ANZUS membership by the island countries is recorded in John W. Henderson, *Area Handbook for Oceania* (Washington, DC: US Government Printing Office, 1971), pp. 269-270.

8. Henry S. Albinski, "The US Security Alliance System in the South-West Pacific," Paper presented at the International Studies Conference, Philadelphia, March 1981.

9. Ralph Premdas and Michael C. Howard, "Vanuatu's Foreign Policy: Contradictions and Constraints," *Australian Outlook* 39(December 1985).

10. Greg Fry, *A Nuclear-Free Zone for the Southwest Pacific: Prospects and Significance* (Canberra: Australian National University, Strategic and Defence Studies Centre Working Paper No. 75, 1983) provides this history.

11. This argument is developed more fully in my "Regionalism, Strategic Denial and South Pacific Security."

12. *Ibid.*, p. 178, note 40.

13. David J. Doulman, "Some Aspects and Issues Concerning the Kiribati/Soviet Union Fishing Agreement," Pacific Islands Development Program Seminar Paper (Honolulu: East-West Center, May 1986).

14. Paul Dibb, "Soviet Strategy towards Australia, New Zealand and the South-West Pacific," *Australian Outlook* 39(August 1985).

15. A recent survey of the Soviet Union's interest specifically in the Pacific Islands is given in R. A. Herr, "The Soviet Union in the South Pacific," Briefing Paper (Canberra: Australian Development Studies Network, October 1986).

16. Dibb, "Soviet Strategy."

17. See, for example, Daniel Tumarkin, "USSR: the Unknown Northern Neighbour," in *Foreign Forces in Pacific Politics* (Suva: Institute of Pacific Studies, University of the South Pacific, 1983), pp. 143-149, and Alexander Malyashkin, "USSR, the Pacific," *Pacific Islands Monthly* (January 1978), pp. 15-16.

18. Albinski, "US Security Alliance System"; Dibb, "Soviet Strategy"; R. A. Herr, "Some Aspects of Regional Security in the South Pacific," in Stuart Inder, ed., *Pacific Islands Yearbook*, 13th ed. (Sydney: Pacific Publications, 1978); and Dalton A. West, "Soviet Union and the Pacific," in John Henderson, Keith Jackson and Richard Kennaway, eds., *Beyond New Zealand: The Foreign Policy of a Small State* (Auckland: Methuen, 1980).

19. Dibb, "Soviet Strategy," p. 72.

20. Michael Danby, "Fishing for friends in the islands," *Australian*, 17 February 1987.

21. *Speech by Mikhail Gorbachev*, p. 29.

22. *Ibid.*, p. 36.

23. R. A. Herr, "What's Happening to the Neighbourhood," *Island Magazine* 24(Spring 1985), pp. 52-54.

24. Danby, "Fishing for friends in the islands."

25. Stuart Inder, "Russia in the Pacific to stay but its progress is slow," *Bulletin* (Sydney), 30 September 1986, p. 101.

26. Danby, "Fishing for friends in the islands."

27. "Vanuatu/Soviet Union Fisheries Agreement," Australian Department of Foreign Affairs, *Backgrounder* 557(4 February 1987), p. 1.

28. "Soviets give pledge on military intentions," *Mercury* (Hobart), 5 March 1987.

29. "Australia - South Pacific Relations," *Australian Foreign Affairs Record* 57(May 1986), pp. 384-385.

30. "South Pacific," *Radio Australia News Summary*, 16 October 1986, p. 3.

31. Ross Peake, " Tuvalu ban on fishing by Soviets," *Australian*, 26 February 1987.

32. Peter Young, "Australia beefs up defences to counter Soviets in Pacific," *Weekend Australian*, 21-22 February 1987.

33. Rowan Callick, "PNG seeking a wide ranging treaty," *Financial Review*, 23 February 1987.

34. Robert Keith-Reid, "The Japanese join the party," *Islands Business* (January 1987), pp. 10-16.

35. "Libyan, USSR influence a 'great worry' to Pacific," *Mecury* (Hobart), 17 February 1987.

36. Peake, " Tuvalu ban on fishing by Soviets."

37. Bruce Loudon, "Tonga in flirtation with Moscow," *Weekend Australian*, 21-22 February 1987.

38. After this article was written, the Fiji Labour Party won the elections in April 1987 in coalition with the National Federation Party, but the new coalition government was overthrown in a military coup on 14 May 1987; editors.

39. "Move for Pacific peace force," *Financial Review*, 27 May 1986.

11

Afghanistan

Amin Saikal

The term *glasnost* has assumed a central place in Soviet politics since Mikhail Gorbachev's assumption of power from an aged leadership generation. Giving it a wider meaning than mere "openness," Gorbachev has sought to deploy the term in aid of self-legitimation, domestic social and economic revitalisation, and foreign policy rationalisation. To this end, he has already unfolded a number of initiatives in a blaze of Western-style publicity to set himself apart from the late Leonid Brezhnev, to chart a way for the Soviet Union out of its chronic social and economic stagnation, and to seek a better international image for the USSR, that of a constructive world power. His widely publicised speech of 28 July 1986 in Vladivostok, largely made in this context of more general innovation, constitutes the most comprehensive elaboration yet made of present Soviet policy towards Afghanistan. Gorbachev articulated a broad outline of what his leadership wanted in Afghanistan and how it desired to resolve the problem - a problem which he had earlier on 25 February 1986 described in his political report to the 27th Congress of the Communist Party of the Soviet Union (CPSU) as a "bleeding wound."[1] His declarations that his leadership was genuinely willing to negotiate a political settlement of the problem and to withdraw Soviet troops on such a basis from Afghanistan as soon as possible may have given rise to a degree of optimism among Western analysts and observers about an early resolution of the problem. However, any such optimism soon proved to be quite premature, for little progress has thus far been made towards a viable settlement.

AFGHANISTAN QUAGMIRE

What has confounded the Soviet leader's initiatives for a political solution has been primarily the fact that they have not as yet signalled a change in the basic objective for which the Soviets invaded Afghanistan in the first place in late December 1979. That objective was to secure the long-term survival of the puppet regime of the minute "People's Democratic Party of Afghanistan" (PDPA), which had seized power, with Soviet blessings, in a bloody coup in April 1978, but ever since has proved totally unfit to rule the predominantly Muslim, ethno-tribal Afghanistan. The PDPA has been disabled by its own factional fighting, and by the nationwide opposition, headed by the Afghan Islamic freedom fighters, the *mujaheedin*. As long as this remains the case and the Kremlin continues to disregard the internationally-backed demand of the Afghan people for the immediate, unconditional withdrawal of all Soviet troops and for the right to self-determination, Gorbachev's *glasnost*- based initiatives, which have come to include the promotion of a process of "national reconciliation," are unlikely to lead to a viable settlement of the Afghan conflict and therefore the withdrawal of Soviet troops in the near future.

Needless to say, the Afghanistan problem is one of the most painful legacies of the Brezhnev era to confront the Gorbachev leadership. The human, material and political costs of its Afghan war may not as yet have become overburdening for Moscow. But they have reached such a level as to prompt Gorbachev to identify Afghanistan as a continuing drain on a notable volume of Soviet resources, and to cause growing concern among the Soviet popoulace. Whereas the total Soviet troop casualties, killed and wounded, in the war with the *mujaheedin* since the Soviet invasion are estimated by Western intelligence sources at about 35,000, the Soviet material costs of the war rose sharply towards the end of 1986 to an average of more than $ 15 million a day, with the loss of one plane of some kind or another almost daily.[2] Although it is extremely difficult to tap the extent of the Soviet public's displeasure with the war, numerous eyewitness accounts and increasingly frequent Soviet media and press reports in the last two years have indicated it to be quite considerable. Also, an unofficial poll conducted by human rights activists in Moscow in 1984 found that 62 percent of respondents did not support the war, and more significantly, that 41 percent of Communist Party members did not either.[3]

Moreover, the episode has continued to serve as a blot on the Soviet Union's international reputation, acting as an important obstacle to improvement in the country's foreign relations, most notably with Pakistan and many other Islamic states, China and the West, particularly the United

States. Islamabad has viewed the Soviet invasion with deep apprehension, given the implications for Pakistan's security of Soviet troop concentrations in Afghanistan. As well as hosting about three million Afghan refugees and supplying the Afghan resistance with logistic backing and access to outside aid, it has forged a *de facto* strategic alliance with Washington and Beijing. Tehran has strongly objected to the Soviet invasion, and has sheltered about 1.5 million Afghan refugees and provided some assistance to elements within the resistance. Similarly, Washington and Beijing have held Moscow guilty of "expansionism" and have supplied arms, though in limited quantities, to the *mujaheedin*. It must be noted that the *mujaheedin* have persistently met most of their arms needs from what they have been able to salvage from Soviet and Afghan troops; and that the continuation of their struggle, which has proved to be popular and self-propelling, is not necessarily dependent on outside assistance. But the limited foreign arms, which began to arrive after the Soviet invasion, and not before it, as Moscow claims without any evidence, and which have come to include since mid-1986 a number of American Stinger missiles, reducing dramatically the *mujaheedin's* vulnerability to Soviet airpower, have helped the resistance to minimise its own losses and maximise those of the enemy.

To date the Soviets and their Afghan surrogates have not been able to build a viable PDPA government in Kabul, capable of managing its own affairs - to achieve, in other words, anything more than "socialism in one suburb"[4] - or to expand their original shaky hold on the capital and on a number of other main cities and strategic points. By even the PDPA's own admission the *mujaheedin* still have managed to control roughly two-thirds of the country,[5] with wide access to the major urban centers, above all Kabul. In fact, despite the Soviets' increasingly frantic efforts within a strategy of forward fighting pursued since 1984 to expand their security belts and hit the *mujaheedin* and their popular sanctuaries as hard as possible, as well as to block their supply-infiltration routes, particularly on the border with Pakistan, Kabul had never come under as much *mujaheedin* pressure as it did during 1986.[6] The Soviets once again, as in previous years, were not able to immunize even their embassy and residential compounds. For example, the main Soviet ammunition store near Kabul was blown up by the resistance on the night of 26-27 August,[7] illuminating the city with a brightness compared by witnesses to that produced by the detonation of a nuclear weapon. Amongst serious analysts of the Afghan situation, it is widely believed that without the presence of Soviet troops the PDPA regime could not survive for more than a brief interval. Its demise is most likely to come through its own factional fighting rather than any *mujaheedin* assault in the first instance.

Given this situation, which has made the prospects for total Soviet domination of Afghanistan look increasingly bleak, particularly in view of Moscow's reluctance for a variety of reasons to boost its troop deployment substantially beyond its present level of about 120,000, the Gorbachev leadership seems to have worked round to the view that the only way the Soviets could militarily conquer Afghanistan would be on the total ruins of the country, and at much greater cost than is presently the case for the Soviet Union. Gorbachev, whose priorities evidently appear to be different from those of his predecessors and who is keen to make a break with the Brezhnev era, has therefore good reasons to seek, if he can, a way out of the Afghan problem as soon as possible.

However, given the complexity of the problem and the importance of the Soviet ideological and pragmatic stakes in it, he has found it necessary to seek a settlement of the conflict on the basis of a conciliation of different and conflicting interests. He has apparently envisaged that a balance can be struck between what the Soviet Union as a world power can accept in Afghanistan and what could be tolerable to the Afghan people and the international community. Evidently, this has led him to search for a solution which could satisfy both sides to some extent, and enable the Soviets either to end their military involvement or stabilise it at the lowest level possible, with an option if necessary to *afghanise* the war. Early signs of such a "solution" actually emerged in the second half of 1985, when Moscow, shortly before the November superpower summit in Geneva, stepped up its publicity about a more serious willingness to negotiate a political settlement of the Afghan crisis. In an unprecedentedly frank editorial in its issue of 21 December, *Pravda*, while upholding the sanctity of the PDPA regime, for the first time admitted that the PDPA rule was not as popular, secure and faultless as Moscow had hitherto described it to be, and called for a more level-headed approach to a resolution of the Afghan problem. It stated: "[b]y no means everyone in Afghanistan, even among the working people, has accepted the April [1978] revolution" and the PDPA policies. Describing the size of the opposition as "considerable," it continued: "[t]here have been negative repercussions from the mistakes made during the first stage of the revolution," as "social reforms" were accelerated "without due regard for the real situation and the country's specific social and national features." Furthermore, it said that "it is necessary to create the atmosphere for a positive dialogue between public and political forces, including those that still hold views that are hostile to the revolution..."; and that such "reconciliation presupposes certain compromises." The editorial ended by calling on the international supporters of the Afghan resistance, most notably Pakistan and the United States, to respond constructively to the problem and terminate their aid to the *mujaheedin*.[8]

VLADIVOSTOK SPEECH

However, neither this nor Gorbachev's political report to the 27th Congress of the CPSU provided a clear and coherent exposition of the type of solution that the Kremlin was entertaining. This had to await Gorbachev's Vladivostok speech. In this address, which was essentially designed to outline Soviet Pacific interests but at the same time dampen regional, especially Chinese, concern over Soviet involvement in Indochina (specifically Kampuchea) and Afghanistan, Gorbachev provided the clearest inkling yet of what he desired to do about the Afghan problem. He conveyed three main points upon which a Soviet troop withdrawal was dependent.[9]

First, he stressed that the leading role of the PDPA was not negotiable. He described the April 1978 coup as a "national-democratic revolution" and implied its irreversibility under the PDPA leadership, against which all armed hostilities had to stop. He warned that "if intervention [i.e. the *mujaheedin* struggle and outside support for it] against Democratic Afghanistan continues the Soviet Union will not leave its neighbour in the lurch. Our internationalist solidarity with the Afghan people [i.e. the PDPA], as well as the security interests of the Soviet Union rule that out absolutely."

Second, he emphasised that at the same time the PDPA's rule had to be strengthened and its power base needed to be expanded through a policy of not mainly military pacification and total party monopolisation of power but of "national reconciliation," "up to the point of creating a government with the participation" of those opposition forces prepared not to question the legitimacy of "the April [1978] revolution" (and therefore the PDPA's leadership) and to "participate sincerely in the nationwide process of constructing a new Afghanistan."

Third, he intimated that only in conjunction with these two elements, and when a "political settlement is finally worked out," not necessarily with the *mujaheedin* but primarily with Pakistan, would the Soviet Union pull out all of its troops. Even then it would be stage-by-stage, according to the timetables which "have been agreed with the Afghan leadership." He preferred the "political settlement" to be reached within the framework of the UN-sponsored indirect-proximity Geneva talks, which have been conducted in various stages between the PDPA regime and the government of Pakistan since mid-1982 with the aim of finding a solution to the Afghan crisis.

To demonstrate the sincerity of his moves for a political settlement, he also proposed to pull out six Soviet regiments - one tank, two motorised infantry and three anti-aircraft regiments (about 7,000 troops in total) from Afghanistan before the end of the year.

What the Soviet leader's proposals essentially constituted was little or no change in the original Soviet goal in Afghanistan but a change in the Soviet strategy for achieving this goal. On the one hand, he sanctioned as imperative his predecessors' basic objective: to ensure the long-term survival of the PDPA regime and for that matter Soviet influence in Afghan politics. On the other, while finding his predecessors' strategy of long-term, low-cost military pacification and uncompromising reliance on the PDPA as the sole ruling body very unproductive, he posited a modification of this strategy by stressing one qualitative difference. That difference was to put more stress on political means, with certain marginal concessions, rather than military means, to advance Soviet objectives.

This change of emphasis was plainly designed to enable the Soviets gradually to level off their military operations in response to the dividends expected from Moscow's political initiatives inside Afghanistan and at the international level. It was also seemingly hoped that this, combined with careful Soviet-PDPA punitive actions in the form of destabilising cross-border raids and infiltrations by the PDPA's secret police, KHAD,[10] into Pakistan's North-West Frontier Province (NWFP), where the bulk of the Afghan refugees live and *mujaheedin* have their headquarters - actions which have markedly increased in the last year - would induce Pakistan to negotiate a settlement with the PDPA regime, dropping its support for the resistance.

The Kremlin has regarded a settlement with Pakistan as crucial to any kind of resolution of the Afghan problem, for it would also undermine the support of other *mujaheedin* supporters. What interests Moscow most in a settlement with Pakistan would be a "non-interference" agreement, backed by international guarantees. It has several reasons to be quite optimistic about the possibility of achieving such an *agreement* (although not necessarily a workable settlement), especially if Moscow succeeds in bringing about certain changes through its political initiatives in Afghanistan and in the international arena.

First, the Geneva talks have so far been exclusively conducted between the PDPA and Pakistani governments, with only the endorsement of Moscow and Washington. Pakistan has not insisted as a precondition for the success of the talks on the inclusion of the Mujaheedin or their other main outside supporters, namely Iran (which, like the *mujaheedin*, has rejected the Geneva talks on the grounds that no one has the right to speak on behalf of the Afghan people except the *mujaheedin* leaders) and China. The Kremlin has indeed preferred to keep the talks to the very end at such a bilateral level.

Second, the talks have to date focused only on such issues as an agreement of "non-interference"; international guarantees of this agreement; repatriation of Afghan refugees; and a timetable for the withdrawal of Soviet troops. Reportedly, substantial progress has been made on the first three issues and a settlement has for some time hung on a resolution of the last. Moscow has lately undertaken to solve the latter by moving to offer a more "attractive timetable," whose attractiveness would necessarily have to depend on the success of Gorbachev's initiatives with regard to the situation on the ground in Afghanistan.

Third, the growing burden of the Afghan problem, and its potential for partisan exploitation, have equipped Pakistan's sizable left and center-left opposition parties, which generally have favoured a solution of the Afghan problem along similar lines to those desired by Moscow, with further ammunition to focus public discontent on President Mohammad Zia ul-Haq's regime, pressuring it to become amenable to Gorbachev's settlement intiatives.[11]

Consequently, since the beginning of 1986, the Soviets have pursued a two-tiered objective in keeping with the policy lines set out in the Vladivostok speech. One is to strengthen the PDPA rule, with organic, structural ties with the Soviet Union; and the other is to seek to create certain conditions conducive to the political settlement desired by the Kremlin.

Strengthened PDPA Rule

In respect of the first objective, while intensifying their military operations more than ever before against the *mujaheedin* throughout the country, with stress on the provinces bordering Pakistan and indeed the border itself,[12] the Soviets launched a vigorous campaign to overhaul the PDPA under an effective leadership, and to give greater salience to the structure of its relationship with the Soviet Union. One of the fundamental problems confronting the Soviets all along in Afghanistan has been the in-fighting between and within the two deeply entrenched rival factions of the

PDPA - the Khalq, which had gained dominance before the Soviet invasion, and the Parcham, which the invading Soviet forces placed in ascendency over the Khalqis. In the wake of their invasion, the Soviets had killed their insubordinate former comrade, the Khalqi President Hafizullah Amin, and replaced him with his arch-rival, the Soviet loyalist and head of Parcham, Babrak Karmal.[13] This they contrived to do even though the latter with several of his top colleagues, including the current PDPA leader, Dr Najibullah, had been expelled from the party and had gone into exile to Eastern Europe shortly after the coup of April 1978. Indeed, the Soviets have legitimised their invasion on the basis of a claim that their forces were invited to Afghanistan; but they have never plausibly explained exactly who invited them. The Khalqis to this day deny any knowledge of such an invitation, as it proved to be immensely to their cost; and Karmal and his collegues could not credit themselves with it either, since they had no authority to issue any such invitation, given their status as expelled and outlawed members of the PDPA.

Whatever the case, the Soviet action only exacerbated the Parcham-Khalq rivalry, leading to growing bloodshed between them, and to Khalqi underground activities against the Soviets to the detriment of Moscow's efforts to create a viable PDPA government. As events subsequently showed, Karmal too proved ineffective for the Soviets in containing this factionalism and expanding the PDPA's power base. Yet, Moscow had to live with his disreputability as "the Soviet-installed leader of the PDPA," with whose government neither Pakistan nor other countries outside the Soviet bloc were keen to have any direct dealings.

The Soviets tried for several years to improve Karmal's image, but to no avail. Towards the end of 1985, when Gorbachev decided to change tack, Moscow began to criticise his leadership openly and embarked on a discreet process of replacing him with someone who could prove to be more effective, particularly in view of Gorbachev's pending initiatives. But the choice of a replacement was indeed limited, given the fact that there were only a few PDPA leaders that the Soviets can trust in a party which has no more than 3,000 committed members in a country of over 16 million people, although it has officially claimed 120,000.[14] For several reasons, they settled on Dr Najibullah, a Parchami activist loyal to Moscow since the late 1960s, and Chief of the KGB-run KHAD following the Soviet invasion.

First, he had proved to be totally dedicated to the goal of Soviet communist rule in Afghanistan. As Chief of KHAD, he had instrumentally helped the Soviets to transform that organisation into the most brutal and efficient governing force, which the Soviets have increasingly deployed to act as the core operative mechanism of PDPA rule and Soviet control in Afghanistan. Second, at the age of 39, he had gained a reputation as the PDPA's most shrewd, cunning and brutal tactician, possibly capable of handling the types of political manœuvres which came to underline Gorbachev's Vladivostok initiatives. Third, unlike most of the Parchami leaders, including Karmal, he is a full Pushtun, a member of the largest ethnic group, whose support has historically been crucial to the survival of any Afghan government and which has provided some of the best *mujaheedin* fighters.

Thus, he was perceived as the one best equipped to bolster the KHAD-based PDPA rule, to implement Gorbachev's initiatives and, at the same time, to free Moscow of the liability of Karmal and to present the PDPA leadership as more acceptable to the outside world, especially Pakistan. While at first promoting him to the Secretariat of the PDPA on 21 November 1985, and subsequently giving him growing public prominence, most of all as a "revolutionary patriotic Pushtun," the Soviets engineered his final takeover of the party's leadership from Karmal on 4 May 1986 during a three-day plenum of the Party's Central Committee, which was held in Kabul amid unprecedentedly tight Soviet security and attended by the Soviet Ambassador. Karmal was allowed to retain his position as President of the Revolutionary Council, formally the supreme legislative body of the state, but not for very long. In November, he was stripped of all his party positions, joining the ranks of the Kremlin's other forgotten Afghan comrades, Hafizullah Amin and his predecessor, Nur Mohammed Taraki. Karmal has since been flown to Moscow for "medical treatment," reportedly after attempting to flee to Pakistan.[15]

Seizing Gorbachev's *glasnost* as a device which could also work for him, Najibullah started his job with unprecedented openness about the shortcomings of PDPA. Over the next two months, he criticised the party's failure to expunge factionalism and corruption (which has indeed reached epidemic proportions, as party members have sought to secure their own well-being above everything else); to expand its territorial control beyond one-third of the country; to bolster the depleted Afghan Army, which has dwindled to less than half of its pre-invasion strength of 60,000 due to desertions and refusal to fight; and to win mass support. He even declared: "[w]e are weak in the tactical and practical sphere. Most of the grand thoughts and plans get drowned in mere words and remain on paper."[16]

This was accompanied by substantial purges from the party of "undesirable elements" (who turned out to be mainly Khalqis, and Parchami supporters of Karmal) and their replacement by Najibullah's supporters. The latter came to include not only several of his more bloodthirsty KHAD *protegés,* but also two of his close and tainted associates, Abdul Wakil and Mohammed Rafi, who by the end of the year assumed the foreign affairs and defence portfolios. Moreover, he launched a vigorous drive to tighten the conscription laws to ensure the ready recruitment into the Army of all males of ages 18-50 from at least the limited areas under the Soviet-PDPA control. The KHAD was given even wider powers in order to allow it formally to implement this measure as forcefully as possible, while the regime and the Soviets continued to disregard detailed reports from the UN Human Rights Rapporteur and Amnesty International about large-scale violation of basic human rights in Afghanistan.[17]

Meanwhile, Najibullah promised to use his "experience" as chief of KHAD to crush the resistance in order to secure the PDPA as the lasting "guide" and "light" in the country; and proclaimed that "[a]ll our work will be based on the continued strengthening and development of friendship with the great Soviet Union, the party of the great Lenin and the heroic and generous Soviet people."[18] This was to give wider credibility not only to the intensified Soviet-PDPA military offensives, involving most of Afghanistan for much of the past year, with constant pressure maintained on the Afghan-Pakistan border, but also to a continued systematic push for strengthening all-round organic, structural relations between the regime and the Soviet Union, as background to the implementation of Gorbachev's initiatives.

For example, in addition to an acceleration of efforts by thousands of Soviet civil and KGB-military *apparatchiki* to run, shape, and build the PDPA administration along Soviet lines of governance, and to train PDPA supporters in the art of Soviet-type socialist state-building, in June 1986 the Soviets completed the construction of a new complex as the Social Science Institute of the PDPA's Central Committee in Kabul. The objective of this Institute, which like many other educational institutions in the capital is largely run by the Soviets, is to train committed party activists, wholly dedicated to the goal of communist rule.[19] On 25 July, in addition to hundreds of mature-age Afghans who have been dispatched (many of them by force) over the last few years to the USSR for training as future PDPA cadres, a further 200 Afghan children were sent to that country for the same purpose, bringing the official total to 6,500 since 1980. Furthermore, on 15 September an 800-strong delegation was dispatched to Tashkent to participate in the second Afghan-Soviet Youth Festival.[20]

In the economic sphere, where the PDPA regime has become totally dependent on the Soviet Union, and has even received observer status at

COMECON meetings, a new trade agreement was signed in mid-February 1986 between the regime and Moscow for 1986-1990. According to official figures, whereas the trade between the two sides increased by 200 percent in volume from 1980 to 1986, during the time-span of the new agreement trade is projected to increase by a further 30 percent.[21] To highlight the degree of the regime's economic integration with the USSR, in a *joint communiqué* in late April, following an official visit by the regime's Prime Minister Sultan Ali Keshmand to Moscow, the two sides praised the level of "Soviet-Afghan economic cooperation" and "noted that in recent years it has been filled with new content and has become solid and stable." "They expressed mutual interest in the development and strengthening of cooperation on a long-term ... basis" in both economic and social spheres. The Soviets also expressed readiness to provide further assistance in all fields of the regime's activities in the future. The two sides also pledged "to continue to devote constant attention to Soviet-Afghan ties in the fields of culture, education, public health and sports"; and "to promote the expansion of contacts between Soviet and Afghan organizations and institutions with a view of more thorough familiarisation with the life, labour, experience and achievements of the two countries' peoples."[22] The Kremlin gave further assurances of such structural linkages during Najibullah's visit to Moscow in December 1986 and the visit to Kabul in early January 1987 by the Soviet Foreign Minister, Eduard Shevardnadze, and the Kremlin's top foreign policy adviser, Anatoly Dobrynin.

At the same time, the Soviets pressed on with efforts to strengthen their defence system for daily operations against the resistance, and develop their strategic bases for wider and longer-term purposes. For instance, they continued not only to strengthen their two large bases in Bagram (outside Kabul) and Shindand (near Herat in the west), but also pushed for the expansion of the third one in Kandahar (in the south) and construction of new but smaller ones in other parts of the country. It has been from these bases that Soviet airpower has been deployed against the resistance and that the Soviets have carried out long-range reconnaissance flights over neighbouring Pakistan and Iran as well as right across the Persian Gulf coastline. In addition to the four major SIGINT (signals intelligence) sites which they have constructed at a total cost of more than $25 million in strategic locations on the Afghan borders with China, Pakistan and Iran, essentially to spy on and monitor military movements in these countries, there were reports of efforts for the construction of more such sites.[23]

Political Settlement

It was against this background, and in fulfilment of the basic Soviet objective, that Moscow also sought to promote conditions for a policy of political settlement and troop withdrawal as another aspect of Gorbachev's Vladivostok initiatives. Thus, whatever it has initiated in this respect has necessarily been in compliance with and limited by the basic Soviet objective. Central to its efforts has been to present the PDPA regime as legitimate, with a view to impressing upon the Afghan people and the world community the need to accept the long-term survival of the regime as an historical fact and therefore abandon their support for the resistance. It has sought to do this via what it has called a process of "national reconciliation."

The Soviets started putting this process to test well before Gorbachev's Vladivostok Initiative. For example, amid increasing Soviet peace overtures, in January 1986 the PDPA regime announced an expansion of its Revolutionary Council by 79 members in order to give greater representation in the government to "all social forces," including the "clergy," and described several new members as "non-party," although the past association of most of them with the PDPA was unquestionable. This was followed by the regime's staging of a *Loya Jirgah* (Great Tribal Council) and several smaller *jirgahs* to convey that tribal, particularly Pushtun, support was increasing for it. It did not admit that half of the people attending the *jirgahs* were party members and the remainder paid citizens, whose economic destitution under the PDPA rule has been acute. In the period since July 1986, the announcement of such measures has become more frequent. The most important ones included a declaration by Najibullah that the party's Central Committee would be expanded from 79 to 147 to provide again for larger representation from the provinces. In September, he foreshadowed the establishment of a National Reconciliation Commission to "normalise" the situation in Afghanistan and thwart "imperialist counter-revolutionary intervention and fratricide." In October, the regime claimed that the first stage of "local elections" had been "concluded successfully in all provinces."

Meanwhile, Moscow backed these measures and its own peace gestures by implementing Gorbachev's promise about the withdrawal of six Soviet regiments. In a flurry of publicity but with opportune timing, it begun pulling out those regiments shortly before the superpower summit at Reykjavik in October - a "withdrawal" which was completed by the end of the month. The PDPA and Moscow hailed this as a significant "good-will step," evidence of their desire for a political settlement. This was further supported by a declaration by Gorbachev during his visit to India on 24 November that "we stand for a non-aligned and independent Afghanistan .... We are not going to stay there for ever"; and that the Soviet Union would withdraw its troops as soon as "the question of the political settlement of the situation *around* [not inside] Afghanistan" is resolved.[24]

However, by the end of the year it was clear that neither Moscow's appointment of Najibullah, nor its reconciliation efforts, nor its partial troop withdrawal had improved the situation for the PDPA regime or the prospects for a settlement. The displacement of Karmal by Najibullah backfired in many ways. Najibullah's criticisms of the PDPA rule under Karmal, and his purges to rid the party of Karmal supporters and staunch Khalqis, not only alienated further the vengeful Khalqis, but also split the Parcham between the Karmal and Najibullah supporters. As the Karmal supporters sought to form their own sub-faction, there were sporadic demonstrations by them in Kabul, resulting in violent clashes. Even a senior Soviet commentator, Alexander Bovin, has acknowledged the extent of "dissensions, feuds and bloody clashes within the ruling party" under Najibullah.[25]

Although unable to use his KHAD agents effectively against the *mujaheedin,* Najibullah certainly made good use of them in suppressing his Parchami opponents, at the cost of many lives. This did not end the Karmal faction; it simply forced many of its members to engage, like the Khalqis, in underground opposition activities. Subsequently, unconfirmed reports implicated them in several anti-Najibullah actions, including an abortive attempt on his life on 22-23 November 1986; and a power plot on 16 January 1987, which forced Soviet forces to stage a heavy security clamp-down in Kabul. Meanwhile, upon Najibullah's assumption of leadership, his own Pushtun tribe, from which he has been estranged since childhood, held a *jirgah* and denounced him as a "traitor"; while the *mujaheedin,* who have identified him as one of the most vicious PDPA figures, responsible for the loss of thousands of Afghan lives during his tenure as Chief of KHAD, vowed not to have any dealings with him, but to fight him to the end. Also, given the circumstances of his rise to leadership, the Soviets had little success in presenting him as a more legitimate leader than Karmal.

Similarly, the Soviet-PDPA reconciliation measures did not prove effective. The Afghan people had become too familiar with such measures and had heard them all before in one form or another. They regarded them as nothing more than further deceptive devices. The regime's claims of success looked equally absurd in the face of its own admissions that it has accomplished little in implementing the plans that it has had on paper; that it has failed in the area of gaining "mass support"; and that it has not controlled much more than one-third of the country. Nor could the Soviet partial troop withdrawal amount to much. The resistance and its outside supporters (at whom the measure was really directed) dismissed it as yet another exercise in propaganda and public relations for several reasons. First, it involved one tank and three anti-aircraft regiments, which had proved superfluous in the conditions of guerrilla warfare and in the face of the *mujaheedin's* total lack of airpower. Second, it had questionable impact on overall Soviet military strength, particularly in view of the facts that Moscow has never disclosed the exact number of its troops and that it rotates its troops regularly in Afghanistan. Indeed, Western sources alleged that prior to the withdrawal the Soviets had increased their troops to make up for it.[26] Third, and most importantly, it did not tally, as with every other Soviet peace gesture, with what the Soviets have been actually pursuing inside Afghanistan.

When by the end of the year all these steps, like the Soviet military intensification, failed to achieve the desired objectives, the Soviets found it imperative to come up with their most striking peace plan to date, presumably as the second stage of implementing Gorbachev's Vladivostok initiatives. During and after a two-week visit to Moscow in December, Najibullah announced what appeared to be a Soviet-designed settlement plan. As the details of the plan filtered out, it became clear that it mirrored little more than what Gorbachev had declared at Vladivostok. The plan once again called for a process of "national reconciliation," creation of a "coalition government of national unity," and an overall settlement agreement between the PDPA regime and Pakistan. The only major innovation in this plan was a call for a six-month "ceasefire" from mid-January 1987 and an implicit Soviet-PDPA recognition for the first time of the *mujaheedin* as torch-bearers of a popular resistance, and not simply as the "imperialist-backed bandits" which they had hitherto been labelled.

While asserting the PDPA's "deep respect" for the religion of Islam, stressing that his team was "different" from those of his communist predecessors, and proclaiming a "general amnesty" for the opposition forces, Najibullah called on the surviving officials of former Afghan regimes living abroad, and the *mujaheedin* leaders, to cease their anti-regime activities and enter dialogue with his leadership to formulate a new constitution, elect a national assembly and participate in the governmental process. However, in line with Gorbachev's Vladivostok speech, all this was made conditional on the "irreversibility of the April [1978] revolution" and therefore the PDPA leadership; and on the "strengthening" of Afghan-Soviet ties.[27]

Given these preconditions, which are precisely those that have underpinned the Afghan resistance, the immediate rejection of the whole plan by the seven main groups of the *mujaheedin,* whose consent would be crucial to the success of any settlement, was virtually guaranteed. Nor has the plan so far received a warm reception from Pakistan and other outside supporters of the resistance to the extent necessary to cause much optimism about its chances of success. Even if Moscow succeeded in extracting an agreement from Pakistan, something which is always a possibility, without a direct endorsement of it by the *mujaheedin,* such an agreement is most unlikely to end the Afghan conflict and permit the withdrawal of Soviet troops in the near future. The Soviets lack a government which can stand on its own feet in Kabul, and the *mujaheedin* would always be able to wreck a settlement which did not meet the demand of the Afghan people for the unconditional withdrawal of all Soviet troops and for their right to determine their own future. Indeed, one wonders what can have led the Gorbachev leadership to think that there is a chance of conciliation between the PDPA and the *mujaheedin* after so many years of bloodshed, hatred and animosity, and particulary in view of the fact that there was no meeting of minds between them in the first place. Any prudent *mujaheedin* leader or prominent official of a former regime would be taking an enormous personal risk by participating in a PDPA-led government. If the Gorbachev leadership really desires a *viable* settlement of the Afghanistan problem and an end to the costly and humiliating Soviet military involvement in that country, the best option for it would be to formulate a solution not by seeking to address the obvious *symptoms* of the Afghan problem but the central *cause* of it: that is the illegitimacy of the PDPA regime. Until this is done, there is little prospect of peace in Afghanistan.

NOTES

1. Mikhail Gorbachev, *Political Report of the CPSU Central Committee to the 27th Party Congress* (Moscow: Novosti Press Agency Publishing House, 1986) p. 86.

2. Confidential sources. For a discussion of different estimates, see Henry S. Bradsher, *Afghanistan and the Soviet Union* 2nd ed. (Durham: Duke University Press, 1985), pp. 270-271; for an American figure of $ 11-18 million expenditure a day, see the *Friday Review of Defense Literature* 9(March 1987), p. 5. On plane losses, see intelligence reports cited in the *Washinton Times*, 30 March 1987.

3. *Strana i mir* [Munich], (October 1984). Further information on Soviet public opinion can be found in *The Soviet Public and the War in Afghanistan: Perceptions, Prognoses, Information Sources*, AR 4-85(Munich: Radio Free Europe/Radio Liberty, June 1985).

4. This apposite phrase is to be found in William Maley, "Political Legitimation in Contemporary Afghanistan," *Asian Survey* (forthcoming).

5. Cited in William Maley, "Prospects for Afghanistan," *Australian Outlook* 39(December 1985).

6. For Soviet admissions of the pressure to which Kabul was subjected, see *Pravda*, 21 July 1986, p. 6.

7. *Afghanistan Chronology: July 1985-October 1986* (London: Foreign and Commonwealth Office, November 1986), p. 7.

8. For a translation, see *Current Digest of the Soviet Press* 37(15 January 1986), pp.18-19.

9. For a translation of the speech see BBC, *Summary of World Broadcasts*, 30 July 1986, SU/8324/C/1-17. This speech is reporduced in the Appendix.

10. *Khadamat-i ittila'at-i dawlati*, or State Information Service. In January 1986, it became a ministry, but it continues to be identified by its old acronym.

11. For background see Amin Saikal, "The Pakistan Unrest and the Afghanistan Problem," *World Today* 40(March 1984).

12. For details see "The Continuing War in Afghanistan," *Strategic Survey 1986-1987* (London: International Institute for Strategic Studies, 1987), pp.133-140, and especially pp. 135-136.

13. See Joseph J. Collins, *The Soviet Invasion of Afghanistan: A Study in the Use of Force in Soviet Foreign Policy* (Lexington: Lexington Books, 1986), chs. 5-6.

14. Richard F. Staar, "Checklist of Communist Parties in 1985," *Problems of Communism* 35(March-April 1986), p. 65. The figure of 120,000 was also claimed by Karmal in a January 1985 speech; BBC, *Summary of World Broadcasts*, 17 January 1985, FE/7851/C/3.

15. Confidential diplomatic source.

16. BBC, *Summary of World Broadcasts*, 16 May 1986, FE/8260/C/1-2.

17. See *Situation of Human Rights in Afghanistan* A/41/778(United Nations General Assembly, 31 October 1986), and *Afghanistan: Torture of Political Prisoners* ASA 11/04/86(London: Amnesty International, November 1986).

18. For a condensed text of this speech, see *Current Digest of the Soviet Press*, 38(4 June 1986), p. 22.

19. Najibullah observed at the opening of this institute that "we see a sound basis for the future of the PDPA Central Committee's institute both in the productive development of scholarly and practical ties with, and in the extensive help it continually receives from, Party educational institutions in the USSR and in the other fraternal socialist countries ...." See *Current Digest of the Soviet Press* 38(23 July 1986), p. 17.

20. *Afghanistan Chronology: July 1985-October 1986* (London: Foreign and Commonwealth Office, November 1986), pp. 7-8.

21. *Current Digest of the Soviet Press* 38(19 March 1986), p. 27.

22. For a translation of the *communiqué*, see *Current Digest of the Soviet Press*, 38(21 May 1986), pp. 13-15.

23. See Amin Saikal, "Soviet Policy Toward Southwest Asia," *Annals of The American Academy of Political and Social Science*, 481(September 1985), pp. 104-116, and Desmond Ball, "Soviet Signals Intelligence," *The International Countermeasures Handbook*, 12th ed. (Palo Alto: EW Communications, Inc., 1987), p. 85.

24. For an edited text of Gorbachev's remarks, see BBC, *Summary of World Broadcasts*, 25 November 1986, SU/8425/C1/1-10.

25. BBC, *Summary of World Broadcasts*, 17 February 1987, SU/8494/A3/3. See also Anthony Hyman, "Tribal rivalry adds to Kabul disarray," *Times*, 25 November 1986.

26. See Craig Karp, *Afghanistan: Seven Years of Soviet Occupation* , Special Report No. 155 (Washington, DC: US Department of State, Bureau of Public Affairs, December 1986), pp.10-11.

27. For an edited version of Najibullah's speech, see BBC, *Summary of World Broadcasts*, 5 January 1987, FE/8457/C/1-8.

12

Kampuchea: Soviet Initiatives and Regional Responses

Carlyle A. Thayer

On 28 July 1986 CPSU General Secretary Mikhail Gorbachev delivered a major address in the Soviet Far Eastern city of Vladivostok. The speech was equally divided in its discussion of domestic and external questions. The main foreign policy thrust of Gorbachev's speech was aimed at China, where potentially significant conciliatory signals were made on two of the three obstacles China has set on the normalisation of its relations with the USSR.[1] This chapter focuses specifically on Soviet initiatives on Kampuchea arising from Gorbachev's Vladivostok speech, and regional responses to these initiatives.

It can be argued that the significance of Gorbachev's Vladivostok speech for Indochina, and a possible settlement of the conflict in Kampuchea, lies in what was not said rather than what was. While Gorbachev's speech contained no basic change in the USSR's previously announced public position that Kampuchea was an issue best left to China and Vietnam,[2] it did signal a Soviet willingness to play a role, however indirect and ambiguous, in achieving a settlement. What was left unstated, was how Moscow intended to encourage Sino-Vietnamese reconciliation. This led to a period of anxiety on the part of the Vietnamese which was only assauged later in the year.[3] Vietnamese anxiety was aroused when Gorbachev and then his Deputy Foreign Minister, Mikhail Kapitsa, omitted in public remarks the caveat that Sino-Soviet normalisation would not be at the expense of a third country, meaning Vietnam.

Significantly, Gorbachev listed Kampuchea first among the five conflict areas which the General Secretary singled out for possible resolution under his umbrella Helsinki Conference formula.[4] His comments on the Kampuchean conflict were brief and deserve citation in full:[5]

> Summing up, I want to stress again that we are in favour of including the Asian-Pacific area in the general process of creating an all-embracing system of international security, which was spoken of at the 27th CPSU Congress. How do we envisage this in concrete terms? First of all, questions inevitably arise of a regional settlement. I will speak of Afghanistan separately. Now I am going to deal with Southeast Asia and Kampuchea.
>
> The Khmer people have made terrible sacrifices. This country, its town[s] and villages were more than once subjected to American bombing. Through its suffering it won its right to choose its friends and allies, and it is unacceptable to try to draw it back into the tragic past and decide the future of this state in distant capitals, or even in the UN. Much here, as in other problems of Southeast Asia, depends on the normalisation of Sino-Vietnamese relations. This is the sovereign affair of the governments and leaderships of the two countries. We can only express our interest in seeing the border between these socialist states becoming again a border of peace and good neighbourliness, and a comradely dialogue renewed, with unnecessary suspicions and distrust being removed. The moment now seems propitious, and the whole of Asia needs it.
>
> In our opinion, there are no insurmountable obstacles to the settlement of mutually acceptable relations between the countries of Indochina and ASEAN. Given good will and conditions of non-interference from outside, they could settle their problems for the good of general Asian security at the same time.

Gorbachev's Vladivostok speech commenced a new phase of heightened Soviet diplomatic activity in Asia. The party heads of the three countries of Indochina were separately invited to the Soviet Union. Senior Soviet officials in turn visited Thailand[6] and Indochina to brief local leaders, to gauge regional reactions, and to exchange views. Gorbachev himself travelled to India, while his Foreign Minister embraced Thailand, Australia, Indonesia, Laos, Kampuchea and Vietnam in a single whirlwind trip. Senior Soviet officials attended party congresses in Laos and Vietnam. In 1987, Moscow hosted the Foreign Minister of Thailand, Vietnam's new party boss, Nguyen Van Linh, and the Prime Minister of Malaysia.

Senior Soviet officials continued to meet with their Chinese counterparts in a continuation of the normalisation process. Initially, the Soviet Union rejected but later agreed to discuss the Kampuchean question. At the same time, there were hints that Soviet diplomats sought to achieve a greater objective: the reconstitution of a socialist community in Asia with China as an active participant.

Quite clearly, in the year after Gorbachev's Vladivostok speech, Southeast Asia entered a period of cautious optimism with respect to the prospects for a negotiated settlement of the Kampuchean conflict. Laos undertook initiatives designed to improve relations with Thailand and China. Some observers saw these moves as harbingers of a possible improvement in Sino-Vietnamese relations. Vietnam, for its part, sent out secret peace feelers to Prince Norodom Sihanouk in an effort to entice him into "national reconciliation" talks with the regime in Phnom Penh. India undertook quiet diplomatic soundings; while Indonesia renewed its efforts to find a framework for discussions suitable to all parties.

INDOCHINESE REACTIONS

Vietnam

At the very moment that Gorbachev was delivering his speech, Truong Chinh, then Secretary General of the Vietnam Communist Party (VCP), was in Moscow on "vacation" at the invitation of the Central Committee of the CPSU.[7] They later met on 12 August in an atmosphere of "complete mutual understanding, fraternity and cordiality," according to official accounts, after which Chinh departed for Hanoi.[8] Soviet and Vietnamese reports of this meeting suggest that a wide range of issues were discussed, such as trade, and economic, scientific and technical matters, in addition to Gorbachev's Vladivostok address. After Truong Chinh expressed Vietnam's determination to overcome "certain [domestic] difficulties," Gorbachev reaffirmed the USSR's continued support and assistance to the Socialist Republic of Vietnam (SRV). (In December at the sixth congress of the Vietnam Communist Party, the head of the CPSU's delegation announced a doubling of Soviet economic assistance to Vietnam over the next five years.)

The two party leaders also reached an "identity" of views on all international matters discussed, including relations with China. According to TASS: "[t]he Soviet Union and Vietnam reiterate their readiness for the normalisation of relations with the PRC, which would be of much importance for the improvement of the situation in the Asian-Pacific region...."[9]

Truong Chinh also took the opportunity to issue a *pro forma* endorsement of Gorbachev's Vladivostok speech. The party's newspaper reported: "Comrade Truong Chinh expressed the stand of our party, government and people to support wholeheartedly the latest initiatives put forward in the very important statement by Comrade Gorbachev in Vladivostok to normalise the situation in the Asian-Pacific region, lead this region's development in the general direction of establishing a global security system, and favour the convening of an Asian-Pacific conference with the participation of all countries in the region to achieve the above goal."[10] On his return to Vietnam, Truong Chinh's support of the Soviet position not unexpectedly received the endorsement of the VCP Politburo.[11]

However, close observers reading between the lines noted that Truong Chinh had received a "cool reception" while in Moscow. Publicly, the relationship appeared normal, while in private, the Vietnamese had misgivings. According to veteran Indochina watcher Nayan Chanda, "[t]he communique issued at the end of his talk avoided the standard phrase about both sides achieving 'complete identify of views.' Also conspicuous by its absence in the communique was the standard assurance that Sino-Soviet normalisation would not be at the expense of 'third countries'."[12]

Vietnam and the Soviet Union share a particularly close relationship which involves the coordination of their respective foreign policies. Therefore it should not surprise that the official Vietnamese media chose to report and endorse the broad outlines of Gorbachev's Vladivostok speech uncritically. Vietnam's domestic radio broadcast extensive extracts from the speech, both party and army newspapers carried supportive editorials, the Vietnam Peace Committee issued a general statement of approval, while no less a figure than Pham Van Dong, then a member of the VCP Politburo, granted an interview to TASS to offer his endorsement.[13]

On 14 August a symposium was held in Hanoi "in support of the new peace initiatives" set out by Gorbachev in his Vladivostok speech. The symposium was jointly sponsored by the the Vietnam Fatherland Front Central Commitee, the Committee for Solidarity and Friendship with Other Countries, and the Hanoi branches of the Vietnam Peace Committee and the Vietnam-USSR Friendship Association. According to VNA, "the participants warmly welcomed the Soviet leader's peace initiatives and expressed their determination to do their best to contribute to the cause of peace, security, and equitable cooperation in the region."[14]

The first Vietnamese media reactions came just two days after the speech. In contrast, one western magazine reported that its editors and correspondents in Moscow had to wait until 1 August before an accurate, coherent translation of Gorbachev's address was provided to them.[15] However, as one Hanoi-based diplomat stated in conversation with the author, while the Vietnamese had been briefed beforehand on Gorbachev's Vladivostok speech, they certainly were not privy to the full text before delivery.

Vietnam's initial reportage of Gorbachev's speech was mainly factual; both radio and press carried the key paragraphs on Kampuchea, cited above, when reporting to their domestic audience. The Vietnamese media also highlighted a specific reference made to Vietnam, namely, that Vietnam was a major country in Asia and the Pacific alongside the USSR, USA, and other countries of the region.

Vietnamese media endorsement was also couched in general terms. For example, on 30 July an editorial in *Nhan Dan* declared: "[o]ur people warmly welcome and fully support Comrade Gorbachev's 28 July statement and the Soviet Union's correct position and series of important new proposals for establishing new fair relations and creating an atmosphere of peace and stability in the Asian-Pacific region, in response to the aspirations and interests of various nations in the region." *Quan Doi Nhan Dan,* the army's newspaper, chimed in with similar terms:

> [t]he Vietnamese people and armed forces warmly welcome and fully support the 28 July statement by Comrade Gorbachev with the aim of consolidating peace and security and promoting broad and equitable relations among the nations of Asia and the Pacific. This statement is a great encouragement to the revolutionary and socialist forces and forces of national independence, democracy, progress, and peace in this largest region of our planet.

It was left to Pham Van Dong, acting in his capacity as Chairman of the Council of Ministers, to give the official Vietnamese government view: "[t]he Socialist Republic of Vietnam fully supports the Soviet Union's initiatives and will coordinate its actions with the Soviet Union to implement those noble objectives." When asked specifically for his views on Gorbachev's "concrete initiatives and proposals aimed at solving regional issues [i.e. Kampuchea]," Dong answered:

> The essential things of these proposals are peace, security and cooperation which have become a historical trend in Asia and the Pacific, and the world as a whole and Comrade Mikhail Gorbachev has worked out concrete measures to turn this trend into reality .... It is [the] right time for all nations in Asia and the Pacific to embark on constructive dialogue aimed at settling all regional issues on the basis of honouring each other's independence and sovereignty, shirking confrontation, limiting and reducing weapons and military activities.

Vietnamese anxieties about Sino-Soviet and Sino-Vietnamese relations can be illustrated with reference to *Nhan Dan's* editorial of 30 July. "If China genuinely and sincerely wants peace and better relations with its neighbouring countries," the paper stated, "it should immediately give up its policy of hostility toward Vietnam and the other Indochinese countries and sit down with Vietnam to discuss and settle the outstanding problems in their bilateral relations, in order, first of all, to stabilise the situation along the common border and create favourable conditions for the normalisation of relations between the two countries."

The Vietnamese media, in contrast to the Soviet press, left no doubt as to who was to blame for continuing tensions. *Nhan Dan* observed, "[t]o realise its neo-globalism, US imperialism has put forward its extremely reactionary doctrine for Asia and the Pacific, with the aim of maintaining its imperialist position, developing hegemonism, and impeding and opposing revolutionary movements and the on going new changes in this important, increasingly important, region." Turning to China, the same newspaper declared: "the responsibility for the worsening relations between the two countries and the continuing tension along the Vietnamese-Chinese border rests completely with China."

Quan Doi Nhan Dan took an even tougher line. It alleged that the United States was trying to draw the countries of the Asian-Pacific region into "a close NATO-type military alliance." It also accused the United States of colluding with the "Chinese expansionists to oppose Vietnam, using Thailand as a sanctuary for the Khmer reactionary remnants in exile to wage a guerrilla war against the PRK."

Laos

Laos too offered a general endorsement of Gorbachev's Vladivostok speech in a pattern similar to that of Vietnam. However, it differed markedly in its treatment of relations with the United States and China. Laos took the opportunity offered by Gorbachev's Vladivostok speech, to initiate diplomatic manœuvres aimed at improving relations with its two neighbours, Thailand and China.

The first public reaction to Gorbachev's Vladivostok speech was made by Kaysone Phomvihan at a session of the LPDR Council of Ministers. According to Vientiane Radio, Kaysone "affirmed his vigorous support for the Soviet Union's peace initiatives."[16] On 8 August, Kaysone left Laos for a month-long visit to the USSR, at the invitation of the CPSU Central Committee.[17] On his last day there, Kaysone was received by Secretary General Gorbachev.[18]

Meanwhile, Soviet Deputy Foreign Minister Igor Rogachev visited Laos, arriving on 19 August. He was received by the Lao Foreign Minister on the following day.[19] According to Vientiane Radio, "Comrade Phoun Sipaseut also expressed full support for the new, creative proposal on the improvement of the situation in the Asian-Pacific region as noted in the speech delivered in Vladivostok by Comrade Mikhail Gorbachev."[20]

Rogachev then held a working session with his Lao counterpart, Deputy Foreign Minister Soulivong Phasitthidet, after which the two officials declared that they had "reached unanimity on all issues raised for discussion."

Further Lao endorsement was solicited on 23 August, when LPDR President Souphanouvong received Vladimir Gussak, the USSR *Charge d' Affaires,* to "highly commend ... the Vladivostok statement of 28th July" among other Soviet initiatives.[21] In mid-September, a special seminar on Asian-Pacific peace and security was convened in Vientiane for key officials similar to that organised in Hanoi. The task of explaining recent changes in Lao policy was left to Thongsavat Yamani, chairman of the State Committee for News Agency, Newspapers, Radio and Television.[22]

PRK Reactions

Kampuchea's first public reaction to Gorbachev's Vladivostok speech was reported by Sarpordarmean Kampuchea (SPK), the regime's official news agency. "The Kampuchean people," it stated, "warmly welcome Soviet leader M. Gorbachev's speech at Valdivostok as another vivid expression of the Soviet Union's deep concern for the destiny of mankind."[23] SPK's brief summary highlighted Gorbachev's remarks that "Kampuchea has regained its right to choose friends and allies for itself." SPK then reitereated long-standing policy: "the three Indochinese countries are willing to foster the relation of good neighbourliness with Thailand, thus turning the Kampuchean-Thai and Lao-Thai borders into borders of peace and friendship, and solving the problems concerning their relations with Thailand through negotiations." On China, SPK referred to the *communique* of the eleventh meeting of the Indochinese Foreign Ministers encouraging the resumption of Sino-Vietnamese talks aimed at the normalisation of relations.

Several days after the SPK transmission, an editorial in *Pracheachon,* the official organ of the KPRP Central Committee, provided the PRK's first official endorsement of Gorbachev's initiatives in very general terms, virtually ignoring the specific references highlighted earlier. The newspaper proclaimed that "the Cambodian people enthusiastically greet and fully support the latest peace initiatives and proposals of Comrade General Secretary Gorbachev made on 28 July ...."[24]

Soviet Deputy Foreign Minister Igor Rogachev, after visiting Laos, paid a working visit to the PRK from 21-23 August, to personally brief Kampuchea's leaders. After meetings with Hun Sen, Chairman of the

PRK Council of Ministers and Foreign Minister, and the First Deputy Foreign Minister, Kong Korm, it was announced that "the two sides completely agreed on issues of common interest and on international problems."[25]

Heng Samrin then paid a month long visit to the Soviet Union, where he was received by Andrei Gromyko on 5 October. Samrin's visit followed that of his Lao and Vietnamese counterparts, Kaysone Phomvihan and Truong Chinh. Soviet sources indicated that Gromyko expressed the USSR's desire for a political solution to the conflict in Kampuchea, and that such a solution should result from a dialogue with China and ASEAN.[26] Soviet endorsement for "national reconciliation" talks was further elaborated in July 1987 (see below).

CGDK Reactions

Democratic Kampuchea, one of the three components of the Coalition Government of Democratic Kampuchea (CGDK), reacted first to Gorbachev's Vladivostok speech. On 4 August its radio station termed Gorbachev's proposed conference on peace and security in Asia and the Pacific "a rotten proposal which the Soviet Union has tried to sell for decades, ever since the late Brezhnev's time. No one wants such rotten goods."[27] The DK radio commentary rejected any notion that the Vladivostok speech signalled new flexibitily on the Soviet Union's part. It ended with a restatement of the Coalition Government's public position: "concerning the Cambodian problem, the Soviet Union must stop giving aid to Vietnam. It must pressure Vietnam to accept the CGDK's eight-point proposal for a political settlement of the Cambodian problem." Subsequent radio commentaries also stressed the demand that the Soviet Union demonstrate its sincerity by withdrawing support from Vietnam and by endorsing the CGDK's eight points.[28]

On 18 August the CGDK Foreign Ministry reacted to Gorbachev's speech with an official denunciation.[29] According to this statement, "Soviet propaganda ... has tried to hoodwink the world into believing that this speech reflects a new change in Soviet policy towards this region and the Cambodian problem .... On behalf of the CGDK, the CGDK Foreign Ministry vehemently condemns these dirty tricks." Gorbachev's Vladivostok proposals were seen as essentially defensive, as the CGDK statement pointed out:

1. The fact that Mikhail Gorbachev has forced himself to speak about the Cambodian problem and lied about his desire for good relations with the countries in the Asian-Pacific region cannot be regarded as proof of a change in Soviet policy. Gorbachev has been compelled to speak about the Cambodian problem because Vietnam has become bogged down in Cambodia, a fact that can no longer be concealed.
2. Gorbachev's speech proves that the Soviet Union has been compelled to help redress the Hanoi authorities' extreme isolation resulting from their aggression in Cambodia.
3. Gorbachev has forced himself to speak about his desire for good relations with countries in the Asian-Pacific region because the Soviet policy of supporting the Vietnamese aggression against Cambodia has shaken the Soviet strategy of aggression and expansion in the Asian-Pacific region and has isolated the Soviet Union itself even more seriously in the Asian-Pacific region.

REGIONAL RESPONSES

Laotian Initiatives

On 5 August, the LPDR Council of Ministers issued a statement calling for an improvement in relations with Thailand. The Lao statement read in part, "it is now a favourable time for the LPDR and the Kingdom of Thailand to join in adopting appropriate measures to resume talks with a view to normalising and improving in all respects the relations between the two countries."[30] The Council statement was followed by a personal letter from Kaysone Phomvihan to the Thai Prime Minister, Prem Tinsulanon, which repeated this call. The Lao *volte face* was received sympathetically by Prem who replied in a letter dated 19 September. Discussions were quickly arranged at the UN that month, and agreement was reached for a meeting of technical delegations to be held in Vientiane at a later date.[31]

Laos' diplomatic moves to improve relations with Thailand received endorsement from the Indochinese Foreign Ministers, who met in Hanoi from 17-18 August.[32] The final *communique* of their thirteenth meeting declared the ministers' full support for Kaysone's efforts to do his "utmost at national as well as regional level" to improve relations with Thailand. This was the first sign of improvement in Thai-Lao relations since the downturn in 1984 over the disputed three border villages.[33]

In mid-November, the LPRP held its fourth national party congress. This conclave was attended by, among others, Geydar Aliyev (CPSU), Pham Van Dong (VCP) and Heng Samrin (KPRP). Kaysone Phomvihan used the occasion to endorse Soviet "peace initiatives" flowing from Gorbachev's Vladivostok speech. The Political Report, delivered by Kaysone, stated:

> We regard the improvment of relations between the USSR and China, the normalisation of the relations between Vietnam and China, and the establishment of relations acceptable to both sides between the Indochinese and ASEAN countries, and other measures advanced by the Soviet Union, as actions that will certainly make significant contributions to peace and security in the Asian-Pacific region. We will do our utmost together with the SRV and the PRK to speed up the negotiations between the countries of Indochina and ASEAN. We are ready to cooperate with ASEAN and other countries in the region to turn it into a zone of peace, stability, friendship and cooperation.[34]

In addition, Kaysone also called for an improvement in relations with China and the United States.[35] "As for China," he intoned, "we are sincere about being friendly with the Chinese people. We consistently reiterate that we will never abandon our efforts to maintain this friendship .... We hope that the relations between our country and the PRC will return to normal...."

What prompted this change? According to one weekly, "observers said Kaysone's push for better ties with Peking, Washington and Bangkok plainly echoed the peace initiative for Asia mooted in July by Kremlin chief Mikhail Gorbachev in Vladivostok. But Laos' softening diplomatic stance, they added, was also prompted by a need for economic aid and to boost its international trade."[36]

Immediately after the fourth congress, Lao initiatives bore fruit. In late November, high-level technical discussions were held with Thai officials who journeyed to Vientiane.[37] The press release issued after the meeting set the stage for further discussions and a resolution of some of the outstanding issues (such as lifting a Thai ban on the sale of so-called strategic goods to Laos, curbing propaganda directed against each other, security cooperation, the repatriation of refugees, and the opening of more border check points).[38] The second round of talks were held in Bangkok from 24-28 March 1987 at which Laos was again represented by its Deputy Foreign Minister, Souban Salitthilat.

China, for its part, reacted immediately to the Lao initiative by welcoming Kaysone's call in positive terms. This resulted in a visit by Vice Foreign Minister, Liu Shuqing, who arrived in Vientiane on 20 December for discussions with Khamphai Boupha, Lao First Deputy Foreign Minister. This was the first such contact at vice ministerial level since 1979. At the conclusion of Liu's five-day stay, Xinhua reported that there had been a "frank exchange of views on issues on which their views are different." However, "both sides believed the talks would lead to a better mutual understanding" and the vice foreign ministers had agreed to meet in Beijing "at an appropriate time."[39]

Indochinese Foreign Ministers

The most significant meeting in Indochina to be held following Gorbachev's speech in Vladivostok was the thirteenth conference of Foreign Ministers of the Indochinese countries held in Hanoi from 17-19 August, attended by Hun Sen, Phuon Sipaseut and Nguyen Co Thach.[40] According to one analysis: "there was no hiding the evidence that Moscow, impatiently determined to improve relations with Peking, had convinced Hanoi that it would be wise to mend fences fast."[41]

The final *communique* described Gorbachev's Vladivostok speech as "very important" and "the first-ever [integrated] peace programme concerning Asia and the Pacific." It also reiterated a long-held formulation that a "trend has emerged towards dialogue among states with different social systems." In a conciliatory signal, perhaps resulting from Soviet influence, the *communique* referred to "large public opinion calling for the withdrawal of Vietnamese forces" and stated that the three countries of Indochina "are prepared to discuss an early political solution." One Asian newsweekly, perhaps overstating the case, observed with respect to other sections of the *communique:* "[p]erhaps most important of all, Ho Chi Minh's successors appeared at last to have conceded the futility of trying to gain Chinese recognition of Indochina as Vietnam's own bloc or sphere of influence."[42]

A delegation of the VCP Central Comittee's International Department, led by Phan Dinh Vinh, visited Kampuchea from 21-28 August to map out future diplomatic moves. Vinh was received by Hun Sen, who, in addition to being a member of the KPRP Politburo and PRK Foreign Minister, also heads the KPRP International Department.[43]

Vietnam's Diplomatic Gambits

After the 1986 UN General Assembly session, Vo Dong Giang, Vietnam's Deputy Minister of Foreign Affairs, stopped in Bangkok *en route* home where he held talks with his Thai counterpart, Praphat Limpphan. In Bangkok, Giang told reporters that the Thai Deputy Foreign

Minister had called for an improvement of relations and a settlement of mutual differences. This, he said, was a "positive signal."[44] Giang reportedly presented the Thais with seven scenarios, and suggested that both sides meet in Hanoi or Bangkok for discussions. Giang stated that his offer was a "new approach because it refers to different accesses" to a solution. Did this signal a change?

Giang offered what he termed a clarification in wording of point five of Vietnam's January 1985 proposal. A withdrawal of Vietnamese military forces could occur "at the same time as there is a complete end to any support to the Pol Pot clique" (previously a Vietnamese troop withdrawal was paired with "the exclusion of the Pol Pot clique"). Giang also refined what Vietnam meant by "the elimination of the Pol Pot clique." He said: "[o]f course that doesn't mean beheading them. It means the cessation of all assistance from outside. [Without] assistance and support from outside they cannot exist as a political and military organisation."[45]

Journalists quoted Thai officials as admitting that Giang had introduced one new element: Vietnam "would accept anything coming out of national reconciliation talks." Asian diplomats interviewed by *Asiaweek* saw Giang's remarks as a major development, a sign that Moscow was putting pressure on Vietnam over the Kampuchean issue.[46]

It would appear that Hanoi and Phnom Penh agreed to approach Norodom Sihanouk at this time, in an effort to entice him into "national reconciliation" talks with PRK officials. These diplomatic soundings took several forms and were accompanied by hints of flexibility in Hanoi's formula for a peaceful settlement of the Kampuchean conflict. The first reported Vietnamese approach took place through Karl Fischer, Austrian delegate to the United Nations, who was asked to deliver a message to Sihanouk. This letter was handed over on 26 October, and reportedly accepted a Khmer Rouge presence (minus Pol Pot) in proposed talks between anti-Vietnamese resistance forces and the PRK. This was to be followed by two further phases: talks between the two Kampuchean sides with Vietnam, and finally, an international conference.[47] Senior Thai officials revealed that Hanoi had intimated that it would accept Khieu Samphan, CGDK vice president, as a party in talks between the resistance coalition and the PRK.[48] On 12 November, Sihanouk publicly rejected this Vietnamese diplomatic probe. He proposed, instead, a meeting between himself and either of Vietnam's leaders, Truong Chinh or Pham Van Dong. The PRK's Heng Samrin or Hun Sen could be included in the Vietnamese delegation.[49]

Vietnam's second approach was reportedly made through Jean-Christophe Öberg, Sweden's Ambassador to Algeria and, more importantly, former Ambassador to Thailand and Vietnam. Öberg was asked to pass on a proposal to Sihanouk suggesting that he make contact with an unidentified Vietnamese official in Paris. Öberg later met Sihanouk in Paris on 4 December, where the matter was discussed. However, when the matter became public, the Swedish diplomat denied making "any formal proposal" at all.[50]

In January 1987, Sihanouk made public the details of yet another secret approach involving Nicolae Ceaucescu, President of Romania. According to press accounts, Vietnam allegedly proposed that negotiations be held between the PRK and the three CGDK partners in order to set up a quadripartite government in Phonm Penh. After the formation of this government, Sihanouk averred, Vietnam would enter into direct negotiations with it to arrange a cease-fire and the withdrawal of Vietnamese forces. Immediately after this proposal was aired in public, Vietnam's Foreign Ministry denounced the report as an "ill-intentioned fabrication." Nevertheless, Vietnam's denial also indicated that Vietnam had been in communication with Romania on the Kampuchean question.[51] Other alleged Vietnamese intermediaries involved unnamed French figures, and an unidentified ambassador to the DPRK.

Vietnam's diplomatic gambits appeared to have had some effect. On 7 May 1987, Sihanouk announced that he was taking a year's leave of absence from his post as President of the CGDK. Sihanouk gave as his reason, recent Khmer Rouge attacks on his forces. Later, Sihanouk stated that he was motivated by his desire to seek a peaceful resolution to the nine-year old conflict. Vietnam then intensified its pressures to arrange a meeting with the PRK's Hun Sen in either Bucharest, Paris or Pyongyang.[52]

China

The first major Soviet delegation to visit China after Gorbachev's Vladivostok speech was led by Nikolay Talyzin, First Deputy Chairman of the USSR Council of Ministers and Chairman of the State Planning Committee. This delegation, which arrived in Beijing on 8 September for a week-long visit, held talks with Yao Yilin, PRC Vice Premier, and Song Ping, PRC Minister in Charge of the State Planning Commission. These talks were mainly concerned with trade, and economic, scientific and technical cooperation.[53]

In the midst of these discussions, Igor Rogachev, Soviet Deputy Foreign Minister, held talks with his counterpart, Qian Qichen. After the Soviet delegation departed, it was revealed that Gorbachev's Vladivostok speech had been discussed. TASS quoted Talyzin as stating that during conversations in Beijing, Chinese representatives had said that Gorbachev's Vladivostok speech "contained a number of new and positive elements which they had hailed."[54]

Within a week of the delegation's departure, it was announced that Rogachev, after paying a working visit to Indochina, would lead a USSR delegation to the PRC for the ninth round of talks aimed at normalising relations. In the meantime, the Foreign Ministers of both countries met on 25 September at the United Nations, for "an extensive and frank exchange of views."

It was at the ninth round of Sino-Soviet talks in early October that the USSR agreed for the first time to place Kampuchea on the agenda.[55] Moscow also apparently turned down a Chinese request to exert pressure on Vietnam to withdraw from Kampuchea. On Rogachev's departure, his Chinese counterpart Qian Qichen noted that there had been "no substantial change" in the Soviet position on Kampuchea.[56] However, Xinhua quoted a Soviet negotiator as suggesting that "the problem may be resolved in another round of talks."[57]

On the eve of the next round, Chinese Vice Foreign Minister Qian Qichen told a news conference in Beiijing that "[r]ecently the Soviet Union expressed agreement to discuss the questions of obstacles to normalising relations," (which included the presence of Vietnamese troops in Kampuchea).[58] The Kampuchean issue was discussed in the course of the tenth round of normalisation talks held in Moscow. But it was obvious in remarks made by both sides that prospects for a settlement were unlikely in the immediate future and that Kampuchea would continue to be an irritant, if not an obstacle, in the development of their bilateral relations. TASS reported, for example, that "Qian Qichen set out the PRC's known approach to matters of Soviet-Chinese relations, linking it with the conflict in Indochina and other regional problems."[59]

India

India has close relations with the USSR and Vietnam, and virtually stands alone among non-communist states in its diplomatic recognition of the PRK. In October, Prime Minister Rajiv Gandhi, after a visit to Thailand and discussions with Prem, agreed to raise Kampuchea in discussions with Gorbachev.[60] The following month, from 25-26 November, Gorbachev travelled to India in his first visit. Nothing in the press reports, various speeches and official *communique* indicated that the Kampuchean issue had been discussed extensively.[61] Nonetheless, shortly thereafter, India embarked on a series of low-key diplomatic probes.

On 19 January, the Indian Minister of State for External Affairs K. Natwar Singh paid a brief working visit to Moscow where he met with Foreign Minister Eduard Shevardnadze. A TASS report that "topical international issues" had been discussed indicated in somewhat elliptical fashion that the Kampuchea issue had been raised.[62] Singh also visited Hanoi where he agreed to visit Southeast Asia to make further soundings.

Speculation on India's role surfaced again in February-March 1987 with the visit of India's Deputy Foreign Minister to Southeast Asia (Indonesia, Thailand, Brunei, Malaysia and Singapore), and diplomatic reports that Indian officials had detected "new changes" in Vietnamese attitudes on the Kampuchean conflict.[63] In May, Anatoly Dobrynin visited New Delhi for discussions with Singh which touched on Kampuchea. In June, India's External Affairs Minister visited Moscow, and early the following month, he revisited Laos (1-2 July), Kampuchea (3-6 July), Vietnam (6-8 July), and Thailand (9 July) where he held discussions with high-ranking officials.[64] Singh urged regional states to engage in dialogue with Vietnam, arguing that Hanoi's attitude was easing, that it would meet its 1990 deadline for withdrawal of troops, and that it its aims were limited to ensuring that any government which emerged in Kampuchea would not be anti-Vietnamese.

Vietnam's Sixth Party Congress

In December 1986, prior to the VCP's sixth congress, Truong Chinh journeyed to Moscow on his second trip in three months. Once again he held wide-ranging discussions with Gorbachev. According to an official account, both leaders reached "total unanimity" of views on domestic and foreign issues. Nayan Chanda quoted analysts as concluding that Chinh and Gorbachev "reached a compromise by which Gorbachev gave his blessings to the party congress plans, in return for Hanoi's backing for his Asian initiative."[65]

None of the reports or speakers at Vietnam's sixth party congress indicated that any radical shifts would occur in Vietnam's foreign policy, especially on the Kampuchean question. Rather, the Central Committee's political report reiterated long-standing views: Vietnam would maintain its close ties with the Soviet Union and develop its "special relationships" with Laos and Kampuchea as the cornerstone of its foreign policy.

Nayan Chanda also assessed the implications of the sixth congress for a settlement of the Kampuchean issue in negative terms.[66] He noted that the 1990 date set by Vietnam for the withdrawal of its troops from Kampuchea was omitted from the political report, although it was mentioned by Vice Minister Vo Dong Giang outside the congress hall at a press conference. Chanda interpreted the political report's references to Indochinese solidarity as implying "that Hanoi would not accept any settlement that weakens Vietnam's security cooperation with Cambodia (or Laos) and allows hostile countries a foothold there." Furthermore, in Chanda's view, the CPSU delegate "seemed to offer his blessing to the solidarity of Vietnam, Cambodia and Laos." While in Hanoi, CPSU delegate Egor Ligachev twice mentioned that the Soviet Union's desire to seek a normalisation of relations between China and Vietnam would not be at the expense of Vietnam's interests, and neither would the Soviet Union mediate.[67] The matter was, in his view, best solved by dialogue between Beijing and Hanoi.

Immediately after the congress, a meeting was held in Hanoi between Nguyen Van Linh, Kaysone Phomvihan and Heng Samrin. This dealt mainly with economic issues and a proposed summit of heads of party and state set for the following year. One report stated that the three leaders had "agreed that in the new stage, there should be further strengthening of the revolutionary alliance between the three countries, an upgrading, renewal and strengthening of all-round cooperation, especially in economy ...."[68]

Did the sixth congress signal a hardening of the Vietnamese position? In Chanda's view, the congress "set back a timid improvement of atmosphere in recent months. But a closer look suggests that an apparent hardening of positions is tactical and not a prelude to escalation."[69] Chanda also argued that the elevation to the Politburo of two officials with direct experience in Kampuchea "could instill greater realism in Hanoi's approach" and that "[d]omestic political considerations may dictate a hard-line position on Cambodia at this stage." Subsequently, as leadership changes unfolded in Hanoi, and as Vietnamese officials began to focus almost exclusively on the parlous state of the domestic economy, some leading ASEAN officials began to adopt a more upbeat attitude about the possibilities of a negotiated settlement.

An Asian Socialist Community?

According to a former ASEAN Ambassador to Moscow, the foremost aim of Soviet foreign policy enunciated by Gorbachev in Vladivostok was to normalise relations with China. Ultimately, according to this source, the Soviet Union would like to repair the rift in the ideological field and include the People's Republic of China in an expanded Asian socialist community. Not only has Moscow repeatedly stated that China is a legitimate socialist country, but in a reorganisation of its Foreign Ministry, all the socialist countries of Asia - including China - have been grouped into one department in a structure parallel to the socialist countries of Europe, which are also included in one department.[70]

As a first step, a "consultative working meeting" of the deputy foreign ministers from the SRV, PRK, DPRK, LPDR, MPR and the USSR was held in Moscow from 8-9 January 1987. Their press *communique* endorsed Gorbachev's initiatives: "the meeting's participants stressed the extremely important and long-range meaning of the programme for ensuring peace, security and cooperation in Asia and the Pacific which the Soviet Union put forth at Vladivostok."[71]

The only reference to Southeast Asia declared:

> the existing complex situation in Southeast Asia requires countries in the region to seek positive ways to resolve their existing problems on the basis of total respect for the sovereignty, independence and territorial integrity of the countries concerned without outside interference in their international affairs. The many constructive proposals of the Indochinese countries and their policy of promoting dialogue with the ASEAN states for the sake of turning the region into one of lasting peace, stability, good-neighbourliness and cooperation as well as their policy of normalising relations with their neighbouring countries are precisely aimed at achieving these goals.

With respect to China the same statement declared: "those taking part in the meeting were convinced that the normalisation and further development of relations between the PRC and other socialist countries will have a positive effect on efforts to make the Asian-Pacific situation healthy and consolidate peace and security in this part of the world."

In July 1987, a three-day meeting of Asian communist parties was convened in Ulan Bator, Mongolia, at which it was agreed to promote Soviet proposals for a collective security system in the Asian-Pacific region. This was the first ever meeting of this type held in Asia. In an obvious move designed to allay Chinese suspicions, the meeting was held as an open forum with no apparent effort being made by the Soviet Union to push through decisions binding on all participants.[72]

SHEVARDNADZE'S 1987 REGIONAL VISIT

Thailand

Soviet Foreign Minister Eduard Shevardnadze made a brief stop over in Bangkok on 2 March 1987 at the start of his six-nation tour. Kampuchea dominated discussions. The main message he delivered was that Moscow and Hanoi wanted to talk peace, "some aspects" of the Afghanistan peace plan might be useful for Kampuchea, and that the USSR stood ready to guarantee peace there after a Vietnamese withdrawal. Further detailed discussions were left to the future when Foreign Minister Sitthi Sawetsila was scheduled to visit Moscow.

Australia

Shevardnadze visited Australia from 3-5 March for talks with Foreign Minister Bill Hayden and also Prime Minister Bob Hawke. Kampuchea was but one item on the agenda, which also included such weighty matters as East-West relations, arms control, human rights, trade, and Afghanistan.[73] Despite this, Hayden revealed that a surprisingly long dicussion on Indochina and Kampuchea had taken place,[74] and that Shevardnadze "made it clear that he was not here talking for the governments of Indochina," and that it had not been possible "to explore in a conclusive way whether the Soviets could influence an end [to] the problem." Later, Bill Hayden told a press conference that he had explored ways of facilitating a solution to the Kampuchean issue with his Soviet counterpart, that he had stressed the importance of drawing Vietnam into a wider orbit, and that he had also made several suggestions which he hoped Shevardnadze would take up in Hanoi.[75] One of these was that the time was ripe for Vietnam to make some sort of "political act or gesture" to resolve the dispute.[76] Shevardnadze listened politely, according to one account, and took note of Hayden's remarks.

Australia, like India, has continued to play a low-key role in the matter of seeking a negotiated settlement of the Kampuchean conflict. In May 1987, Hayden stopped briefly in Bangkok to discuss Thai Foreign Minister

Sitthi's recent visit to Moscow. Hayden, too, detected some shift in the Soviet position. In June, at the ASEAN post-ministerial dialogue session, Hayden, in reflecting on his March talks with Shevardnadze, said that he thought there was "an important change in mood and tone" in Moscow's discussions about the future of Kampuchea.[77]

Indonesia

Anatoly Zaitsev, new chief of the reorganised Southeast Asia Department in the Soviet Foreign Ministry, visited Indonesia in September 1986 to brief officials there on Soviet foreign policy following Gorbachev's Vladivostok speech. In talks with Foreign Minister Mochtar Kusumaatmadja he arranged an invitation for a visit by his boss, the Soviet Foreign Minister. This eventuated immediately on the heels of Shevardnadze's visit to Australia. During his brief stay, Shevardnadze was content mainly to listen to Indonesian views, leaving future prospects hanging on the forthcoming visit of the Thai Foreign Minister. Mochtar was led to comment, "I think there is a [Soviet] willingness to help solve [the conflict]."[78] Dr Mochtar then revived an old idea, the convening of an informal "cocktail party" involving all Cambodian sides to the conflict, as well as the Vietnamese.

Indochina

After visiting Indonesia, Shevardnadze paid his first visit to Indochina, stopping in Laos and Kampuchea first before travelling to Vietnam. Press and radio reports later indicated that the Foreign Minister had not presented any new Soviet initiatives on ending the war in Kampuchea.[79] In Hanoi, the main topic of discussion was "renovation" in the relationship between the Soviet Union and Vietnam. By this was meant that Vietnam would push ahead with its plans for economic liberalisation and would improve its handling of Soviet economic aid. For his part, Shevardnadze supported the strengthening of the alliance of the three countries of Indochina, as well as their efforts to normalise relations with China.[80]

Since Gorbachev's Vladivostok speech, the Soviet Union has intensified its efforts to normalise relations with China and ASEAN. As both have set the resolution of the Kampuchean problem as a precondition, Shevardnadze's visit to Thailand, Australia, Indonesia and Indochina may be seen as a signal that Moscow is trying to bring about a resolution of that conflict. Certainly Mochtar's assessment of Shevardnadze's regional visit bears this out. The Indonesian Foreign Minister was quoted as stating that Shevardnadze's visit marked the "first concrete steps" towards the implementation of Gorbachev's Vladivostok Initiative. According to Mochtar, it was too much to expect that Shevardnadze could achieve some "drastic or concrete" result just yet. His purpose was first to ascertain how firm the regional countries were that the settlement of Kampuchea was a prerequisite for improved Soviet relations with the region. His visit was only "the first act" in the "Vladivostok process."[81]

THE "VLADIVOSTOK PROCESS"

Thailand

Foreign Minister Sitthi's visit to Moscow (10-14 May 1987), represented Thailand's first detailed probe into the substance of Gorbachev's Vladivostok speech. Sitthi met with his counterpart, Shevardnadze, and President Andrei Gromyko. In the course of a luncheon address, Shevardnadze acknowledged the Soviet Union's interest in resolving the Kampuchean conflict. "We hold differing views on the situation around Kampuchea," he said, "but we by no means consider that the situation is deadlocked, that there are no opportunities for a settlement of the conflict .... I would like to say quite definitely that any proposals and practical steps which lead towards [the] establishment of a just and stable peace in the region will continue to meet with total understanding and support on our part."[82]

According to Thai officials, Shevardnadze's remarks represented a marked change in Soviet attitude if not in policy, since formerly Moscow had refused to discuss the Kampuchean problem. One Thai journalist travelling with Sitthi concluded "[i]t is significant that for the first time ever the Soviet Union said it wanted to see peace in the region and a quick solution to the Kampuchean problem."[83] In his Vladivostok address, Gorbachev suggested that the Kampuchean conflict should be settled between China and Vietnam with no role specified for ASEAN. Now, this line has changed, according to the Thais. Foreign Minister Sitthi was quoted as saying that Moscow genuinely wanted to improve its relations with ASEAN, and that Moscow had promised it would help to settle the Kampuchean problem.[84]

During the Shevardnadze-Sitthi talks, the Soviets alleged that progress in Sino-Soviet normalisation was being held up by the Kampuchean issue.[85] This was considered an encouraging sign by the Thais. Thai officials were also impressed by Shevardnadze's demonstration that he was ready to listen to what Sitthi had to say about ASEAN's position. Thai officials took this to mean that the Kremlin was finally concerning itself with the Kampuchean problem. Senior Thai officials thus saw the Shevardnadze-Sitthi meeting as prelude to further negotiations; but estimated that it would take at least a few more years, if not longer, to settle the dispute.[86]

Vietnam

Nguyen Van Linh paid his first visit to the Soviet Union as newly elected VCP Secretary General at the same time as Sitthi was in Moscow (7-22 May). Linh was accompanied by Foreign Minister Nguyen Co Thach. Linh was received by Gorbachev on 18-19 May. To all outward appearances, the visit appeared "routine," with Soviet aid the main topic.[87] A closer examination suggests that the Soviets continued to try and persuade the Vietnamese to seek an early resolution of the Kampuchean conflict by opening a dialogue with China,[88] and by adopting a more flexible policy on what would constitute an acceptable government of "national reconciliation" in Phnom Penh.

At a dinner speech welcoming Linh, Gorbachev called for a political solution based on "the unification of all their national patriotic forces" in Kampuchea.[89] Later, both Gorbachev and Linh called for an improvement in relations with China, stating that "[t]hey would also greet China's active involvement in the search for ways of solving the complex problems of the Asian continent." Linh later told Gorbachev that Vietnamese military withdrawal from Kampuchea was as important as the elimination of the Khmer Rouge leader Pol Pot and an end to foreign interference in that country.[90]

The Soviet-Vietnam joint statement left no doubt that Hanoi, whatever its earlier misgivings and anxieties, had been brought round to supporting Moscow's efforts to woo China. The joint statement declared: "the search for ways of settling the international aspects of the Kampuchean problem by political means should be conducted with regard for realities in the region and with the involvement in this or that form of all sides concerned." The *communique* then stated, "[t]he participants in the talks pointed to a desire by their countries to normalise and improve relations with the PRC, which would be a major positive factor for stronger stability in Asia and in international life in general. They would also greet China's active involvement in the search for ways of solving the complex problems of the Asian continent. The Soviet side supported Vietnam's initiative for holding Vietnamese-Chinese talks with a view to settling contentious issues as soon as possible."[91]

Vietnam has long been concerned about the pace of Sino-Soviet normalisation and the implications for itself. Hanoi has reacted, in part, by initiating as many as six confidential diplomatic approaches to Beijing since Gorbachev came to power.[92] China has reportedly rejected each one, citing the occupation of Kampuchea as the main stumbling block.

ASEAN

ASEAN Foreign Ministers held their twentieth ministerial meeting from 15-20 June 1987. At the opening session, Singapore's Prime Minister Lee Kuan Yew declared that the chances of a negotiated settlement have increased and that there had been reassessments of positions in Moscow and Hanoi.[93] In Lee's words, "[a]n eventual Cambodian settlement through negotiations, followed by withdrawal from Cambodia, is more likely than continuing Vietnamese defiance."[94] ASEAN ministers were briefed by Sitthi on his recent trip to Moscow.

For the first time, their final *communique* called upon the Soviet Union by name to assist in settling the conflict in Kampuchea by urging Vietnam to reach a negotiated political settlement.[95] Reference to the USSR is recognition of the key role that Moscow can play in pressuring Vietnam to withdraw from Kampuchea. Diplomatic sources say this inclusion also marks a new phase in ASEAN-Soviet relations which have come about as a result of Gorbachev's new approach to Southeast Asia. Kampuchea is now regarded by ASEAN as a "test case" of Moscow's desire to improve relations with ASEAN.

PRK

Continued Soviet interest in playing a role in a negotiated settlement of the Kampuchean conflict was indicated in the aftermath of Sitthi's visit. Hun Sen, chairman of the PRK Council of Ministers, who was "vacationing" in the USSR, was summoned to Moscow on 1 July, for a meeting with Shevardnadze and, shortly after, with Gorbachev himself.

Both officials made clear to Hun Sen their support for a policy of national reconciliation. The joint statement issued after the talks declared: "[the two sides] held that the only reasonable solution is a policy of national reconciliation and cooperation among all the patriotic forces .... and welcomed the active contributions of the countries concerned in the search for ways to settle the Kampuchea issue."[96]

Cocktail Party

Indonesia viewed Nguyen Van Linh's trip to Moscow in positive terms, reading into Gorbachev's public remarks (cited above) a Soviet willingness to include the Khmer Rouge in the process of reaching a negotiated settlement.[97] At the conclusion of ASEAN's twentieth ministerial meeting, Indonesian Foreign Minister Mochtar, citing "some positive developments," announced that he would visit Vietnam later that month.[98] Mochtar's trip had already been postponed three times previously, and thus expectations were aroused.

Mochtar's visit took place from 27-29 July. Discussions were held in Ho Chi Minh City with Nguyen Co Thach; Mochtar also met Nguyen Van Linh and Pham Hung, who had recently replaced Pham Van Dong as premier. Both sides quickly endorsed Mochtar's "cocktail party" formula. For example, the text of the joint press release stated, "[w]ith respect to the Indonesian idea of holding a cocktail party, it was understood that this would be an informal meeting of the two Cambodian sides held on the basis of equal footing, without preconditions and with no political label. At a later stage of this party, Indonesia will invite other concerned countries, including Vietnam to participate."[99]

Had substantial progress been made? ASEAN hawks thought not. An ASEAN special meeting was hurriedly convened in Bangkok on 16 August. At issue was the format of the cocktail party agreed to by Mochtar, in particular the length of time between the first meeting (involving only the Kampuchean parties) and the second (to include Vietnam). Thai and Singaporean officials felt that the Indonesian Foreign Minister had gone too far, and that the format agreed to would make it appear that the conflict in Kampuchea was a civil war, and not a case of Vietnamese aggression. They wanted Vietnam involved in the "cocktail party" at the earliest possible moment. In the end, Mochtar's proposal was modified to read: "one meeting initially among the Cambodian parties, followed immediately by Vietnam's participation."

Thailand was also concerned that no agenda had been agreed. They succeeded in inserting a reference to portions of the CGDK's 1986 eight points into the final ASEAN *joint communique*.[100] These alterations were unacceptable to Hanoi and were quickly rejected.

Malaysia

Prime Minister Mahathir Mohamad was the next Southeast Asian leader to visit Moscow, in a continuation of the "Vladivostok process" of improving bilateral relations with regional countries. Mahathir arrived in early August, and found no difficulty in obtaining Soviet endorsement for a political solution to the Kampuchean conflict. Mahathir was quoted as stating that the implementation of the broad tasks outlined in Gorbachev's 1986 Vladivostok speech required cooperation aimed at reaching "the earliest settlement of regional conflicts." The Malaysia-Soviet *joint communique* echoed these remarks in calling for an urgent political settlement to the Kampuchean conflict which would take account of the interests of all the parties.[101] Whatever hopes were aroused, were quickly dashed as a result of the ASEAN special meeting of 16 August.

CONCLUSION

Soviet initiatives on the vexed question of a political settlement to the nine year Kampuchean conflict must be placed within the broader context of Gorbachev's domestic and foreign policy. As early as the 23rd Congress of the CPSU, and reiterated in his Vladivostok speech of July 1986, Gorbachev has sought to bring about a comprehensive system of international security designed to buy time for his domestic programme of economic reform. Quite clearly, Gorbachev does not want to be caught up in massive new defense expenditures in order to match an American SDI program.

In order to prevent this, Gorbachev must first reach a new arms control agreement with the United States. The pace of Soviet initiatives in this sphere has been positively breathtaking. For example, on the first anniversary of his Vladivostok speech, Gorbachev offered to extend his European "zero-zero option" to embrace all of Asia, thus making an INF agreement with the US all the more likely. Significantly, Gorbachev made his proposal in an interview granted to *Merdeka*, an Indonesian newspaper. This move was quickly perceived by outside observers as a revival of the

"Vladivostok process." In other words, Gorbachev sought to breathe new life into his peace offensive by advancing the notion of a global double zero option.[102]

In his Vladivostok address, Gorbachev proclaimed that the Soviet Union was an Asian-Pacific power. While the Soviet Union has military might in the North Pacific, its political and economic influence lags far behind elsewhere in the region. In order to reform the domestic economy, and especially to develop the Soviet Far East, Gorbachev must prevent the formation of a US-Japan-China bloc aligned against, and hostile towards, the USSR. Accordingly, high priority is set on normalising relations with China, and encouraging mutually beneficial commerce and trade.

One aim of Soviet diplomacy is to restore the unity and coordination of Asian socialist countries, including China. Soviet commentaries directed at China have homed in on the theme that now is the time to improve relations with Vietnam. One broadcast beamed at China stated: "[t]he Soviet Union has openly indicated its concern for the restoration of dialogue between Chinese and Vietnamese comrades for the purpose of eliminating unnecessary mutual suspicion and distrust between the two socialist neighbours. Mediation of the Cambodian issue and promotion of good-neighbourly relations in Southeast Asia hinge, to a large extent, on normalised relations between China and Vietnam."[103]

Is the conflict in Kampuchea an impediment to the attainment of these broad Soviet objectives? For example, China includes the Kampuchean conflict among its "three obstacles" which must be settled before relations with the USSR can be normalised. Yet, as Gary Klintworth's chapter demonstrates, in all spheres, save party-to-party ties, Soviet-Chinese relations have already become "normalised." In one sense, the Kampuchean conflict is a bilateral issue between Hanoi and Beijing. That is why the Soviet Union has repeatedly called on both sides to engage in dialogue to settle the matter peacefully.

Since his Vladivostok address, Gorbachev has shifted ground, and agreed to discuss this "third country matter" with China. In Soviet eyes, the Kampuchean conflict need not remain a zero-sum game between Vietnam and its opponents. Rather, a key feature of Soviet diplomacy has been to use the prospect of a peaceful settlement as a means of enticing China into participating in a new Asian socialist community. In such an arrangement, Kampuchea could remain both "independent" and socialist, and neither Vietnam nor China would lose prestige over such an outcome. ASEAN has likewise made Kampuchea the litmus test for an improvement in its relations with Moscow. To the extent that they now place their hopes on Soviet influence and initiatives to end the conflict, Gorbachev has succeeded in demonstrating that the USSR is indeed an Asian-Pacific power.

NOTES

1. Gorbachev announced that the USSR and Mongolia were examining "the question of withdrawing a considerable number of Soviet troops from Mongolia" and he further offered China the possibility of balanced force reductions along their border; and he also announced the withdrawal of six Soviet regiments from Afghanistan. In a third conciliatory signal, Gorbachev declared that the main channel of the Amur river could serve as the official border with China.

2. This conclusion is reinforced by press conference remarks made later by Mikhail Kapitsa, USSR Deputy Foreign Minister. According to TASS, on 6 August Kapitsa "drew the journalists' attention to the section of Mikhail Gorbachev's speech, in Vladivostok expressing the [sic] interest in the restoration of comradely dialogue between China and Vietnam (as the key to a solution of the Kampuchean conflict)." Neither Gorbachev nor Kapitsa, however, restated the caveat that Sino-Soviet normalisation would not be at the expense of Vietnam. Shortly after the Vladivostok speech, Deng Xiaoping dismissed Gorbachev's "peace initiative" by declaring that "it does not signify a major step in the normalisation of Sino-Soviet relations." Deng further stated that if Gorbachev decided to try to resolve the problem, "a foreign ministerial meeting will be held between China and the Soviet Union ... and a summit meeting will also be considered," thus testing Gorbachev on the third obstacle. Kyodo, 3 September 1986. Richard Nations, "Moscow's New Tack," *Far Eastern Economic Review*, 14 August 1986, pp. 30-40, concluded, "Moscow apparently sees no need for Hanoi to make concessions to the tripartite anti-Vietnamese Cambodian resistance coalition."

3. Nayan Chanda, "Not So Soft on Cambodia," *Far Eastern Economic Review*, 1 January 1987, p. 12.

4. After Kampuchea, Gorbachev nominated the following areas in his priorities: halting nuclear proliferation; reduction of nuclear-armed naval fleets in the Indian Ocean; radical reduction of armed forces and conventional weapons; and discussion of confidence-building measures.

5. The text of Gorbachev's speech in Vladivostok is taken from Soviet Television and Moscow Home Service, 28 July 1986. For an excellent, concise analysis consult: Richard Nations, "Moscow's New Tack," pp. 30-40. The text of this speech may be found in the Appendix.

6. Anatoly Zaitsev, director-general of Southeast Asian Affairs in the Soviet Foreign Ministry, visited Bangkok in early September 1986. Zaitsev stated that Moscow would support a meeting between ASEAN and the Indochinese countries to

"normalise the situation around Kampuchea"; *Nation* (Bangkok), 4 September 1986, p. 2.

7. Vietnam News Agency dispatch from Hanoi, 26 July 1986.

8. Moscow Home Service and TASS, 12 August 1986.

9. TASS and Hanoi Home Service, 12 August 1986.

10. Editorial, "New Brilliant Manifestation of the S.R.V.-USSR Militant Solidarity and Comprehensive Co-operation," *Nhan Dan*, 13 August 1986.

11. Vietnam News Agency dispatch from Hanoi, 19 August 1986.

12. Nayan Chanda, "Weather Eye on Moscow," *Far Eastern Economic Review*, 23 October 1986, p. 24.

13. Respectively, excerpts [trich] were broadcast by Hanoi Domestic Service, 30 July 1986; "Tam Cuong Cao Ca Dau Tranh Cho Hoa Binh, An Ninh Va Hoc Tac Quoc Te" (A Noble Example of Striving for the Cause of International Peace, Security and Cooperation), and "Phat Bieu cua Dong Chi M. X. Gooc-Ba-Chop tai Vla-De-Vo-Xtoc ve Nhieu Van De Quan Trong trong Nuoc va The Gioi," (Speech by Comrade M. S. Gorbachev in Vladivostok about Many Important Problems in the USSR and the World) *Nhan Dan*, 30 July 1986; "Just Stand, Lofty Responsibility," *Quan Doi Nhan Dan* carried by Hanoi Domestic Service, 1 August 1986; Vietnam News Agency, 1 August 1986; and Pham Van Dong interview with TASS carried by Vietnam News Agency (VNA) dispatch from Hanoi, 4 August 1986. Subsequent references are from these sources unless otherwise indicated.

14. VNA dispatch from Hanoi, 14 August 1986.

15. "Soup a la Carte," *Asiaweek*, 10 August 1986, p. 21.

16. Station commentary, "Support the Soviet Union's Initiatives on Peace and Security in the Asian-Pacific Region," Vientiane Domestic Service, 7 August 1986.

17. TASS, 11 August 1986.

18. On 18 October 1986, after reporting on these discussions, Kaysone received the full endorsement of the LPRP Politburo; Vientiane Home Service, 18 October 1986.

19. *Ibid.*, 21 August 1986.

20. *Ibid.*, 22 August 1986.

21. Khaosan Pathet Lao [KPL], 23 August 1986.

22. *Ibid.*, 13 September 1986.

23. SPK dispatch from Phnom Penh, 31 July 1986.

24. Editorial, "Wave the Flag of Praise and Unreservedly Support the New Peace Initiatives and Proposals of the Soviet Union," *Pracheachon;* as broadcast by Phnom Penh Domestic Service, 6 August 1986.

25. SPK, 23 August 1986.

26. "A Thaw Between Two 'Brothers'," *Asiaweek*, 19 October 1986, p. 18.

27. Voice of Democratic Kampuchea, 4 August 1986.

28. Station commentary, "All Countries in the Asian-Pacific Region Continue to Regard the Soviet Union as the Most Dangerous Threat Not to Be Overlooked," Voice of Democratic Kampuchea, 10 August 1986; and "No Matter How Hard the Soviet Union Tries, It Cannot Cover Up Vietnam's Aggression in Cambodia," *ibid.*, 11 August 1986.

29. "Statement of the CGDK Foreign Ministry on Mikhail Gorbachev's Vladivostok Speech and the Points Relating to the Cambodian Problem," Voice of the National Army of Democratic Kampuchea, 18 August 1986.

30. Vientiane Home Service, 25 September 1986.

31. "A Thaw Between Two 'Brothers'," *Asiaweek,* 19 October 1986, p. 18.

32. "Communique of the Thirteenth Conference of Foreign Ministers of Kampuchea, Laos and Vietnam," *Vietnam Courier* (Hanoi), 9(September 1986), pp. 8-10.

33. In late August 1986, the Thai Interior Ministry authorised the governors of border provinces to begin talks directly with their Lao counterparts to settle outstanding problems.

34. "Political Report of the Central Committee of the Lao People's Revolutionary Party Presented at its Fourth Party Congress by Comrade Kaysone Phomvihan, General Secretary," (Vientiane: typescript, November 1986).

35. *Ibid.;* for a discussion consult Reuter dispatch from Bangkok, *Sydney Morning Herald,* 14 November 1986; and Murray Hiebert, "Change at the Top," *Far Eastern Economic Review,* 4 December 1986, pp. 42-43.

36. "Warming Up," *Asiaweek,* 30 November 1986, p. 18.

37. The Thai delegation was led by Arun Phanuphong, adviser to the Prime Minister; the Lao side was led by Souban Salitthilat, Deputy Foreign Minister. The discussions were held from 27-29 November.

38. The press release was carried by KPL, 29 November 1986.

39. Xinhua dispatch from Vientiane, 24 December 1986.

40. Radio Hanoi, 18 August 1986.

41. "End of a Vision," *Asiaweek,* 7 September 1986, p. 12.

42. *Ibid.*, p. 13.

43. VNA, 29 August 1986.

44. *Nation,* 29 October 1986.

45. "Is Pol Pot Dying?" *Asiaweek,* 14 December 1986, p. 40.

46. *Ibid.*

47. "Another Bluff By Vietnam?" *Asiaweek,* 15 February 1987, p. 16.

48. Rodney Tasker, "Offering to the Prince," *Far Eastern Economic Review,* 27 November 1986, p. 28.

49. AFP dispatch from Paris, 10 November 1986.

50. "Another Bluff By Vietnam?"*Asiaweek,* 15 February 1987, p. 16.

51. This episode is recounted in: Vietnam News Agency, 22 January 1987; Voice of the National Army of Democratic Kampuchea, 23 January 1987; Xinhua, 24 January 1987; and "Another Bluff By Vietnam?" pp. 16-17.

52. AP dispatch from Beijing, *Bangkok Post,* 12 July 1987.

53. Two agreements were reached, one on contact between the two state planning commissions, and a revised consular treaty. Talyzin also met with PRC Premier Zhao Ziyang and discussed ways of expanding economic and technological cooperation.

54. TASS, 16 September 1986.

55. AFP dispatch from Beijing, *Canberra Times,* 6 October 1986.

56. "A Crescendo for Withdrawal," *Asiaweek,* 2 November 1987, p. 11.

57. Nayan Chanda, "Communist Compromise?" *Far Eastern Economic Review,* 25 December 1986, p. 15.

58. Xinhua, 3 April 1987; and AP dispatch from Beijing, *Mainichi Daily News,* 5 April 1987.

59. TASS and Xinhua, 20 April 1987.

60. "A Crescendo for Withdrawal," *Asiaweek,* 2 November 1987, p. 11.

61. Text of the *joint communique* was carried by TASS, 27 November 1986.

62. TASS, 19 January 1987.

63. Malaysia's Minister for Foreign Affairs, Datuk Rais Yatim, based his remarks on conversations with his Indian counterpart in New Delhi; Kuala Lumpur Radio, 16 February 1987.

64. *Bangkok Post,* 10 July 1987. He briefied Thai Foreign Minister Sitthi afterwards.

65. Chanda, "Communist Compromise?" p. 15.

66. Nayan Chanda, "Not So Soft on Cambodia," *Far Eastern Economic Review,* 1 January 1987, pp. 11-12.

67. Moscow Home Service, 17 December 1986.

68. SPK, 20 December 1986.

69. Nayan Chanda, "Southeast Asia: More Smoke Than Fire Amid the Maneuvering," *International Herald Tribune,* 22 January 1987.

70. Conversation with A. K. Siddique, former Ambassador of Singapore to the USSR, and present Ambassador to the Federal Republic of Germany; Kiel, 15 July 1987.

71. Text of press *communique* carried by Hanoi Home Service, 11 January 1987.

72. Reuter dispatch from Moscow, *Nation,* 11 July 1987.

73. TASS, 19 February 1987.

74. Mark Baker dispatch from Canberra, *The Age,* 5 March 1987.

75. Patrick Walters, "Soviet Minister Lashes Tokyo," *Sydney Morning Herald,* 5 March 1987.

76. Greg Earl, "Aust Seeks Gesture," *Australian Financial Review,* 5 March 1987.

77. Nicholas Rothwell dispatch from Singapore, *Australian,* 18 June 1987.

78. "Looking for a New Approach," *Asiaweek,* 15 March 1987.

79. Reuter dispatch from Bangkok, *Sydney Morning Herald,* 12 March 1987.

80. Associated Press dispatch from Bangkok citing Vietnam News Agency, *Sydney Morning Herald,* 13 March 1987.

81. Michael Byrnes citing remarks made by Mochtar on a visit to the Philippines, *Australian Financial Review,* 29 April 1987.

82. See the remarks by Shevardnadze to Sitthi; TASS, 11 May 1987.

83. Pornpimol Kanchanalak dispatch from Moscow, *Bangkok Post,* 14 May 1987.

84. *Nation*, 25 May 1987. Later Sitthi stated that Shevardnadze acknowledged that the USSR had a role to play in resolving the Kampuchean problem; Singapore Domestic Service, 17 June 1987.

85. Sompong Kittinaradorn writing in the *Nation*, 28 May 1987.

86. Sompong Kittinaradorn writing in the *Nation*, 18 May 1987.

87. A series of agreements on cooperation in industry and agriculture were signed. The USSR pledged continued cooperation with the SRV. AP and UPI dispatches from Moscow, *Nation*, 21 May 1987.

88. Sompong Kittinaradorn in *Nation*, 5 August 1987.

89. TASS, 19 May 1987.

90. *Bangkok Post*, 22 May 1987.

91. Text of the Soviet-Vietnamese *joint communique* as carried by TASS, 21 May 1987.

92. Sompong Kittinaradorn writing in the *Nation*, 28 May 1987.

93. Cameron Forbes dispatch from Singapore, *The Age*, 16 June 1987.

94. Quoted by Cameron Forbes in a dispatch from Singapore, *Sydney Morning Herald*, 16 June 1987.

95. AAP dispatch from Singapore, *Canberra Times*, 17 June 1987.

96. SPK, 4 July 1987 and *Bangkok Post*, 29 July 1987.

97. Jakarta Home Service, 23 May 1987.

98. Jakarta International Service, 17 June 1987.

99. Hanoi Domestic Service, 29 July 1987.

100. Paisal Sricharatchanya, "New Mix to Old Cocktail," *Far Eastern Economic Review*, 27 August 1987, pp. 8-9.

101. TASS dispatch from Moscow, *Nation*, 6 August 1987.

102. Sophie Quinn-Judge and Robert Manning, "The Missile Message," *Far Eastern Economic Review*, 6 August 1987, pp. 10-11.

103. Commentary by station observer Mulatov, Moscow Radio, 14 August 1986.

Appendix: Text of Speech by Mikhail Gorbachev in Vladivostok, 28 July 1986

Dear comrades,

I have long intended to visit the Far East. And it is not only because a person is attracted to regions where he has not been and by an interest in what he has not yet seen. Without getting to know your great and beautiful land, one's very concept of the homeland, its history, its present and its future, cannot be complete.

The Far East is always associated in our minds with the immense expanses of the Land of the Soviets, striking from the Baltic and the Black Sea to the Pacific Ocean. It is associated with the valour, industry and steadfastness of the people who settled and defended this land, and with the novelty and scale of today's affairs. Vladimir Ilyich Lenin, with especial warmth, called the city of Vladivostok our very own city. The exploit of our fellow-countrymen, of those first pioneers who blazed the trail to the Pacific Ocean, will always remain in folk memory. We shall never forget the stormy nights of Spassk and the Volochayev days, the energetic assimilation of the region during the years of the first five year plans, and the martial labour of the Border troops on these hallowed borders of ours. The bravery and courage of the Far Eastern divisions and the sailors from the Pacific who fought near Moscow and Stalingrad and in the final battles of the second world war in the East will live for ever in the memory of the people.

History is made by people. The Far East means the courageous images of Dezhnev, Khabarov, Nevelskoy. The Far East means the glorious names of Lazo and Postyshev, Sukhanov and the Sibirtsev brothers, Bonivur and Chasovitin, Blyukher and Uborevich. Among those who are fascinating others with their example today, I should like to name Ivan Andreyevich Chuprynin, party veteran and participant in the civil war; Yuri Petrovich Volkov, captain of fishing vessels and Hero of Socialist

Labour; Anatoly Andreyevich Belov, shipwright team-leader and Hero of Socialist Labour; Galina Vladimirovna Merkulova, team-leader of builders and candidate member of the CPSU Central Committee; and Nikolay Nikolayevich Dubinin, People's Teacher of the USSR.

The Far Eastern region glorified by Arsenyev and Fadeyev has always been and will remain a region dear to the heart of the Soviet man. I am glad to have an opportunity to visit the Maritime Kray and to acquaint myself with your life and work, with what is being done in this region today and will be done tomorrow; the more so as in the plans defined by the 27th CPSU Congress a special place is assigned to the Far East as to Siberia.

These days I have had quite a few business-like and interesting meetings, both planned and non-planned at factories, on ships, in institutes and, finally, simply in streets and squares. I should say that these meetings were necessary, frank and friendly. The talks proceeded frankly on every topic. That is how it should be when the matter concerns deeds, what is more, the deeds of today which are connected with restructuring.

As for our meeting today, it is taking place in connection with a very solemn occasion - the presentation of the Order of Lenin to the city of Vladivostok. Vladivostok has been awarded this highest decoration for the success of the working people of the city in economic and cultural building and for the great contribution to the development of the economy of the Far East. I am fulfilling with great satisfaction this mission of the Central Committee of our Party and the Presidium of the USSR Supreme Soviet.

From the bottom of my heart I congratulate all the people of Vladivostok, which now has two Orders. The Order of Lenin on your banner is a well-deserved award. It bears in it the selflessness and strenuous labour of the remarkable people of a marvellous city: sailors, shipbuilders and fishermen; engineers and power workers; builders and transport workers; scientists, doctors and teachers; veterans and young people. This honour is justly shared by the Border Troops and the Troops of the Red Banner Far East Military District and the Red Banner Pacific Fleet. It crowns the glorious feats of many generations, who have done not a little in order to master, defend and transform with their labour the Pacific coast of our country.

Vladivostok today is a modern industrial, cultural and scientific centre, a large port, the soul and heart of the Soviet Maritime Kray, and one of the most remarkable cities of the country. May this award of the homeland become a source of fresh inspiration for all of you. Accept the congratulations of the Central Committee of the Party, the Presidium of the USSR Supreme Soviet and the Soviet government, and their wishes for successes in labour and remarkable new feats in the life of the city, its labour collectives and every family.

Comrades, a little more than a year has passed since the April plenum of the Central Committee, and nearly five months since the ending of the work of the 27th Party Congress. All this time has been filled with active searches for new approaches to the solution of the urgent problems of Soviet society. It has been marked with a principled evaluation of what has been done, both what has been done and what has been left undone. We now have at our disposal an extensive programme of action for the acceleration of the social and economic development of the country for a long time to come: one which takes account of both our own aspirations and the most important trends of world development. We also have the necessary setting out of this programme in detail: the State Plan for the 12th Five Year Plan period, worked out from a profound analysis of the state of affairs and a search for reserves and for ways and means of ensuring the dynamic development of Soviet society.

The time has come to make ourselves responsible for implementing what we intend. Responsible on the widest scale, without making any allowances. The results of the work of the national economy for the first half of this year have already been summed up. They show that positive changes in the economy are gaining force, even if not to the same extent everywhere. We have succeeded in giving greater dynamism to economic processes and in raising the rates of growth of production and labour productivity. Measures for improving the situation in engineering, the fuel and power and agro-industrial complexes, ferrous metallurgy, chemicals and petrochemicals and in several other sectors have begun to have an effect.

Social tasks too have been tackled better. More housing has been handed over for use. The number of facilities for social and cultural purposes being brought into use has increased. In places where the local bodies work dynamically and energetically, the supply of food products, industrial goods and consumer services to the population has improved. Such changes can only be welcomed.

But we shall speak straight, comrades. The pleasing and encouraging improvements have been obtained first and foremost as a result of measures for strengthening labour, state and plan discipline. People have had a more exacting approach to drawing up and fulfilling plans and bringing order into their affairs. They have started to work better. They have edged out drunkenness. And the positive results are already there.

But along with the general favourable indicators of the half-year, in some sectors the rates of growth fell in May and June. A number of ministries failed to cope with their plans. An irregular pace of production and an insufficiently effective use of what we have at our disposal continue to cause considerable difficulties, and quality of output has not shown any marked changes for the better. And you know that this is our common problem.

All this enables one to draw a quite definite conclusion: qualitative changes which would really have consolidated tendencies for accelerated growth have not taken place yet in the country. I think you understand and will agree that they could not have taken place, since the highly important measures of an economic, social, organisational, ideological and other nature have only just started to be implemented and, of course, they cannot produce an immediate effect. Consequently, the increase in the rate of growth of national economy is not - and, perhaps, even cannot yet, as I have already said - be stable.

This means that it is impermissible now to go to one of two extremes. It is naive - and even harmful - to assume that if economic indicators have risen, then the restructuring of our work has been fully embarked on and is progressing at full speed everywhere. This is yet far from being the case. In a whole number of the country's regions and industries they are only talking about restructuring and not setting it in motion. It is equally impermissible to give in to the difficulties of restructuring and the resistance or indifference of those accustomed to living by inertia and working in the old fashion.

It was rightly stressed at the 27th Congress that we are starting on a task which is not simple and that we are posing for ourselves goals which are realistic yet difficult, which can only be achieved if we continually learn from life and constantly assimilate its experience, lessons and new trends. In fact, we are just starting on this work, succeeding in some things and not so well in others. It is becoming more and more clear with time how complicated this task is and how large the volume of matters we are to tackle. But retreat we cannot and will not. There is simply no alternative to the strategy of acceleration. We have already had to speak about this on a number of occasions, and I should like to reiterate it here in Vladivostok once again.

What is meant is not that we should urge or persuade people to actions contrary to the laws of social development or try to bypass somehow or outwit these laws and really existing conditions. In maintaining the course towards restructuring, the party and its Central Committee are proceeding from another premise - from the need to recognise these laws more profoundly and operatively and skilfully take account of them in our activities, and the pressing need to remove all impediments and obstructions, artificially created along these paths.

The tangible, objective results of the first half-year of the Five Year Plan period prove that the Soviet people support the course of acceleration and support it in the most valuable way - by deeds. Here in Vladivostok, just as wherever else I have to be in the course of fulfilling, let us say, my new obligations, I have been asking one and the same question: is everything clear regarding the policy worked out by the party and proposed to the people, or are there any doubts? With great satisfaction I have also heard here, on Far East soil, warm support and approval for the party's policy directed towards the interests of the people, the interests of all Soviet people, every family, the interests of the country's future. It is important to direct this support, this mood of our people for struggle and the surmounting of difficulties with maximum returns and to the utmost effect towards solving the tasks set by the 27th CPSU Congress.

SOVIET FAR EAST DEVELOPMENT

It is from this position, comrades, and I should like to touch upon certain issues to do with the development of the Far East. I should like to consult, even perhaps continue the consultation which I have been having for three days now with you people of the Far East, as to how we can transform this region more swiftly, put its riches at the service of the Soviet people and meet more adequately and fully the demands of the people living here.

The Far East is traditionally called the country's outpost in the Pacific. This is undoubtedly true. But today this view can no longer be regarded as sufficient. The Maritime Kray and the Far East must be turned into a highly developed national economic complex.

I see that you are already mature enough to set about solving these tasks. And I think that possibly you know even better, you who have already lived here for years and even decades, that it is not easy, this work on the large-scale assimilation of the Far East. But since you have greeted the idea so enthusiastically, this means that you are confident that we are up to this task today.

All that has been done in previous years provides a real precondition for this. Major enterprises have been built representing all industries. Mines and electric power stations have been commissioned, as have new railways, ferry crossings and ports. Hundreds of thousands of hectares of land have been improved. The Far East Scientific Centre of the USSR

Academy of Sciences has been set up, with a network of institutes. Qualified modern key workers and specialists have grown up. As a result, over two decades industrial production has almost trebled, and agricultural production has increased by over 50 percent. Today the Far East yields 40 percent of all fish caught in the country. Over the past four Five Year Plan periods 62,000,000 square metres of housing has been built, which is equivalent to the erection of approximately seven cities like Vladivostok. While the growth in labour resources is still not sufficient, nevertheless the population has risen by 40 percent over the past 20 years. Overall, the country's economy has now a broad base on the coast of the Pacific Ocean.

However, in the light of the acceleration policy and from the positions of the 27th CPSU Congress, we must pose a direct and acute question: do the economic and social development, the standard of work of scientific institutions and the scale of their research in the Far East correspond to its growing role and the new tasks set by the party? Is the potential created there being used efficiently enough?

The strategic course towards accelerating socioeconomic development requires the implementation of a new regional policy, too. The party gives a prominent position in this to priority development of the eastern regions. In this connection, we are obliged to look attentively at the prospects for the economy of the Far East, and this must be done rapidly, taking into account the particular significance of the region.

It is important to do this without delay, because the economy of the Far East has started to develop more slowly than the country's national economy as a whole: although it would seem that things ought to be the other way around. As a consequence, the region's share of all-union production is not only failing to increase but even falling. Lagging behind has also increased in the resolution of social problems, particularly in housing construction. I have heard a lot of opinions and requests on this matter addressed to the Party Central Committee and the Soviet government, and these views were just.

It cannot be said that no attention has been paid to the development of the Far East. In recent years the Central Committee and the USSR Council of Ministers have adopted measures which defined the tasks of developing power engineering, non-ferrous and ferrous metallurgy and the coal industry, for the further development of fisheries, forestry, timber-processing, transport and other sectors of the economy, to increase production of rice and soya, for the reconstruction of the countryside and improving the state of affairs in culture.

However, comrades, much of what was mapped out has, unfortunately, been carried out badly. This was a reflection of lack of understanding of the role and significance of the economy of the Far East and, in the final analysis, of political short-sightedness on the part of certain senior officials in the USSR's State Planning Committee for Material and Technical Supply, Ministries of Non-Ferrous Metallurgy, Coal Industry, Power and Electrification, and a number of other ministries. And both republican and local bodies carry a significant and large part of the blame.

The situation has to be improved in a fundamental manner, and a transfer effected from a slowing down of growth rates to their acceleration and from a preponderance of extensive (development) factors to all-out intensification on the basis of scientific and technical progress. It is important to compress the time taken for solving problems and sharply increase the Far East's contribution to the country's economic potential. And this requires above all an accelerated growth in the living standards of people in the Far East, substantial improvement in working conditions, provision of housing, supply of foodstuffs and industrial goods and the development of the whole public service sector. It is obvious that it has fallen behind although it is the sector which affects population settlement and, in the final reckoning, the Far East's pace of development.

It is now a question of elaborating a concept for the long-term development of the Far East within the framework of a unified state regional policy. Specifically, this concept must most likely be embodied in a comprehensive programme. Its aims will be to set up in the Far East a highly efficient national economy complex which will have its own major resource, scientific and production supply base, optimum economic framework and developed public service sector and will be organically included in the system of all-union and international division of labour.

Quite a good deal of work in this respect has been done in the process of preparing the Five Year Plan. It is intensive and its fulfilment will require great efforts. However, it is just the beginning of the task of speeding up the development of the whole region. Without forestalling by any means what must be elaborated in detail by specialists and with the participation of the public at large, I shall just tell you about some of the most important orientations of this work.

First: the Far East's geographical location in itself determines the course for the formation here of a highly developed complex of industries linked with the use of the ocean's resources. For many reasons, the country's fisheries will more and more move to the Far East. The creation here of a powerful fishing fleet has had considerable sums invested in it, but at the same time, the fitting out of shore services is lagging seriously behind. The mechanisation of heavy work is at a low level. As a result of this, a considerable proportion of the expensive ships is lying idle, is not being used efficiently; there is a chronic lack of facilities, repair bases, stores, fishing ports and processing enterprises. In short, serious comprehensive measures are required for the development of the Far Eastern fishing industry. Particular attention must be paid to the production of biologically active substances from marine products. This trend is being actively developed in other countries and has proved its effectiveness.

Secondly, it is a matter of the comprehensive use of the extremely rich natural resources of the region. The attention of the Ministry of Non-Ferrous Metallurgy will have to be drawn to the potential of the Far East. As geologists have established, the region abounds with numerous rich deposits of non-ferrous metals, gold, silver and many other valuable elements and minerals. The mining and processing of them could be considerably expanded if the matter were approached in a business-like manner. We must seriously take up the matter of non-ferrous metallurgy on a large scale in the Far East; we must create here complete production cycles, to produce a variety of end-products. I think that you should not accept the present situation, and I think this should be well understood at the centre, I have in mind both all-union and republican bodies. The Far East must not be looked upon just as a raw material base. The tremendous raw material potential must be used here for building enterprises with complete cycles, to produce here as a minimum semi-finished products, but better still, end-products.

What I have said about non-ferrous metallurgy applies still more to the Ministry of the Timber and Paper Industry, which must decisively begin the intensive processing of timber. In this connection, there are also tasks of the broad-scale economic assimilation of the Baykal-Amur railway zone. A special resolution of the Central Committee and government on this matter is now in preparation. And there you are faced with large scale affairs.

Thirdly, the chronic lagging of the fuel and power complex of the Far East, which is holding up the development of other branches, must be overcome in the shortest possible time. One cannot live without looking into the future, feeling that after all there will be help from the centre with fuel and power. The resources of fuel, hydrocarbon raw material, are colossal here. But talk has been going on for more than a decade, for example, about the use of north Sakhalin gas, but practical work is only just now beginning.

The solution of problems of the exploitation of oil and gas deposits of the Sakhalin shelf has also been dragged out. Meanwhile, hundreds of trainloads of oil are going from Western Siberia to the Far East. We are now obliged to transport millions of tonnes of oil for the life of the Far East from other areas of the country. The fulfilment of the measures sketched out at one time for developing the fuel and power base in the regions East of Baykal and in the Far East is lagging very greatly behind the schedules set.

The Far East can and must satisfy completely its power needs from its own resources. The Far Easterners must work hard on the creation of a reliable base for power construction and speed up the construction of a complex of thermal and hydroelectric stations and the formation of a unified, powerful system of electric power supply. It is necessary to start from the belief that in the future the Far East must not only supply fuel and power to the nearby areas of the country, but also become a sound exporter of them.

Fourthly, the line for the speedy development of the production infrastructure. This of course is not only a Far East problem, but here it is perhaps particularly urgent. Here it is essential to speed up the development of a modern construction industry. I would say that that is the foundation of the plans we have made here, in this region, in the Far East. Now powerful detachments of railway builders have come to you. In a short period they laid the Baykal-Amur railway. They can and must be used, for example, in the reconstruction of old railway lines which today have a low throughput capacity, or they can be switched over to building roads and ports, and other essential facilities.

Marine transport too should be used more efficiently. Its infrastructure should be reinforced and progressive forms of transportation should be developed. In this respect you have experience. Just today I acquainted myself with the activity of Nakhodka's Vostochnyy port - a wonderful modern port which could serve as an example to many. The ferry link to Sakhalin, for example, operates well. Measures must also be rapidly taken in increasing the economic benefit from through navigation along the northern sea route.

Fifth: the solutions to issues of regional scientific and technical policy, including the equipping of enterprises with the very latest technology, taking into account operating conditions in this area, have a largely specific character. It would seem that there are many machine-building enterprises here, many of which have good craftsmen and a good reputation. However, due to a lack of coordination between departments, a considerable part of the Far East's machine-building output goes to the country's European regions, while a counter-flow of equipment comes from there to meet requirements here. These issues must be rapidly examined, the specialisations of machine-building works must be defined more precisely and stress should be placed on the creation here of powerful and technically well-equipped facilities, both for the requirements of the area itself and for export.

Sixth: the opportunities for the export-oriented development of the Far Eastern economy must be fully used. At the present time the region's share in the country's exports is extremely low and very far from its potential capabilities. Here too cardinal changes and new approaches are needed in order to animate trade in both the coastal and border areas, to master progressive forms of economic links with foreign countries, including cooperation in production and joint enterprises, and to create a specialised export base.

Seventhly, at the Party Congress, the residual principle of resource allocation for the development of the social sphere was severely criticised. This is an inveterate disease. Such a practice has also become widespread in a number of the country's eastern areas, including Maritime Kray. About 7,700,000 people inhabit the vast territory of the region. Nearly half of all food products is brought here. In the last 20 years, the production of milk, potato and vegetables per capita in the Far East has dropped. Many heads of krays, oblasts, okrugs, rayons and farms have got used to low harvests, poor milk yields, poor weight gains by cattle, and massive deliveries of fodder from other areas. Even the proposals for the plans for 15 to 20 years ahead envisage the expansion of food supplies to the Far East through supplies from other regions of the country.

I think that this line is a short-sighted one. There is only one way out: to create your own, highly-developed agricultural base and food industry. For this purpose, it is necessary to develop actively, on the basis of intensive technologies, all the branches of the agro-industrial complex, in particular, the fertiliser industry, and to cooperate with neighbouring countries in solving agricultural tasks.

A tense situation has arisen in the region in housing construction and amenity construction, and this is a hindrance to the settlement of those who arrive here for permanent residence, as I have already said. I think that the responsibility for such a situation must be shared by the corresponding economic ministries and departments, both all-union and republican, along with local bodies.

I have reprimanded, comrades, leaders and the kray and of the city, saying that what they are doing today for the development of the social sphere is not enough. In any case, it does not correspond to the need that actually exists here. But I think that while pronouncing these reprimands a considerable part has to be directed at the central departments. Many of them are very lavish when it comes to developing various kinds of production, while being very mean in allocating funds for developing the social spheres. As a result, production capacities are being created but there is nobody to use properly the production potential that has been created. So this is one of those tricks that costs the state dear. That is the political assessment.

You have such a wonderful region, beautiful sea, unique nature, rich in mineral resources. Indeed, I have been immensely impressed by what I have managed to see - here, from the aircraft while we were in the air, and in Nakhoda, when the fog and the clouds all lifted finally, and the bright sun lit up all these hills and valleys, the golden valley, the ocean, everything all around - that made a colossal impression on me. It really is a fine kray.

The Far East must become one of the leading all-union health resorts, a major centre for domestic and international tourism, including oceanic and high altitude tourism. This, incidentally, would also add resources for speeding up the organisation of public amenities for the towns and villages.

Yesterday, I met on the bypass, when we were going to a pioneer camp, a group of holiday-makers. It seemed as if the whole country were there, and there were many who were there again having been many times before, because they had fallen in love with this kray and its nature. And all of them insistently advised that everything be done here to promote widely a leisure centre for the working people.

The cause of the current situation is clear: the unsatisfactory nature of the construction of housing and social and cultural amenities can be explained by the absence of advance work, the lagging behind of the building base and the weakness of building collectives. We can no longer tolerate this. While a turn towards social issues is vitally important for the whole country, for the Far East it is doubly, trebly, important.

How are the difficulties that have accumulated over years to be overcome? As I have already said here, the fault lies with both the centre and in local bodies. Action is to be taken both from the bottom and from the top simultaneously in order to remedy the situation. I can assure you that the CPSU Central Committee and the government will urge decisively the all-union and republican ministries and departments to face the problems of the eastern regions of the country, including your kray.

The Soviet Far East has an unforgettable past, and, I am sure, a glorious future. It is a land of colossal natural riches, huge social and economic potential, and a great international prospect. It depends on you, and of course on the attention of the centre, how we conduct the business, conduct the economy and what results we achieve in this very important region of the country.

I realise that my remarks, and this sharp way, perhaps, of putting the problems, have not sounded very much in keeping with a celebration. But this is the businesslike Leninist tradition: to evaluate what has been done, and to turn one's eyes to the future. This is the most important thing: not to lose sight of the future, to lay now a basis for achieving new positions. The main thing now is to concentrate on the long-term tasks arising for the region from the resolutions of the 27th Party Congress. And I think that even such a solemn pretext as the receipt of a high award is suitable for a critical examination of this matter.

FOREIGN AFFAIRS

These are our common plans and concerns, comrades. They, better than any verbal contrivances, speak of the real intentions of the Soviet Union. And however much the ruling forces of imperialism may try to distort them, we openly and honestly have spoken, and will go on speaking to all peoples and governments: yes, we need peace. Again and again we appeal to them to put a stop to the arms race, to end the nuclear madness, and eliminate nuclear arms, and to search persistently for political solutions to regional conflicts.

A phenomenon of enormous significance is taking place before our eyes. The notion that peace is needed by all is powerfully penetrating the consciousness of peoples even in places where the governments continue to regard weapons and war as a means of policy. It is needed by all precisely since a nuclear war would not be a clash merely between two blocs, between two confronting forces. It will lead to a global catastrophe threatening the destruction of human civilisation.

Our initiatives for nuclear disarmament and a significant cut in conventional armaments and armed forces, for monitoring and improvement of the international situation have been met in different ways. The friendly countries have come out in support of them. The countries of the socialist community quite rightly regard them as an integral part of the common line of socialism in the international arena. And not only because they, these initiatives, were agreed with them, not only out of principled internationalist considerations, but also because both of us, we and they, are preoccupied with one and the very same exclusively peaceful effort - perfection of our societies.

On this basis impetus is being given to the beneficial process of drawing together, economic integration is being filled with new content, specific steps are being taken to create joint enterprises and associations, and living contacts among people are being broadened. In a word, a progressive, mutually advantageous process is taking place which deepens the cooperation and brotherhood between the peoples of the community.

The developing world regards our plans and intentions, both internal and international, with great interest. We note that many countries of that world are willing to continue broadening and deepening economic, scientific and cultural cooperation with the Soviet Union. We are ready for this.

It would be right to say that our plans are regarded seriously and with interest by broad public circles, politicians and representatives of the business world in the West who view things realistically, who are free of the paranoia of anti-communism and who are not bound up with profits from the arms race. They also favour peace and cooperation, the development of healthy economic, scientific and cultural relations with the Soviet Union. We welcome this approach.

But in many capitalist countries, the tone continues to be set by forces, the past and future of which are blinded by hostility towards socialism, imperial ambitions, or which are bound hand and foot to military business interests. And these, as is known, are very greedy and merciless. Yesterday they needed millions, today thousands of millions, tomorrow trillions. Of their own will, they will never start making children's toys instead of missiles. Such is their nature.

The ruling circles of the USA and some of the countries allied to it try to represent our peace initiatives as pure propaganda, or allege that they benefit only the Soviet Union. Yes, disarmament is beneficial to us, if you want to use that term, as it is beneficial for all peoples whose governments spend thousands of millions on the arms race.

But this is only part of the truth, I would even say the lesser part of it. The main truth is that our initiatives are based on profound concern for the fate of mankind. It is absurd and criminal, in the face of the nuclear threat, to act on the old, already dead, concept that what is good for the socialist countries must be rejected. This particularly clearly shows class narrowness, primitive ideological automatism and the growing political influence of militarism. But all the same, I am not inclined to think that the military-industrial complex is omnipotent. We see that the world public is ever more clearly recognising the danger of militarism. We see that in the USA too, in spite of the constant chauvinist injections, realistic attitudes are on the increase. The understanding of the fact that the military threat to the USA comes not from Soviet people, not the socialist countries, not the peasants of Nicaragua, not far-off Vietnamese or Libyans, but from its own arms-makers and the irresponsible politicians and adventuristic military who serve them, is becoming more profound.

We understand, of course, that the ruling circles of imperialism are seriously worried by the international influence of our plans, calculated for accelerated socioeconomic and scientific development. We also know that the arms race that is picking up speed serves not only super-profits and the preparation of war but also, and not least by a long way, other immoral goals, the essence of which is to wear the Soviet Union out economically, to thwart the course of the party for a further improvement of the people's living standards and to slow down the implementation of the social programme. We know who exactly is continuing to cherish hopes of bringing about a planned and methodical destruction of the USSR and of the socialist countries, using for this purpose economic, moral-psychological, propaganda, political and military means.

But we can say that this task was always doomed to failure, and it remains hopeless today too. The time has come to take realities into account and not to shape policies on the basis of illusions and errors. If there are no accords, the world will not feel better, and it will not be at ease. Fear will not go away until certain rulers in the West give up efforts - which may be consoling for them, perhaps, but are fruitless and, the main thing, dangerous - to bring the Soviet Union to its knees, to split the socialist community and to delay our progress.

The time demands insistently a new understanding of the present stage in the development of civilisation, of international relations, of the world; of a world which is contradictory and complex, but is objectively united by ties of interdependence; of international relations in which, even taking into account all differences and clashes of interests, one cannot live any longer according to the millennia-old traditions of the "law of the fist"; of a civilisation demonstrating the unprecedented power of human intellect and labour and, at the same time, its fragility and vulnerability to the forces that have been released by human genius but put at the service of destruction.

All this dictates the necessity of an urgent radical break with many conventional approaches to foreign policy, a break with the traditions of political thinking, with views on the problems of war and peace, on defence, on the security of specific states and on international security. One may understand, in this connection, our radical, in the full sense of the word, global proposals, such as the programme for elimination of nuclear and other weapons of mass destruction in this century, for a complete ban on testing nuclear arms, for banning chemical weapons, for cooperation in the peaceful use of space and a whole number of other proposals which concern the whole world and all countries.

ASIAN-PACIFIC SECURITY

The main problem that has been confronting mankind today is the problem of survival; it is equally acute and urgent for Europe, Africa, America and Asia. It takes a different shape, however, for each part of the world. And so since I am here in Vladivostok, it is natural to look at world political issues from the Asian-Pacific angle. Such an approach is justified on many counts. Above all because a large part of our country's territory lies east of the Urals, in Asia, Siberia and the Far East. It is here that many all-union tasks put forward by the Congress will be solved. Consequently the situation in the Far East as a whole, in Asia and the adjacent oceanic expanses, where we have for a long time been permanent residents and sailors, is for us a national, state interest.

Many major states are situated on this huge expanse, almost half the earth, including the USSR, the USA, India, China, Japan, Vietnam, Mexico and Indonesia. There are states here considered to be medium-sized, but according to European measures, fairly large - Canada, the Philippines, Australia and New Zealand, and together with them dozens of comparatively smaller and quite tiny countries. Some of them have a history of millenia or many centuries. Others were formed in modern times, and many came into being very recently.

Asia, which woke up to a new life in the 20th century, has enriched world progress with its diversified and unique experience of the fight for freedom and independence. This is not only history. This is a living legacy making one of the important fundamentals of the current political realities in this part of the world.

Every country has its own social and political system with all the thinkable tinges, its traditions, achievements and difficulties, its mode of life and its beliefs, convictions and prejudices, its own understanding of spiritual and material values. Each of them has something to be proud of and something to uphold in the treasure house of human civilisation.

This impressive diversity, this colossal human and socio-political massif calls for apt attention, study and respect. We know well from our own Soviet experience what an immense creative force the revived sense of national dignity becomes, what a constructive role is played by the national identity of a people in its organic inter-relationship with other equal and free peoples. This process is on the rise in Asia and the Pacific now: everything is in motion here, far from everything has settled. The new is mixing with the old, the way of life which seemed unshakeable only yesterday is giving way to the whirlwind of changes - social, scientific and technical, and ideological. This is, I would say, yet another period of renaissance in world history, the period harbouring a huge potential of progress. And this is true not only with regard to Asia and Oceania.

Which way will socioeconomic and political development take? What processes will prevail in inter-state relations? These issues will largely determine the destinies of the entire world.

Socialism is an integral factor in the grandiose and complex changes in this region. As a result of the Great October Socialist Revolution and the victory over fascism and Japanese militarism, as a result of the great Chinese revolution, after a new social order was established in Mongolia and in the land of Korea, whose people displayed unusual steadfastness in the struggle for a socialist future for their motherland, and then in Vietnam and Laos, socialism won a firm position in Asia.

But it was here that it had to face the most brutal and cynical opposition. The most vivid example of this is the example of Vietnam. Its heroic experience, and the lessons of its victory over imperialism, have yet again highlighted the unconquerable strength of the ideas of freedom and socialism.

It was here, here in Asia, that the concept of nonalignment was born, a movement which now includes in its orbit over 100 states. It strives to give its answer to the challenge of the time, actively supports ending the division of the world into military blocs, and searches for its own ways of reducing the nuclear threat. Rejecting exploitation, the politics of conquest and neo-colonialism, and condemning them, the nonaligned movement turns to humanity with an appeal for unity and cooperation in the struggle against the hunger and scandalous poverty of hundreds of millions of people.

The acknowledged leader of that movement is great India, with its moral authority and traditional wisdom, with its own particular political experience and huge economic potential. We assess highly the contribution it has already made to the cause of asserting the standards of equitable coexistence and justice in the international community. The friendly relations between the USSR and India have become a stabilising factor on an international scale.

Japan has turned into a power of front-rank significance. The country which was the first victim of American nuclear weapons has covered a huge distance in a short time, and displayed striking accomplishments in industry and trade, education, science and technology. These successes are due not only to the meticulousness, self-discipline and energy of the Japanese people, but to the three non-nuclear principles on which its international policy is officially based, although recently - and one cannot fail to draw attention to this - they, like the peaceful tenets of the Japanese constitution, are being circumvented more and more obviously.

But we see in Asia-Pacific much else too: peoples' dignity outraged by colonialism; the consequences of poverty, illiteracy and backwardness. At the same time profound prejudices preserve conditions for mistrust and enmity between peoples, including those living within one state. Imperialism gambles on these difficulties and survivals of the past. As a result, local conflicts and ethnic and religious strife flare up and there is political instability.

Everywhere where independence becomes a tangible international quantity, and where a threat arises to the exploitative interests of imperialism, it resorts to its favourite methods: economic blackmail, intrigues and plots against the leadership of the country concerned. It interferes in internal problems, supports separatists, and finances or actually arms counter-revolution and terrorists. The Punjab and the Tamil problem which they also want to turn against India; the undeclared wars against Kampuchea and Afghanistan; the annexation of Micronesia; interference in the Philippines; and pressure on New Zealand - these examples alone are sufficient to show how the contemporary mechanism of imperialist intervention and dictate works.

The experience of history and the laws of growing interdependence, the demands for integration of the economy incline us to seek ways towards accord and towards setting up open links between states within the region and outside it. These states have tens, hundreds of problems crying out to be resolved, both those inherited from the colonial past and those arising from the contradictions of current development. But they are being dragged into blocs, which limit their freedom to dispose of their own resources, compel them to inflate their military budgets, drag them into the arms race and the militarisation of the economy and all public life. All this deforms the processes of internal development, creates tension and of course hinders the normalisation of relations between nations and states.

The Soviet Union is also an Asian-Pacific country. This vast region's complex problems are familiar to it; it is directly touched by them. It is this which determines the balanced and large-scale view it takes of a gigantic part of the world which contains a mass of such varied states and peoples. Our approach to this part of the world is based on recognition and understanding of the realities existing here. At the same time our interest is not a claim to any kind of privilege and special position; no egoistic attempt to strengthen our security at someone else's expense; no seeking advantage to the detriment of others. We see our interest in pooling efforts, in cooperation which accords full respect to the rights of each people to live as it chooses and to resolve its own problems independently in conditions of peace. We are for building jointly new and just relations in Asia-Pacific.

I have recently had quite a few meetings with leaders of European states and various political figures from European countries. One cannot help comparing the situation in Asia with that in Europe. The Pacific region as a whole is not yet militarised to the same extent as the European region. Yet the potential for its militarisation is truly enormous and the consequences extremely dangerous. To be convinced of this one only has to glance at the map. Some of the major nuclear powers are located here and powerful land armies and mighty navies and air forces have been created. The scientific, technological and industrial potential of many countries on the western and eastern sides of the ocean makes it possible to boost any arms race. The situation is aggravated by the continuation of conflicts. Let us not forget that it was in Asia that American imperialism waged the two biggest wars since 1945, in Korea and Indochina. For four decades there has been no period lasting several consecutive years when the flame of military confrontation has not blazed, now in one spot in the Pacific area, now in another.

For better or for worse the Helsinki process of dialogue, talks and agreements is in operation in Europe. This introduces some sort of stability and reduces the probability of armed conflict. This does not exist or virtually does not exist in the region which we are discussing. If there has been some change of late, then it is not for the better. Since the second half of the 1970s the USA has undertaken large-scale measures to increase military forces in the Pacific Ocean. It is under its pressure that the militarised Washington-Tokyo-Seoul triangle is taking shape. And although two of the three states in the region which possess nuclear weapons - the PRC and USSR - have pledged no first use the USA has sited delivery vehicles for nuclear weapons and nuclear warheads in one of the crisis zones - on the Korean peninsula - and also delivery vehicles for nuclear weapons on Japanese territory. It has to be noted that militarisation and the growth of the military threat in this part of the world are beginning to gather dangerous speed. The Pacific Ocean is turning into an arena of military and political confrontation. That is what gives rise to growing concern for the peoples who live here. It also alarms us, from all points of view, including that of the security of the Asiatic part of our country.

The Asian-Pacific strand of the Soviet Union's foreign policy is a component part of the overall platform of the CPSU's international activity, worked out by the April plenum and the 27th Congress of the party. However, the platform is not a plan which can be applied to any situation, but rather principles and a method based on experience.

Using this as a starting point, how could one conceive of a process of forming international security and peaceful influence in this vast region?

First and foremost, the Soviet Union, in accordance with the principled line of the Congress, will aspire to give more dynamism to its bilateral relations with all countries situated here without exception. We will comprehensively strengthen friendship and we are stepping up our diverse ties with the Mongolian People's Republic, the Democratic People's Republic of Korea, the Socialist Republic of Vietnam, the Lao People's Democratic Republic, and the People's Republic of Kampuchea. We see our relations with our friends, relations built on the principles of equal rights and solidarity, as a component part of overall security in Asia-Pacific.

At present, for example, the question of withdrawing a considerable number of Soviet troops from Mongolia is being examined with the leadership of the MPR. We are ready to expand our ties with Indonesia, Australia, New Zealand, the Philippines, Thailand, Malaysia, Singapore, Burma, Sri Lanka, Nepal, Brunei, the Maldives Republic, all young and independent participants in the political life of the region. With some of them - Papua New Guinea, Western Samoa, the Kingdom of Tonga, Fiji, the Republic of Kiribati, the Republic of Nauru, Tuvalu and the Republic of Vanuatu - we already have diplomatic relations.

Speaking in a city from which, as they say, one could reach out a hand and touch the People's Republic of China, I should like to dwell on the most important issues in our relations with it. These relations are of particular importance for several reasons, starting with the fact that we are neighbours, that we have the world's longest land frontier and that for this very reason we are predestined, as are our children and grandchildren, to live side by side from this day forward and for all time. But of course that is not the only point. History has entrusted the Soviet and Chinese peoples with an exceptionally important mission. A great deal in international development depends on the two largest socialist states.

In recent years there has been a noticeable improvement in our relations and I want to confirm that the Soviet Union is ready at any time and at any level to discuss with China in the most serious way matters concerning supplementary measures to create an atmosphere of good-neighbourliness. We hope that in the near future the frontier which divides us, I should like to say which unites us, will become a zone of peace and friendship.

Soviet people regard with understanding and respect the aim put forward by the CCP of modernising the country and building in the long term a socialist society worthy of a great people. As far as one can judge, our priorities and those of China are similar: the acceleration of socioeconomic development. Why not support one another and cooperate in realising our plans, where this is evidently to the benefit of both? The better our relations are, the more we can exchange experience with one another.

We take pleasure in noting that a positive change has taken place in economic links. We are convinced that the mutually complementary nature of the Soviet and Chinese economies which has been historically established offers great opportunities for expanding these ties, including in the border regions. A number of major problems in cooperation are knocking at the door. We do not, for example, want the Amur frontier to be regarded as a water barrier. May the basin of this mighty river be a means of uniting the efforts of the Chinese and Soviet people in using the very rich resources and for water management projects there, for the common benefit. An inter-governmental agreement on this matter is already being jointly drawn up. The official border could pass along the main channel. The Soviet government is preparing a positive response on the matter of cooperation in building a railway to link the Xinjiang Uygur Autonomous Region and Kazakhstan. We have proposed cooperation with the PRC in space, which could include the training of Chinese cosmonauts. There are big opportunities for mutually beneficial exchange in the sphere of culture and education. We are ready for and sincerely desire all this.

As concerns relations with Japan, signs of a change for the better are taking shape here, too. It would be a good thing if this change were to take place. The objective position of our two countries in the world is such that deeply intensified cooperation on a healthy and realistic basis is required, in an atmosphere of calm unburdened by the problems of the past. A start has been made this year. There was an exchange of visits by foreign ministers, an exchange of visits at summit level is on the agenda.

Economic cooperation is of mutual interest. This relates first and foremost to our coastal regions, where business contacts with Japanese firms have already been established. Establishing joint enterprises in neighbouring and geographically close regions of the USSR and Japan could also be discussed. Why not also establish long-term cooperation in research into and comprehensive exploitation of ocean resources, and combine programmes for the peaceful study and use of space? The Japanese apparently have a method of making relations dynamic, which is called economic diplomacy. Let this serve the cause of Soviet-Japanese cooperation.

In the Pacific region, the Soviet Union also borders on the USA. A close neighbour, in the literal sense of the word: the distance is only seven kilometres, just the distance between the Soviet Big Diomede and the American Little Diomede islands. The USA, we clearly take this into account, is a great Pacific power because, first of all, a significant part of the country's population lives on the shores of that ocean. The western part of America is playing a growing role in the country's life and is distinguished by its dynamism.

And also because the USA undoubtedly has important economic and political interests in the region, there is no doubt that without the USA, without its participation, one cannot solve the problem of security and cooperation in the Pacific zone in a manner satisfactory to all the states in the region. For the time being, unfortunately, Washington is not manifesting any readiness for this; it is not even contemplating a serious conversation on the subject of the Pacific. If this theme is touched upon, then it is led out onto the well-trodden path of the Soviet threat and sabre-rattling to strengthen this myth.

Our approach to relations with the USA is known. We are for peaceful, good-neighbourly relations on an equal footing, for mutually advantageous cooperation for which, incidentally, there are quite a few opportunities both in the Far East and the Pacific.

As I'm talking about the USA, two words about the most important thing today in our relations: ending the arms race. After the Geneva meeting the Soviet Union put forward many major proposals on all the problems of reducing and eliminating arms and on verifying this process. We have not seen any movement from the other direction: we, in essence, have been regaled with the same fare as before Geneva.

In order to overcome this marking time, we have done even more to meet the other side. In my letter in June to the US President we put forward new, major, compromise proposals. During my visit here, in the Far East, I have received a reply from President [Ronald] Reagan. It calls for thought; we have begun studying it. We shall deal with this with responsibility and attention. For us, what is important first and foremost is the extent to which the proposals contained in the letter correspond to the principle of equal security; do they allow us to arrive at effective joint solutions in the field of ending the arms race and preventing its extension to space? It is in accordance with this that we shall determine our future steps.

As far as a new Soviet-American summit meeting is concerned, I can repeat that we are for such a meeting but are resolutely opposed to the accord reached at the last meeting in Geneva being interpreted as allegedly boiling down to a promise to meet in the future as well. No. The main thing that we agreed on then, and what we signed, was an agreement that we should strive for the normalisation of relations between the USSR and USA and an improvement in the international situation, and that we should speed up the course of the talks on arms reduction. This is what the new meeting should serve as well.

We often hear from abroad various kinds of conjectures about violations by the Soviet Union of its armed might in the east of the country - about a build-up by the Soviet Union of its armed might in the east of the country. I state with all responsibility that we are neither doing nor shall do anything in excess of what meets the minimal requirements for our defence and the protection of our friends and allies, especially taking into account the American military activity not far from our and their borders.

This holds true in the fullest measure as regards medium-range missiles as well. Those who do not want an easing of tension in the world continue to claim that we can allegedly redeploy our SS-20 missiles from west to east and from east to west. Therefore I recall once again that we propose the *liquidation* in Europe both of American and Soviet medium-range missiles - their liquidation and not their redeployment anywhere else. Clearly that could not fail to serve the interests of the countries of Asia as well.

I should also like to say that the Soviet Union is a convinced advocate of disbanding military groups, renouncing foreign bases in Asia-Pacific and withdrawing troops from others' territory. The USSR is a member of the Warsaw Treaty, but that is a European defensive alliance and it acts strictly within its contractual geographical framework. In our turn we resolutely oppose the USA's attempts to extend NATO's competence over the entire world, including Asia-Pacific.

Our thoughts on security in the Asian-Pacific region are not made up out of thin air. They take into account experience - past and present. The principles of *Panchsheel* and Bandung have not sunk into oblivion and the positive examples of the truce in Korea, the 1954 Geneva conference on Indochina and the [1966] Indo-Pakistan agreement in Tashkent, live on in diplomatic experience. At the present time too we can see the efforts of a number of states to tackle in a practical way common economic problems and attempts to settle conflicts somehow.

There is much of positive value in the activity of ASEAN and in bilateral contacts. After the idea of a Pacific Ocean community was rejected, the idea of Pacific Ocean economic cooperation is under discussion. We have approached it with an unprejudiced attitude and we are willing to join in deliberations about the possible foundations for such cooperation if, of course, it is conceived not according to a bloc, anti-socialist plan imposed by someone, but as a result of free dicussion without any kind of discrimination whatsoever. The already fairly extensive arsenal of scientific and political projects on the issue of creating a new world economic order and on the experience of integration in West and East could be a good basis for such discussion.

We would propose a Pacific conference along the lines of the Helsinki conference, with the participation of all countries gravitating towards the Ocean, as an objective, if rather remote one. When and, of course, if, there is success in agreeing to its convocation, it will be possible to agree on where it should be held as well. One possibility is Hiroshima. Why should not that town - the first victim of nuclear evil - become a distinctive Helsinki for Asia-Pacific?

Security Proposals

Summing up, I want to stress again that we are in favour of including the Asian-Pacific area in the general process of creating an all-embracing system of international security, which was spoken of at the 27th CPSU Congress.

How do we envisage this in concrete terms?

First of all, questions inevitably arise of a *regional settlement*. I will speak of Afghanistan separately. Now I am going to deal with Southeast Asia and Kampuchea. The Khmer people have made terrible sacrifices. This country, its town and villages were more than once subjected to American bombing. Through its suffering it won its right to choose its friends and allies, and it is unacceptable to try to draw it back into the tragic past and decide the future of this state in distant capitals, or even in the UN.

Much here, as in other problems of Southeast Asia, depends on the normalisation of Sino-Vietnamese relations. This is the sovereign affair of the governments and leaderships of the two countries. We can only express our interest in seeing the border between these socialist states becoming again a border of peace and good neighbourliness, and a comradely dialogue renewed, with unnecessary suspicions and distrust being removed. The moment for this now seems propitious, and the whole of Asia needs it.

In our opinion there are no insurmountable obstacles to the establishment of mutually acceptable relations between the countries of Indochina and ASEAN. Given goodwill and conditions of non-interference from outside, they could settle their problems for the good of general Asian security at the same time.

There is the possibility of not only getting rid of the dangerous tension on the Korean peninsula but of beginning a movement along the path of solving the national problem of the whole Korean people. If one starts from truly Korean interests, there are no rational grounds for rejecting the serious dialogue being proposed by the DPRK.

Secondly, we are in favour of putting a barrier on the path of the proliferation and build-up of *nuclear weapons* in Asia-Pacific. It is well known that the USSR has bound itself not to increase its medium-range nuclear missiles in the Asian part of the country. The USSR supports the declaration of the southern part of the Pacific Ocean as a nuclear free zone, and calls on all the nuclear powers, either unilaterally or multilaterally, to guarantee its status. Implementation of the DPRK proposal for the creation of a nuclear-free zone on the Korean peninsula would be a serious contribution. The idea of creating such a zone in Southeast Asia has attracted the attention it deserves.

Thirdly, we propose starting talks on reducing the activity of *naval fleets,* first and foremost of ships equipped with nuclear weapons, in the Pacific Ocean. A limitation on competition in the sphere of anti-submarine weapons would help to strengthen stability, in particular an accord to refrain from anti-submarine activity in certain zones of the Pacific Ocean. That would be a significant confidence-building measure. And in general I should like to say that if the USA were to renounce a military presence, say in the Philippines, we should not be found wanting in a response. We are, as previously, also decisively in favour of renewing the talks on turning the Indian Ocean into a zone of peace.

Fourthly, the Soviet Union ascribes great importance to the radical *reduction of armed forces and conventional weapons* in Asia down to the limit of reasonable sufficiency. We are aware that it is necessary to resolve this issue in parts, gradually, starting with one particular region, say the Far East. In this context, the USSR is prepared to discuss with the PRC specific steps aimed at a balanced reduction in the level of land forces.

Fifthly, the Soviet Union considers that the time has long since been ripe to put onto a practical footing the discussion of *confidence-building measures* and the non-use of force in the region. It is possible to start with simpler measures, for example, with measures for the security of maritime communications in the Pacific and also for preventing international terrorism. It would be possible to hold a conference to discuss and work out such steps in one of the Soviet coastal cities. By the way, in time it would also be possible to resolve the question of opening up Vladivostok to visits by foreigners. If it really proves possible to change the situation in the Pacific for the better, Vladivostok could become a major international centre, a seat of trade and culture, a city of festivals, sporting meetings, congresses and scientific symposiums. We should like to see it as our wide-open window to the East. And then may it be, to use the phrase of our great Pushkin, that all flags will come to us as guests.

In conclusion, a word about Afghanistan. It was stated from the rostrum of the 27th Congress that we are prepared to send home the Soviet troops who are in this country at the request of its government. As you know, the party now firmly keeps to the principle that action should lie behind words.

Having thoroughly evaluated the situation which has arisen and in consultation with the government of the DRA [Democratic Republic of Afghanistan], the Soviet leadership has taken a decision which I will officially announce today. By the end of 1986, six regiments - one tank regiment, two motorised rifle regiments and three anti-aircraft regiments - along with their established equipment and weapons will be returned from Afghanistan to the homeland. These units will return to the regions of their permanent deployment in the Soviet Union, and in such a way that all those for whom this may be of interest may be easily convinced of this.

In taking such a serious step - about which we have informed beforehand states which have an interest, including Pakistan - the Soviet Union is striving to hasten a political settlement, and to provide yet further stimulus towards it. The USSR also takes as a starting point the fact that those who are organising and implementing armed intervention against the DRA will understand correctly this unilateral step which we have taken and evaluate it in the proper manner. The response to it must be the curtailment of outside interference in the affairs of Democratic Afghanistan.

Some progress has been achieved recently at the Afghan-Pakistan talks which are being conducted through representatives of the UN Secretary-General. As soon as a political settlement is finally worked out, the return of all Soviet troops from Afghanistan can be speeded up accordingly. The timing and stages of their return have been agreed with the Afghan leadership. However, all those who encourage and finance the undeclared war against Afghanistan and from whose territory it is waged should know that if intervention against Democratic Afghanistan continues the Soviet Union will not leave its neighbour in the lurch. Our internationalist solidarity with the Afghan people as well as the security interests of the Soviet Union rule that out absolutely.

We support the line of the current Afghan leadership towards national reconciliation, expanding the social base of the April [1978] national democratic revolution right up to the point of creating a government with the participation of political forces which have been outside the country but are ready to participate sincerely in the nationwide process of constructing a new Afghanistan.

Comrades, the present generation has inherited many difficult and agonising problems. In order to move forward towards solving them we must get rid of the burden of the past and seek new approaches, guided by responsibility to the present and the future. The Soviet state calls upon all Asian-Pacific countries to cooperate for the sake of peace and security. Anyone who aspires to these goals, who hopes for a better future for his people, will find in us benevolent interlocutors and honest partners.

Mankind is living through a difficult, dramatic time but it has a reserve of toughness which enables it not simply to survive but to learn to live in a new civilised world, in other words, to live knowing no threat of war, to live in conditions of freedom when the highest criterion of all will be the good of man and development of the potential of the human personality. But that requires persistent struggle against the common enemy. Today, as never before, it is important to mobilise the potential of common sense, partnership and reason existing in the world, in order to halt the slide towards disaster. Our resolution to do everything incumbent on us to this end is immutable: all can be sure of this, the peoples of all countries and states.

Such, in brief, is the state of our affairs to date; such, in general outline, is the international situation in whose development the role of the Asian-Pacific part of the world will be growing more and more. From all this we must draw practical conclusions, in order to act with still more energy in restructuring our life for the better.

In history there are no direct analogies, but there do occur similar situations, and that is why, for us, the fruitful experience of the past is so valuable and instructive. In his article on the fourth anniversary of the October Revolution, Vladimir Ilyich Lenin wrote:

> We have now begun the necessary restructuring of our economic policy. We already have in this field some small and partial, it is true, but nevertheless we do have some undoubted successes.
>
> We are already finishing the preparatory class in this field of a new science. Firmly and persistently learning, checking our every step against practical experience, not fearing to repeatedly rework what we have started, to correct our mistakes, carefully examining their significance, we shall pass on to the higher classes and we shall get through the whole course.

That comrades, is Lenin's advice, Lenin's analysis, with its inherent profundity, sobriety and self-criticism. This is the advice how we should act in the present situation, how to carry out the restructuring, in order to get through the entire course successfully and bring the country out on to qualitatively new frontiers. It is our duty to make use in full measure of this wise advice of Lenin's.

I wish you great successes and achievements in the implementation of our common plans, happiness, health, all the best in life. Taking this opportunity, I should like to thank all those in the Far East once again for their expressions of trust and support, advice and wishes, for the warmness of their hearts. Thank you, comrades.

Contributors

DAVID CHARLES has been Australian Labor Party Member of Parliament since 1980, and is Chairman of the Subcommittee on the South Pacific of the Parliamentary Joint Committee on Foreign Affairs and Defence.

GRAEME GILL, Senior Lecturer in the Department of Government at the University of Sydney, has held previous teaching positions in Politics at Monash University and at the University of Tasmania. His main field of interest is Soviet domestic politics and Soviet development, and he is currently working on a full-length study of the origins and development of Stalinism. He is the author of *Peasants and Government in the Russian Revolutioon* (1979), and *The Soviet Union Under Gorbachev* (Legislative Research Service, Discussion Paper No. 5, 1985-1986).

STUART HARRIS, FASSA, has been Secretary of the Department of Foreign Affairs since 1984. He was Director of the Bureau of Agricultural Economics from 1968-1973, Deputy Secretary of the Department of Overseas Trade from 1973-1975, and Professor of Resource Economics at the Australian Agricultural Economics Society in 1970-1971. He has edited *Resource Development and the Future of Australian Society* ((1982), and *Australia's Antarctic Policy Options* (1984).

RICHARD HERR is Senior Lecturer in Political Science at the University of Tasmania, where he has taught international relations for the past 14 years. His primary research interest is on regional relations in the South Pacific, in which field he has published widely in recent years.He has also served as a consultant to the governments of South Pacific states on organisational issues including fisheries, offshore minerals and institutional options.

PAUL KEAL is Research Fellow with teaching responsibilities in the Department of International Relations, Research School of Pacific Studies, Australian National University. He has previously been a Visiting Fellow in World Order Studies at Princeton University, Lecturer in Politics at La Trobe University, and a Research Fellow in the Strategic and Defence Studies Centre, Research School of Pacific Studies, Australian National University. He is the author of *Unspoken Rules and Superpower Dominance* (1984), *Japanese Defence and Australian Interests* ((Legislative Research Service, Discussion Paper No. 8, 1985-1986), and *Japan's Role in United States Strategy in the Pacific* (Working Paper No. 106, Strategic and Defence Studies Centre, Australian National University, 1986).

GARY KLINTWORTH joined the Australian Department of Defence as a Research Analyst in 1971, working on East Asian affairs with a focus on China. Presently, he is Defence Fellow at the Strategic and Defence Studies Centre, Research School of Pacific Studies, Australian National University, where he is investigating China's modernisation and the strategic implications for the Western Pacific. He has produced a range of publications, assessments, conference papers and estimates for the Australian government on China, the Koreas, Japan, Hong Kong, Taiwan, Kampuchea, Indochina, and strategic developments in Northeast Asia and Southeast Asia. He has written Strategic and Defence Studies Centre Working Papers on *Mr Gorbachev's China Diplomacy, Kim Il-sung's North Korea at the Crossroads,* and *Vietnam's withdrawal from Cambodia.*

ROBYN LIM has been Lecturer and Senior Lecturer in Political Science at the University of New South Wales since 1973. She was Australian Studies Lecturer in Japan in 1981, and Academic-in-Residence in the Department of Foreign Affairs in 1986. Her publications are mainly in the area of Southeast Asian strategic issues, Philippine politics, and Australian-ASEAN relations.

AMIN SAIKAL, Lecturer in Political Science at the Australian National University, has been a Visiting Fellow at Princeton University , Cambridge University, and the Institute of Development Studies, University of Sussex, and holds a Rockefeller Foundation Fellowship in International Relations. He is author of *The Rise and Fall of the Shah* (1980), and his recent publications have concentrated on Afghanistan.

EVGENI SAMOTEIKIN is Ambassador of the Union of Soviet Socialist Republics to Australia, Papua New Guinea, Fiji and Vanuatu. He was educated at the Moscow State Institute of International Relations, and the Diplomatic Academy of the Ministry of Foreign Affairs. He holds the degree of Doctor of History, and served in the diplomatic service from 1952-1964. From 1964-1982 he was Adviser on foreign policy matters to L.I. Brezhnev, and took up his position in Canberra on 6 May 1983.

RAMESH THAKUR is Senior Lecturer in Political Studies at the University of Otago. He taught at the University of the South Pacific before joining Otago University, where he has been since 1980. He is the author of *Peacekeeping in Vietnam: Canada, India, Poland and the International Commission* (1984), *In Defence of New Zealand: Foreign Policy Choices in the Nuclear Age* (1984 and 1986), and *International Peacekeeping in Lebanon: Multinational Force and United Nations Authority* (1987). He has written more than 40 articles for various journals around the world, and also writes occasionally for newspapers in New Zealand.

CARLYLE A. THAYER has been Senior Lecturer in Politics in University College of the Australian Defence Force Academy since 1986. Before that, he served in Vietnam, and then lectured in the Faculty of Military Studies, Royal Military College, Duntroon in Australia. He has been a Visiting Fellow at Yale, a Visiting Scholar at Harvard and a Defence Fellow at the Australian National University. His main interests are in Southeast Asian comparative politics and international relations, and he has published extensively on contemporary Vietnam.

Index of Names